TWILIGHT OF THE

Wagners

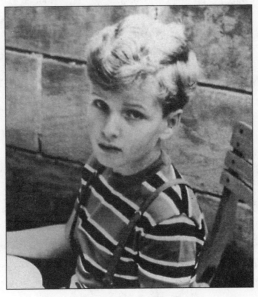

THE UNVEILING

OF A FAMILY'S LEGACY

Gottfried Wagner

ENGLISH TRANSLATION BY DELLA COULING

Picador USA

NEW YORK

Picador® is a U.S. registered trademark and is used by St. Martin's Press under license from Pan Books Limited.

For information on Picador USA Reading Group Guides, as well as ordering, please contact the Trade Marketing department at St. Martin's Press.
Phone: 1-800-221-7945 extension 763
Fax: 212-677-7456
E-mail: trademarketing@stmartins.com

DESIGNED BY ABBY KAGAN

Library of Congress Cataloging-in-Publication Data

Wagner, Gottfried, 1947–
    [Wer nicht mit dem Wolf heult. English]
    Twilight of the Wagners : the unveiling of a family's legacy / Gottfried
    Wagner ; English translation by Della Couling
        p.   cm.
    Includes bibliographical references and index.
    ISBN 0-312-19957-0 (hc)
    ISBN 0-312-26404-6 (pbk)
    1. Wagner, Gottfried. 1947– . 2. Opera producers and directors—
Biography. 3. Wagner family. 4. Wagner, Richard, 1813–1883—Family.
5. Bayreuther Festspiele. 6. Antisemitism—Germany. I. Title.
ML429.W134A3   1999
782.1'092—dc21
[B]   99-19715
                                                                             CIP

First published in Germany by Verlag Kiepenheuer & Witsch, Köln, 1997

First Picador USA Paperback Edition: May 2000

10 9 8 7 6 5 4 3 2 1

FOR MY WIFE, TERESINA;

MY SON, EUGENIO;

AND MAMMA ANTONIETTA

Contents

Acknowledgments

My thanks to Eberhard Wagner, Karl Lubomirski,
Dorothea Hug-Lauener,
Michael Wieck, Ralph Giordano, G. Jan Colijn, Michael Shapiro,
Abraham Peck, and Christian v. Ditfurth.

I also thank my mother, Ellen Drexel-Wagner,
for allowing me to consult her diaries and photos.

Introduction

ABRAHAM J. PECK

wilight of the Wagners is a book that Gottfried Wagner had to write, a book about his coming of age, in an age dominated by the shadow of Auschwitz. It is about family matters and family secrets: the secret of a father and uncle who smiled and walked with their "Uncle Wolf," known to the rest of the world as Adolf Hitler; the secret of a grandmother who worshiped "der Führer," and was a Holocaust denier until the day she died; the secret of a great-uncle whose writings laid the foundations for National Socialist racial thought, and the secret of a great-grandfather, a genius of the opera world, a pillar of modern German culture, whose personal and published views on Jews and Judaism anticipated the anti-Semitic direction of Adolf Hitler and National Socialism by more than eight decades.

And yet Gottfried Wagner could have taken his place amid the glitter and glory of the Festspielhügel, the Festival Hill in Bayreuth that is the monument to Gottfried's great-grandfather, Richard, outshining only the historic "grandeur" of the bust of the composer done by Hitler's favorite sculptor, Arno Breker.

For the first years of his life, Gottfried Wagner lived and breathed the air of the Wagner mystique, living in a corner of the Villa Wahnfried, the place where, befitting its name, Richard Wagner found peace from all of his manias.

But Gottfried did not find peace there, only the growing realization after his ninth year that great-grandpa's music had something to do with the horrible newsreels of the liberation of the Buchenwald concentration camp in April 1945 and the thousands of dead and dying bodies of its Jewish inmates. Indeed, the need to know the truth about this connection proved to be a mania that has been a part of Gottfried ever since. Knowing that truth has indeed set him free, but not without the most dire consequences. Gottfried Wagner is an outcast, banned from his family home. He can hardly find work in his field of operatic artistic direction, and he has chosen to live outside of Germany in a kind of self-imposed exile.

That was the Gottfried Wagner I met at Stockton College, New Jersey, in 1991, where he had been invited to address the Scholars' Conference on the Church Struggle. It was quite an event to have the great-grandson of Richard Wagner speak to this group about Wagner, his music and his anti-Semitism.

Only written questions were allowed after the end of his talk. And Gottfried, like the majority of Germans who deal with the question of German-Jewish relations in the present and in the future, ended by saying essentially that he hoped that his contribution would be a step toward reconciliation.

I asked in my written question whether it was the place of anyone but those murdered in the Holocaust to grant such reconciliation, something that was of course impossible.

I could see that Gottfried was taken aback by the question. Most Germans who have contact with Jews in any positive way turn the event into what they call "a step toward reconciliation." I believe my question made his view of what we were trying to do a very different one. He and I sat up till the early morning hours discussing this and many other subjects.

From that point on we have both examined ourselves in terms of what has been called the "black box" within the sons and daughters of Holocaust survivors. It is a phrase the author Helen Epstein coined in 1979 in a book called *Children of the Holocaust*, the first one to deal with the mostly American children of survivors. This black box contains all the emotions, all of the conflicts that make up the life of survivors and their children.

What Gottfried and I have found is that we both carry a kind of black box within us. And although over the years we have opened it slowly, our discussions have allowed us to really open this black box to a much greater degree than we could have ever imagined. Like Pandora's box, it is uncertain what ultimately will emerge from this. But we continue to focus on the most important thing that separates Jews and Germans: namely the question of family history, what Germans call *Familiengeschichte*.

When it comes to talking about the family histories of Germans and Jews, especially during the Holocaust years, and listening to them and understanding them, every step is difficult and painful, especially for the German side. I believe that for Gottfried and me, that part of the black box has been opened fully and honestly. It is a step in a direction—not necessarily toward reconciliation—because we both reject this term.

Yet, we seek to understand that we have separate, but nonetheless related, legacies that have been left to us by the event we call the Holocaust, which in many respects has poisoned the psyches of our parents and certainly affected our humanity. What we seek is the opportunity to prevent some of that poison from being passed on to our children; to Eugenio, the orphan whom Gottfried saved from the hellhole of post-Ceauşescu Romania, to Abby and Joel, my two American-born children, who will soon be adults.

Family history is a special problem for the sons and daughters of Holocaust survivors. They have often grown up in the eye of a hurricane, surrounded by the shadows of the Holocaust. But many have asked next to nothing about the suffering of their parents or the absence of grandparents, uncles, and aunts. They fear the trauma inherent in their parents' reply.

I am one of those sons. But unlike many, I did ask. I learned as a young boy that there was a reason for the absence of my uncles, aunts, and cousins. Indeed, because I had a father who was obsessed with his own experiences during the Holocaust years, from his time in the ghetto in Lodz, Poland, from 1940 to 1944 to his imprisonment at Buchenwald and Theresienstadt, I developed an unusual knowledge, at a very early age, of my fathers' tormentors.

In a way, this macabre cast of Nazi guards, commandants, and physicians became more real to me than the shadowy figures who had been the murdered members of my family.

All told, there were fourteen uncles and aunts, six on my father's side and eight on my mother's. But for most of my life they have remained only names. I cannot identify them by facial features, idiosyncrasies, or any other characteristics that make up the pleasures of the extended family.

Since Gottfried and I cofounded the Post-Holocaust Dialogue Group, it has become painfully clear to us on many occasions that we have not come as far as we had imagined at the beginning of our encounter. As Gottfried has stated, we have not yet reached the kind of "objectivity" necessary to free us from the shadows of the past. He continues to feel shame at the thought of what happened to my family and the role the Wagner family played in its suffering. He feels angry and powerless because of his inability to provide his family with the sense of mourning necessary to begin the steps toward understanding. This is a symptom that other thoughtful Germans of Gottfried's generation exhibit—the necessity of bemoaning how difficult it is for them to be Germans, to suffer under the burden of history and the sense of homelessness and rootlessness that accompanies such a state.

Our Post-Holocaust Dialogue Group has not yet left the harbor of neuroses that continues to keep it close to the shore of our deepest doubts and demons. Yet we feel it is necessary to go on, as do the other members of our group.

That there are no such things as heroes anymore is a sad lament of our time. But Gottfried and I believe there are heroes.

We both have found a hero in the German-Jewish writer Ralph Giordano. No postwar German publication has aroused so much controversy as his 1987 book *The Second Guilt, or the Burden of Being German*. The book is a clear, concise, and brilliant indictment of German history since 1871. But instead of simply detailing themes such as nationalism, the *völkisch* movement, Prussianism, or the stab-in-the-back legend as the primary forces giving rise to the Nazi state, Giordano focuses on a key issue that succinctly combines all of the above themes into one: the loss of a "humane orientation." This loss, according to Giordano, comes from "the depth of the founding of the German nation-state in 1871, and must be understood as the real indictment of the generation responsible for the creation of the Third Reich." The Nazi state must be seen as a continuation of the systematic dehumanization of the German nation and not its beginning.

"How can this generation breathe?" asks a young woman from Hamburg in a letter to Ralph Giordano. She wonders how the generation of the first guilt, the murderers, can continue to face each day, but is no less concerned for the generation of the second guilt, the generation, including Gottfried's family, which suppressed and forgot the crimes of the first.

It is that part of the family history that is such an impediment to the creation of a meaningful dialogue between Germans and Jews.

But family history, in spite of its ability to keep Germans and Jews from dialogue, has at least in one case brought them closer together.

In 1923, Adolf Hitler's attempt at a Nazi revolution in Bavaria failed. A few months after the abortive coup, Hitler appeared before a court on trial for treason. He recalled in his testimony that "when I stood for the first time before Richard Wagner's grave, my heart swelled with pride. He was one of the three greatest Germans nearest to the Volk." Hitler had become close to the Wagner family and visited them just a few months earlier at Villa Wahnfried in Bayreuth. The town became for Hitler a kind of musical capital of the Nazi revolution. His showmanship was based on operatic devices from the Wagner opera house in Bayreuth. He used torchlight parades, mob choruses, ever-rising climaxes, and grand gestures of Nordic heroes to mesmerize his audiences.

Hitler was sentenced to five years in the fortress prison at Landsberg am Lech, near Munich. He spent only nine months there. Yet he managed to complete the greater part of a manuscript that he dictated to his faithful secretary, Rudolf Hess. The manuscript was an account of his past, present, and future plans for Germany and its "great enemy," world Jewry. Hitler received the paper upon which he dictated his manuscript from Winifred Wagner, Gottfried's grandmother, who visited him in prison.

Is it a coincidence that Gottfried was born in Bayreuth as the great-grandson of Richard Wagner and I was born in Landsberg am Lech as the son of Holocaust survivors? Whatever the circumstances, we have been drawn together because we share a common desire to understand each other's burden as a result of who we are and the consequences of our family history.

The starting point of our dialogue, Gottfried has written, "is the common tragic memory of our past, which will forever be a part of our children's existence." Is the possibility for dialogue worth the encounter? I was never certain of this until I met Gottfried. He represents for me the beginning of Germany's efforts to recapture its sense of a "humane orientation" as it is understood in the work of Ralph Giordano.

The beginning of Germany's misguided path into tyranny and inhumanity may be tied to the generation of Gottfried's great-grandfather, Richard, and to Richard Wagner himself. And what more appropriate representative of the need to reclaim for Germany its humane orientation than the great-grandson of the man who helped to lose it?

I tremble, as does Gottfried, at the thought of all the shadows that lurk over us. But we also know that our post-Holocaust world has not changed enough to allow us to withdraw from the challenge. We see the Holocaust all around us. We see it in the brutalities that occur in national and international conflict, in the apathy with which we can view the victims of war, both young and old, and in our lack of trust in law, religion, medicine, and technology as important and immutable foundations of our civilization.

The Holocaust is a German and Jewish nightmare that will not go away, because we will not let it. It must be on the agenda of Germans and Jews to confront the Holocaust with an intensity and ferocity of purpose that will keep it there for generations to come.

Gottfried Wagner did not have to write this book or lead the life he has led. But he *has* written it, and *Twilight of the Wagners* reflects the pain, the torment, the intensity, the honesty and the hope that has made him who he is.

The Holocaust has shaped us both. It is responsible in many ways for who we are and what we have become. But we are responsible for helping to shape the way it is remembered by future generations. With the publication of this autobiography, Gottfried Wagner has assumed his responsibility.

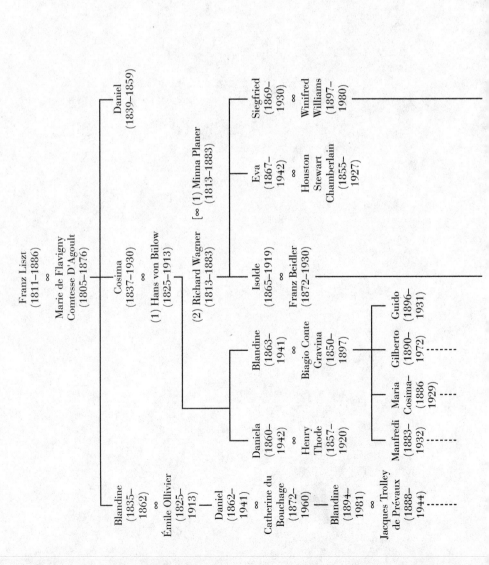

Wagner Family Tree

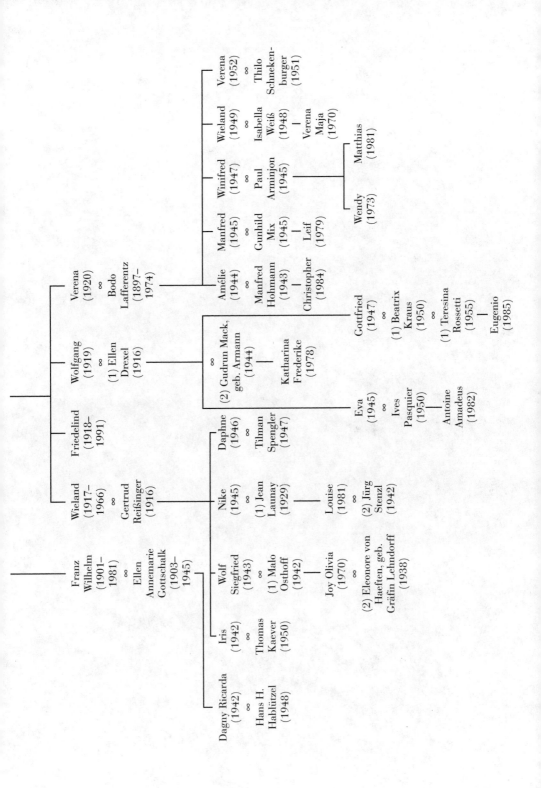

1

Villa Wahnfried

From the moment I was born in Bayreuth, on 13 April 1947, it seemed I was predestined to follow Wagner family tradition. I was introduced to the world at large, via birth announcements, as Gottfried Helferich Wagner, son and heir of Wolfgang Wagner. The choice of my Christian names was already an indication of some future leading role in the family business. Gottfried is the name of Elsa's brother, the ruler of Brabant, in the opera *Lohengrin* by my great-grandfather Richard Wagner, and also the third Christian name of my uncle Wieland Wagner. My other Christian name, Helferich, was the third name of my grandfather, Siegfried Richard Wagner, and a name Richard Wagner himself had invented for his only son.

This rather droll manner of giving names was typical of family tradition. In a letter to King Ludwig II, dated 9 February 1879, Richard Wagner wrote: "The son, now still so young, shall, when he has reached male maturity, know exactly who his father was. Nothing more. Then he may decide. This is also more or less the fashion in which we shall raise him. The boy will not be forced to do anything at all; we shall merely support and guide his inclinations quite freely. We are not at all aiming to turn him into an 'artist': I have only indicated one direction to him through the names which I have appended to his surname: two names mark him out as my son—Siegfried Richard Wagner; but I have added 'Helferich,' i.e., the 'helpful,' to this."[1]

I was christened on Richard Wagner's birthday, 22 May. As godparents my father chose his mother, Winifred Wagner, and Bodo Lafferentz, my aunt Verena's husband. Winifred Wagner, together with the staunch Nazi Heinz Tietjen, general intendant of the Prussian State Theaters, had run the Bayreuth Festival from 1930 until 1945. On orders from Hitler, Lafferentz, as a colleague of Robert Ley, head of the Labor Front, had safeguarded the organization and material interests of the Bayreuth Festival from 1940 to 1944 through the National Socialist organization Kraft durch Freude [Strength Through Joy].

What looked, and was intended to look, from the outside like a peaceful family idyll was in reality quite different. The main focus of interest for Wolfgang and Wieland Wagner was the Bayreuth Festival, the annual production of Richard Wagner's stage works. Founded in 1872 on the composer's fifty-ninth birthday, the festival had been dormant since the end of World War II because of economic and political difficulties. In 1951 it began again, directed, as always, by a member of the Wagner family. In order to devote themselves undisturbed to preparations for this event, my parents took my elder sister, Eva, and me to the Etzerschlössl children's home in Berchtesgaden, a sort of upscale boarding house for the children of well-to-do families. Before leaving us my father explained the reason for our sojourn: "The festival will be starting soon now and it is very important. We must all make every sacrifice for the future and you, as a boy, will just have to grin and bear it. If you're good, you'll get some lovely presents."

I have never understood what was meant by the "sacrifices" our family was supposed to make for the festival, except that in this, the first of the many places I was sent off to during my childhood and youth, I felt miserable. It created in me an aversion to the hectic activity of the festival preparations and even to the "lovely presents"—new clothes, a puppet theater, expensive toy cars—that my parents bought to try to salve their guilty consciences.

Both of my parents' lives were wrapped up in the Bayreuth Festival and its obligations. My father was the second son of Siegfried and Winifred Wagner, both of whom directed the festival, Siegfried from 1904 until 1930 and Winifred from 1930 until the war temporarily shut it down in 1944. As a young man my father assisted Tietjen, the Nazi-influenced artistic director of the festival, and in 1951 he and his older brother, Wieland, became its codirectors. Throughout all of his work at Bayreuth he has remained loyal to the vision of Richard Wagner, his grandfather, and worked to secure the festival's financial base. My mother's life was similarly wedded to the theater, though she would rather perform than direct. By her early twenties she had become a successful ballet dancer, performing mostly in large opera houses. She met my father in Berlin in 1942. After their marriage she gave up her career and dedicated herself to my father's, until their divorce in 1976.

Shortly before the solemn reopening of the festival my sister— two years my senior—and I were brought back to Bayreuth, where my parents would present the public with the image of a happy family. I longed not to be packed off to the children's home in Berchtesgaden once more; but in my family's view, it was my role, my duty, to do whatever was necessary and good for the Wagner legacy and the success of the festival. As my father's successor, I was required from birth to obey him as he and Wieland led another generation of Wagners toward my great-grandfather's vision of supreme art and culture. So I tried, even at the age of four, to be exactly what the grown-up world expected of a "genuine" shining example of a Wagner: I didn't answer back and didn't interrupt the adults' conversations. I kept my stories of the children's home to myself: I was taught to think of myself as privileged, living in the midst of the monumental achievements and goals of my illustrious ancestor and his progeny.

A cult of Richard Wagner and his ideology imbued nearly every aspect of life in my family and the theater community surrounding it. This cult placed Richard Wagner at its center, imbuing his legacy with quasi-religious images—many of which came from his own works—and venerating him as a cultural messiah. My first image of the Wagner cult in Bayreuth was a photograph of the Wagner bust by Arno Breker, Hitler's favorite sculptor. It struck me at once as heroic and menacing. Another impression was made by Zdenko von Kraft, a devoted Wagnerian, who in 1951 wrote the following poem, "Genius," for the festival book on the opening of the new era:

> *Many have passed on, many will come*
> *Yet ever faithful a new circle forms,*
> *What was once flame burns ever hotly*
> *The glow of the spirit shines undimmed*
> *For what the best of their time have perceived*
> *Is close to God, it endures and lasts.*
> *Who counts moons, thankfully counts death;*
> *The unforgettable knows naught of years,*
> *That are, that come and were before us,*
> *Are only leaves on the flourishing vine*
> *That winds about exalted beauty,*
> *That binds us together in a noble way.*
> *For this is the last word of art,*
> *What is common to all is its strength,*
> *What is valid to all creates its works,*
> *What is holy to all feeds its fruitfulness,*
> *And where it inflames a genius,*
> *He has announced himself for the whole world,*
> *Whether the paths of error or pain,*
> *Whether a cobbler's workshop or the trials of gods—*
> *Man's final word means death,*
> *But the seer says a redeeming "Grace!*
> *And so he refines the last things*
> *To a mysteriously beautiful Ring."*[2]

I have never understood the New Bayreuth euphoria, but managed as a dutiful four-year-old to appear thrilled by Beethoven's Ninth Symphony under the baton of the famous conductor Wilhelm Furtwängler, and by my uncle's *Parsifal*. I was taken aback by the tumultuous applause of the audience: I had not been at all pre-pared for such a spectacle in the Festspielhaus and didn't dare admit how frightened I was of Wieland Wagner's dark world of Parsifal and the Holy Grail.

I acknowledged with a smile the constant reminders of how much I looked like Richard Wagner, the "Master of Bayreuth," and the reassurances of what a great future I had before me. Like my father, my uncle, and others before me, I was supposed to behave like a "real Wagner," worshiping at Bayreuth's temple of Wagnerian redemption. I was taught to believe that one day Wagner's works and ideas would save the world. I could make little of the contrast between the devotion demanded within the family to Richard Wagner's art and the overwhelming, spontaneous display that the members of the Bayreuth artistic tribe seemed to find appropriate on public occasions. I felt at home neither in the monumental world of the Festspielhügel—the hill on which Wagner's theater, the Festspielhaus, is situated, a few miles northwest of Bayreuth—nor in the children's homes I was put into again and again as sacrifice for Richard Wagner's "art of mankind." I envied children allowed to grow up in families that did not depend on Richard Wagner for their salvation—surely a more normal environment than what I knew.

During those first seven years I lived with my parents in what was known as the gardener's house, part of the Villa Wahnfried estate, which my great-grandfather had built in the 1870s. We shared the first floor of the small brick house with the gardener, Düret, and his family. The nursery window in our apartment looked out over the front façade of the Villa Wahnfried, the estate's central building and Richard Wagner's famous home. British bombers destroyed much of the main house on 5 April 1945, and U.S. Air Force officers used it as a casino until 1957, an American flag flying overhead. The view from my window showed part of the villa that had survived the war, including the Wagner house's motto: "Here where my fancies [*Wahnen*] found peace [*Frieden*], this house I name Wahnfried."

In front of the Villa Wahnfried, perched on a high plinth, was a bust of King Ludwig II, who had financed many of Richard Wagner's years as a composer. This statue was surrounded by a pine hedge where I liked to hide and watch undisturbed the many tourists passing in and out of the front part of Wahnfried Park. There too I waited for the right moment—that is, once my father had left the park—to start up a conversation with Uncle Wieland's family, or with American officers.

I was forbidden to talk to my cousins or to enter the partly reconstructed Siegfried Wagner House, where my uncle Wieland's family lived until 1966. (The house was not finally rebuilt and refurbished until 1976, when it was reopened for its one hundredth anniversary and made into a museum.) Though the main house, designed by Wilhelm Neumann in 1872, contained a concert hall, a library, a rotunda, and eventually an annex for the Führer, the house my immediate family occupied was modest, and a constant reminder of the animosity between my father and his brother.

My father gave his orders in a stern voice, and the penalties for disobeying him were steep. He was strong and choleric and he refused to accept any objections to his authority. When he discovered me playing with my cousins, he threatened to beat me again, and I believed that he would. I learned to hide myself—in the cupboard, under the bed, in the hedge, around the statue of King Ludwig—in order to avoid my father's anger. My father never discussed his rules: he gave orders and I had to obey. Afraid of being beaten, for he was a very strong man, I pretended to agree with him, cultivating an internal life of dissent that I hid from him and the adult world.

My father never explained to me exactly why I was not supposed to play with Iris, Nike, Daphne, and Wolf-Siegfried, whom we all called Wummi. He spoke disparagingly of his brother and his family, especially the children, referring to their bad manners—not the right company for my sister and me. I soon realized that these accusations were untrue. I was also forbidden to play with other children who visited the park.

In a way I led a double life: with my parents I was the obedient son, but given the opportunity, I broke the paternal laws. As soon as I saw that my father had left Wahnfried Park, I would leave my hiding place in the hedge, climb over the wall dividing the Villa

Wahnfried and the gardener's house, and enjoy wild games and what to me seemed boundless freedom with Wieland's children. As soon as my father returned, I would clamber back over the wall and scramble anxiously back into the hedge. Once my father had disappeared into the house, I slipped across the lawn next to the entrance drive, my allotted playground. Despite all my precautions, my father caught me now and again during these escapades, which meant a sound beating. But these beatings only served to strengthen my resolve to leave my parents' home and the Wagner bombast and the Festspielhügel as soon as possible.

My family life appeared monotonous and regimented when I compared it to the easy hours I spent with the "Wieland children." My father dictated the hours during which I could play and which friends I could have. He forbade my friends from entering our garden house or his villa beside the Festspielhaus. I began to rebel, lying to him about where I was going, making up stories about school meetings. When he discovered my disobedience, he beat me even more severely. My father labeled me the "little Russian," recognizing in me sinister qualities of disobedience which he believed were typical of "the Russians." My rebelliousness worsened with my elder sister Eva's, constant efforts to exercise control over me. If she caught me doing anything wrong, she reported it to my father. As my mother also blindly subjected herself to her husband's will, I was alone in my family. My father beat me until I was sixteen years old and finally rebelled: I told him that if he beat me one more time, he would never see me again.

There were a few bright spots, like my fifth birthday, when my father did allow me to play with Wieland's children. He had given me a bright blue car built of heavy iron with a moped motor, and without prior explanation he sat me behind the steering wheel, put my sister on the backseat, and started up the motor. The thing drove off, I tore round the fountain in the Wahnfried garden and lost control. The trip ended abruptly in the rhododendron bushes near Richard Wagner's grave. Swearing furiously, my father dragged me from the car and the afternoon of birthday games was over. I never got in the car again.

Even at that time, I already felt the tensions between my father and my uncle, primarily about who did what on the Festspielhügel. Their differences of opinion frequently exploded into noisy quarrels, and as even the children heard the mutual exchange of contemptuous remarks, family unity was gradually destroyed. The Wieland party and the Wolfgang party grew further and further apart. Eventually, they didn't even congregate at Christmas or Easter, either in Villa Wahnfried or in my grandmother Winifred's spacious house in the Fichtelgebirge, the mountains to the east of Bayreuth. (My grandmother lived in this first-class "exile villa" from 1945 to 1957, when she moved back into the Siegfried Wagner House, where she lived until her death in 1980.)

During one of my own illicit visits to Villa Wahnfried, Christmas 1952, I was overawed by a gigantic Christmas tree standing in the hall, decorated only with red apples and beeswax candles. I suppose it was then that I wondered why the Wagner family did not stick together, especially at Christmastime, which, as I had always been told in the Bayreuth kindergarten, was a festival of love and peace. I asked my father to pray with me at the time, but he mockingly refused.

The family was now firmly divided into the "Wielands" and the "Wolfgangs." My father was denigrated by his brother as a simpleminded manager, whereas Wieland was generally regarded as an artist. It seemed there were "gifted" and ungifted" Wagners, a label that was to remain for decades and even color media reporting.

To escape at least occasionally from family tensions, my parents, my sister, and I spent weekends in a small house near Neunkirchen, a few kilometers from Bayreuth, set in beautiful countryside. These weekends, together with the regular trips to children's homes, were at that time my parents' only diversions. Their work on behalf of Wagner's theater and legacy required so much of their time and energy that even when we were in Bayreuth with them, surrounded by the theater's business, they rarely told us children anything about it—their work claimed so much of their attention.

In order to escape from such enforced isolation, I disobeyed my father more and more frequently. I thought it ridiculous that I was forbidden to enter the Siegfried Wagner House. At the beginning of the 1950s, there were regular "big parties" on weekends, where American officers would celebrate noisily. They sang and danced, and there was always plenty to eat and drink. It was at these parties—which I observed from the outside, peering in through the window—that I first heard dance bands, jazz, and all the music of the 1940s from North America, which my father dismissed as "nigger music." I enjoyed the warm, lively atmosphere, and instead of listening piously to homemade Holy Grail music, I sat in raptures in the Wahnfried garden in front of the Siegfried Wagner House music-room window and tapped my feet to the boogie-woogie of the "uncultured Yanks," as they were called in my family.

Once, one of the black employees noticed me. Suddenly remembering my father's objections, I went to make my escape, but the big, powerfully built African American saw I was afraid and approached me. With a broad smile and the words "Have fun," he handed me a piece of wedding cake and an orange, at that time luxuries, and not just for me. Why should I be against "Yanks" and "Negroes"?

The year 1953 was to be important for me for two reasons: first, my father staged his first production and also designed his first set for the Festspielhaus; and second, I started school. Father had chosen *Lohengrin* for his Bayreuth debut, and during his intense preparations he expected even more consideration and respect from us children than ever before for the great idea of the festival. When he was working at home, we had to keep absolutely quiet; any noise disturbed him. Come rehearsals in June, there was only one subject of conversation: his *Lohengrin.* The sheer fascination of the preparatory work, first on the rehearsal stage, then on the main stage of the Festspielhaus, compensated a little for the subjection of the whole family to the cause. The hectic life at rehearsals and in the workshops was exciting. But having constantly to pose for photographers—to illustrate the family enterprise—soon became annoying. I was placed in every conceivable pose next to the papier-mâché swan prop and made to smile sweetly again and again.

My father categorically forbade me, without giving reasons, from sitting in on my uncle's *Rheingold* rehearsals, which were taking place at the same time. Such a ban seemed completely incomprehensible to me; but as I was thrilled just to take part in the theatrical work of the Festspielhaus, and did not want to jeopardize this privilege, I didn't argue. At my insistence, my father briefly recounted to me the fairy tale of the good Lohengrin, who comes down to earth from the wonderful world of the Grail as a king's son to free the good Elsa from the wicked Ortrud and Telramund. It struck me as odd that Lohengrin has to leave Elsa because she asks his name and where he comes from, but I didn't pester any further once my father answered my curiosity with: "The music explains everything anyway." I didn't understand that. I also suspected that something wonderful and unearthly was happening in the *Lohengrin* act-one prelude; but I could not grasp why Elsa dies after Lohengrin's return to his father, Parsifal, in the Grail world, and why her brother, Gottfried, previously turned into a swan by the wicked Ortrud, now had to go to war as "leader of Brabant" against the terrible "enemies in the east."

It was not so much whether I understood *Lohengrin* as the fact that it made me uneasy. And yet I assumed that I would take the nonspeaking role of the boy Gottfried. It was a blow when I learned that my father had given this role to the son of the bass Ludwig Weber, who was singing King Heinrich. The boy was only a little older than I. Father's explanation—"I don't want you to be given preference in getting a role just because you are my son"—left me unconvinced: my cousin Wummi, four years older than I, was allowed to play one of the Nibelung dwarfs in *Rheingold*. But Father had decided, and at that time he remained unalterable.

Looking back now, I see that my father considered me a potential rival. He was afraid of living in the shadows of both his artistically talented brother and a possibly gifted son. He wanted to be the last Wagner of consequence, thereby securing his place in Bayreuth history. My mother told me with pain of how he had hoped for a second daughter, and his disappointment when, instead, I arrived.

After the *Lohengrin* premiere we sat with invited guests in the festival restaurant, and there I had my first dealings with the press. In contrast to my cousins, I had been excluded from public life, and I found unsettling the sudden overwhelming interest in me as a Wagner scion and in my opinion on *Lohengrin*. The questions of the tabloids in particular confused me. For example, they wanted to know how I had liked Father's *Lohengrin* and Wieland's *Rheingold*. It was natural for me to find my father's production good, in contrast to most of the critics, who preferred Wieland's directing. About the *Rheingold* I could only say that I hadn't seen it yet.

I was disappointed that my father would not let me sit at the same table with the Wieland children after the *Lohengrin* premiere. Since then, at all such occasions there has been a Wolfgang table and a Wieland table, and we children hardly spoke to one another. We were paraded as the "nice little Wagner children," instructed to greet particularly nicely those who were introduced to us as members of the Society of Friends of Bayreuth—that is, of the festival. I didn't always manage this to my parents' satisfaction, tending to identify whom I liked and whom I did not with childlike naiveté, whether these were influential sponsors or ordinary mortals.

I found my grandmother's behavior on such occasions particularly unpleasant: she could not resist expounding in a very theatrical way on the theme—albeit with variations—of "family resemblance." At the core of this always highly elaborate tale were two sentences: "When you were in my house as a baby and I had guests, I would ask them if they wanted to see Richard Wagner as a baby. Of course they all wanted to see the infant Richard." Nothing could prevent her from parading this joke. Once when I cheekily countered with "Was I really that ugly?," "Omi" thought my retort droll and "typically Wagnerian."

After Father's great performance with *Lohengrin* my sister and I, in new clothes and loaded with new presents, were sent off to Berchtesgaden again. In September 1953 I started school in the nearby village of Maria Gern. This idyllic village school consisted of two classrooms: grades one to four were in one; in the other, grades five to eight. A pretty peasant girl of around twelve, Maria, helped me learn to write, read, and do arithmetic, and lessons were punctuated by long, happy walks in the countryside, during which the teacher, Lösch, taught us the names of the plants. My new school-friends, who mostly came from farming families, were friendly and welcoming; and to better adapt to the new environment, I took up the local upper-Bavarian accent. I enjoyed ringing the bell of the little village church with the other boys, jumping up and hanging on tight to the bell rope, swinging as the bell loudly tolled. In fact, Maria Gern finally saw me play like other six-year-old boys, and I hardly missed my parents and Bayreuth.

But this carefree time was short-lived, and in October I was entered in a second school, this time in Bayreuth. This was the start of a sixteen-year schooling period that would be torture from the first day to the last. Towns, schools, tutors, and teachers changed constantly, and I often had to repeat classes three times. The few high-points were stimulating teachers and friendships with fellow pupils.

My very first school experiences in Bayreuth were nightmarish. It quickly became clear to me what it meant to be different from the other children: I was made fun of for my upper-Bavarian accent and the traditional dress that I had so liked wearing in Maria Gern. And I was a long way behind in my knowledge too. My first teacher in Bayreuth, the kindly and sympathetic Frau Grohm, tried in vain to defend me; she got no help from my parents.

But what separated me most from my fellow pupils was the fact that I was a Wagner going to school in Bayreuth. Of course envy will have played its part in my isolation. First I tried to make the best of the situation, and played the clown. But that didn't make any difference, either. Gradually I began to withdraw into myself, which only made the other children more aggressive. I once was severely beaten up on the way home, and another time I found written on the sandstone outer wall of the Wahnfried garden "Gottfried is stupid," which amused passersby. My schoolwork deteriorated, and my parents arranged extra instruction at home by nannies and private tutors. The number of tutors who strove in vain to improve my school marks grew steadily. I continued to stand out at school not only through bad marks but also through frequent illness and absenteeism.

Neither of my parents ever helped me with my course work: my father was so obsessed with his work for the festival that he had no real friends of his own, let alone time to tutor his son. Dominated by my father, my mother denied her own needs so often that I felt the need to care for her myself. By the age of thirteen I felt as if I were her older brother, in which role I felt only pity for her and the humiliations she endured in my father's house. My mother cried each time I returned to school; my father acted glad to be rid of me, a distraction from his self-centered Wagnerian projects.

In 1954 my father revived his *Lohengrin*, an event that proved less exciting than the meeting with my aunt Friedelind Wagner, my father's elder sister, who came to see the performance in the Festspielhaus. Strange stories circulated in the family about her, which made me curious to get to know her. My father made the most disparaging remarks about her, saying she had been a terribly naughty child and had eventually run away from home to America. When I met this "brazen American aunt" (known as "Maus" in the family) for the first time in the Festspielhaus, my immediate impression was quite different. She resembled us very closely, with her "Wagner nose," but I was more impressed by how she distinguished herself from my father. She wore wide, theatrical dresses which were shockingly colorful and concealed her round, feminine body. She wore her hair in an old-fashioned style, often beneath a hat. I admired her brash, assertive manner. She approached me with a smile and greeted me very affectionately, with warm hugs and soothing words, becoming the only one in the family who ever asked what my interests were and treating me like a boy of my age. "Call me Maus, not Aunt Friedelind," she said. She bore none of the Bayreuth affectation or "Wagner cult" ethic so fervently maintained by the rest of the family, and I listened fascinated as she told me how she had met some "red Indians" in the American prairies. I could have talked to her for hours, but my father soon insisted on driving me home and en route, forbade me any further contact with Aunt Friedelind. This time I didn't accept the edict; I protested and demanded reasons. I didn't get any, however, instead just stonewalling: "It's a long story; I'll tell you one day." I didn't give up, and replied, "Tell me now," to which my father answered: "You wouldn't understand it anyway." Annoyed, he dropped me off at home. I began to suspect that there were a lot of secrets I was not to know about.

Maus knew those secrets, and she was brave enough to expose them in a book she published in 1944, *The Royal Family of Bayreuth*. In that book she made clear how close Hitler was to the Wagner family. She was the only Wagner of her generation who opposed Nazi Germany and the Wagner family's elitism. My father despised Maus, both because she was intellectually and culturally his superior and because she would not let me forget his ties to the Nazi regime. He publicly criticized her book, even at her funeral, which he held at Bayreuth against her dying wishes.

After our first meeting Maus and I saw one another only sporadically between 1959 and 1966, when she was working as director of her Bayreuth Festival Master Classes for music students from all over the world. These summer courses comprised discussions with the students on Wagner operas and productions and took place in a primitive shed right next to my father's home. Father always made fun of Maus and rightly feared her cultural and intellectual standard, for she was fortunate to know and appreciate not only the works of Richard Wagner, but also those of her great-grandfather Franz Liszt and her father, Siegfried Wagner, whom she was the only one in the family to promote. Whenever my father and I talked about her there was a row: I did not share his cutting opinion of my aunt.

After Wieland's death, in 1966, the conflicts between Father and Maus over his style of directing reached such a violent level that in 1972 she finally left and settled in England. I missed her then: during the few conversations we were able to have together she was always frank with me, and right until her death, in 1991, she was always interested in my professional development, coming with a touching pride to the premieres of most of my productions. Maus helped my mother, too, after my parents' divorce in 1976, with great selflessness, which was typical of her plucky character—atypical of the family—and her ethical principles; and yet she did not have much luck at all in her choice of friends, who often exploited her.

It still gives me great pleasure to read my correspondence with Maus now and again. I recognize in it that we—as Wagner descendants in opposition to the Wagner cult, and as family outsiders—actually always liked one another, in spite of all the obstacles, differences of opinion, and Bayreuth intrigues. Maus was the only one in the family enthusiastically to applaud both my journey to Israel and the adoption of my son, Eugenio. I believe I owe it to her to prevent her memory being dragged through the mud, for whatever reasons.

In January 1955 we were able to leave the gardener's house and move into a villa on the Festspielhügel. "Finally we'll be able to live in peace and quiet," said my mother, who was worried about the precarious state of my health. I believe that I was reacting physically to my unstable emotional environment. I was growing rapidly but remained weak and very often sick. Despite having a large room to myself, my situation did not improve, as our villa was only a few meters away from the Festspielhaus and my father now devoted himself day and night exclusively to his work for the Bayreuth Festival and other Wagnerian concerns. Our new home turned into an annex of the Festspielhaus, and my father tolerated nothing but the cult of the Wagner legacy. He had the grounds enclosed by high walls, wooden fences, and hedges, which I could see over only from the second-floor windows. The Festspielhaus was no longer visible from the garden in summer, but I often felt as though I were in a prison. I missed Villa Wahnfried with its big open garden, its proximity to the town, and the forbidden games with the Wieland children.

Moving to another part of the town meant attending the Graser school. Here I was confronted with a very strict teacher, Herr Schäfer, whom I found threatening. I impressed him only once, when I managed to sing without a single mistake a melody he had played on the violin. Of course, I was also fulfilling the school's expectations, which were that anything other than music would not interest a Wagner anyway. "You're not up to much in school, but at least you can sing," was Schäfer's only positive remark about me.

A more-than-welcome change from the dreary monotony of

school was my first big trip abroad, in April 1955. I flew with my parents to Barcelona, where the Bayreuth Festival was on tour with my uncle's productions of *Parsifal* and *Die Walküre.* This first experience of the Mediterranean had a profound and lasting effect on me: not only the luxury hotels, the big gardens, the villas, and the deep blue sea, but also the glittering society inside and outside the opera house. I found it all fascinating. I saw that newspapers, as well as those members of Bayreuth's social elite whom we saw on our vacation, enviously viewed the Wagners as a special dynasty. The Wolfgang and Wieland children were made much of too. Grandmother Winifred declared at every conceivable opportunity "how decently and splendidly these Spaniards stood by us Germans against the Bolsheviks." Enthusiastically she recounted stories of Hitler, praised his Spanish ally the *caudillo* Francisco Franco, and wallowed in memories of the "glorious times" of the National Socialist dictatorship. The hosts applauded heartily, my father remained silent, and I started shouting with the others "Franco-Hitler! Franco-Hitler!" I didn't know what it meant.

In Barcelona everything seemed big and impressive. The reverence paid to all the Wagners went to my head, and I now believed I had a great future in front of me. This burgeoning pride produced a direct effect when we returned to Bayreuth, where I completely lost interest in school, and my marks sank accordingly. I was only interested in the Festspielhaus, and I wanted to take part in everything that happened there. My parents made it unmistakably clear to me, however, that I was only to sit in on Father's rehearsals for the new production of *Der fliegende Holländer.* At the rehearsals for my uncle's *Tannhäuser,* on the other hand, I made sure I was not found out. I quickly discovered various hiding places in the Festspielhaus: over the auditorium, in the orchestra pit, in the prompter's box, under the stage, in the lighting towers, in the flies, or on one of the many roofs. Now I not only could watch my uncle's rehearsals in peace, enthralled, but was also witness to the ruthlessly waged conflict between my father and his brother and the latter's wife, Aunt Gertrud. Tyrannically, Wieland enforced his will in the interests of his work, and my father had to submit to him in front of everybody. Wieland's fits of violent rage, his cynicism, and his damning remarks about people who did not agree with his ideas alienated me just as much as his scornful remarks about my father's productions. Father suffered very much under this: he wanted to be his brother's equal as an artist. I did admire Wieland's directorial work and his sets, which appealed to me more than my father's stagings, but during this time I often felt sorry for my father.

My uncle's frank disparagement of my father's productions led to the formation of two rival factions in the Festspielhaus, who worked and intrigued against one another. The climate became more poisonous, and the rift in the family deepened. During performances we children were no longer allowed to sit together in the family box. Only the Wielands sat there now, while the Wolfgangs sat on the left in the first row of the stalls. In official photos, too, the two families were no longer shown together.

Under these sorry conditions my father's production of *Der fliegende Holländer* was premiered. Wieland and the press, closely allied with him, rated it as badly as they already had the *Lohengrin*. My father, believing I was on his side, took the time to explain the story of *Der fliegende Holländer* to me. It had a similar effect on me as the story of *Lohengrin* had two years before: afraid of the ghostly ship, I could not understand what Senta's suicide at the end of the opera was about and why the Dutchman should then be "redeemed" by this. Naturally, before these festival events, my sister and I were once again packed off to a children's home, this time to the Renée home in Wyk on the island of Föhr in the North Sea, just off Schleswig-Holstein. Saying goodbye to my parents and Bayreuth was easier for me than in former years. I didn't feel at home anywhere, a feeling that didn't change after we got back to Bayreuth, and I was ill more and more frequently.

That year, 1955, we spent the Christmas holidays in the Hotel Wetterstein, Seefeld, in the Austrian Tyrol. It was here that for the first time I met people who were proud of being German. I understood this just as little as the saying "We Germans are somebody again," which was often heard now.

Around this time the adults would heatedly argue about German rearmament. When I asked my father what the Federal Army and the National People's Army, the armed forces of the GDR were, he answered: "The Federal Army are our brave soldiers here, to protect us from the wicked soldiers of the People's Army if they attacked us." I couldn't understand this explanation. But the People's Army of the "Soviet zone" did not worry me in particular. What made the adults anxious in the intensifying cold war, I saw more as a cops-and-robbers story.

I was preoccupied now with National Socialists, seeing for the first time film news bulletins, newspapers, and magazines. During one film presentation at school we saw excerpts from contemporary propaganda material on Nazi Germany, the National Socialist party congresses in Nuremberg, and the world war unleashed by Hitler: goosestepping German soldiers, hysterical mass adulation of the Führer, the war crimes of the Wehrmacht—and all of it to a background of Richard Wagner's music. Shocked by the piles of corpses in the concentration camp of Buchenwald, I told my father about the awful films and especially about the music I had heard in them. "You are still too little to understand all that," he answered. But I refused to be satisfied with this, and he shouted at me to go away and play—or, better still, to finally get down to my homework—instead of asking about things I could not understand anyway. If I had persisted any further with my questions I would have been beaten, so I shut up. But I resolved to get to the bottom of the matter. My next attempt at finding out the truth was aimed at my grandmother, who answered my question of whether there really had been concentration comps in the Third Reich with: "That's all propaganda by the New York Jews, who want to make us and the Germans out to be bad!"

At this time I had another experience that was to influence the course of my life: Wieland's *Die Meistersinger von Nürnberg* of 1956. I had already seen a few illustrations of sets of *Meistersinger* productions of earlier times, but hadn't found them very interesting. When the curtain went up in the 1956 festival season, though, I was stunned: before me was a magical set with constantly changing lighting effects in front of a simple and bright semicircular horizon, with just a few, but wonderful, changes in the different acts. At that time Wieland was my artistic ideal, and I was determined to become a director. When I told my father of this he didn't say a word. I was dismayed when aggressive booing broke out as the curtain came down after the last act. Even my grandmother was among those who found Wieland's production a besmirching of *Die Meistersinger.*

After these events, the end of the festival was hard to take, as a great boredom then descended on the provincial town of Bayreuth. But this time autumn was to bring some diversions. Around then I also began to understand what Winifred meant at her celebrations on 20 April, Hitler's birthday, by "USA": "unser seliger Adolf"—our blessed Adolf—and now I started secretly investigating the family history.

My parents, as was usual after the festival period, had gone on holiday, and so Gunda Lodes, who worked in the telephone exchange of the festival administration, looked after my sister and me. Gunda, with her warmhearted, loving nature, had become a substitute aunt for me, and I have her to thank that my childhood and youth in Bayreuth was not a total nightmare. Gunda's father, the kindly Hans Lodes, had been the caretaker of the Bayreuth Festival for decades. "Grandpa Lodes," as I called him, guided the crowds of tourists through the Festspielhaus and explained in simple words everything essential about the history of the festival and Richard Wagner. My first knowledge of the history of my family I owe to him. Of his wife, Kunigunde, I have equally good memories. She was small, round, good-natured and, like her husband, came from a Catholic farming family. What's more, "Grandma Lodes" made the most wonderful *Bayreuther Glees*—potato dumplings. On weekends the grandchildren Werner and Helmut turned up at the Lodes family home, and finally I could play like other children. Werner, who is six years older than I, became my favorite playmate. I admired him for technical skills that I, a Wagner in training to be an artist, totally lacked. His powers of invention of a steady stream of new games in the garden, and then more and more in the Festspielhaus as well, were limitless. Neighboring children soon joined us, such as Matthias Röntgen, the son of a painter, who lived in a wooden hut on the other side of the Festspielhügel, and Hubert Franz, the son of the forester from the adjoining plot of land.

Of course, before my parents left on their holidays my father had strictly forbidden me to play in the Festspielhaus. Such a prohibition was like a challenge for me to furtively slip the master key to the Festspielhaus that Father had hidden in a secret place into my trouser pocket and to begin my expeditions around the historic building. First I opened all the doors that had been locked to me until then, and behind which, I suspected, lay momentous secrets. My heart thumping, I entered the rooms over the old set-painting workshop, where I found a large plaster model of the Festspielhaus, paintings depicting scenes·from *Der Ring des Nibelungen*, thick tomes on racial theory, festival programs from the years 1933 to 1944, and photos of my grandmother, Uncle Wieland, and my father with the Führer. I also found an enormous oil painting of Hitler with a menacing Alsatian dog. I found boxes of countless handwritten letters, which, being partly written in the old German script, I had difficulty deciphering. Although these finds were lying around dusty, dirty, scattered in wild confusion I carefully picked up each one, piece by piece, and, propping art objects against the wall, examined them.

The plaster model I thought particularly intriguing, but the question was, who would be the best person to answer my questions? I dared not turn to my father, as I was in forbidden territory here. Besides, his previous reaction to my questions on the Nazi films had shown me how loath he was to talk about the subject. Grandpa Lodes, on the other hand, seemed a suitable informant, and so as not to give myself away, I invented an excuse that would enable me to return to the scene legally. I told him I had heard strange noises over the painting workshop, and he immediately whistled up his powerful Alsatian, Bodo, who terrified me and hurried with me in his wake to the painting studio. I urged Grandpa Lodes to climb up the stairs into the lumber room. He contemplated the little footprints on the dusty stairs suspiciously, and although when we entered the room I pretended I had never seen any of it before, he noted drily: "You've already been here." He wanted to know how I had gotten in, and finally I told him the whole story, swore I would never do it again, and started questioning him.

He answered my questions quite readily. "That's a plaster model of the Festspielhaus. After the Final Victory the Führer wanted to have the old Festspielhaus roofed over and used only for very special occasions by very special people. Next to the old Festspielhaus he wanted to have another built, exactly like the old one, to be used for performances." It was only much later that I learned how this plaster model was part of the "monumentalization" of the Festspielhaus by the Nazi architect Emil-Rudolf Mewes in 1940.

"This Führer, was he here often?" I wanted to know.

"The Führer loved Wagner and your family very much."

As Grandpa Lodes talked about the Führer in such a friendly way, I wondered where he was today.

"He's been dead a long time," answered Grandpa Lodes, and firmly took my hand to draw me out of the room. Silently and with a serious expression he locked the doors and then said: "I don't want to see you here again without your dad, otherwise you won't be able to come and see us anymore."

I promised Grandpa Lodes to keep my mouth shut, for the sake of Werner, Helmut, and the wonderful wild games, but I didn't promise that I would not go into the mysterious room again.

After my parents returned, the family investigations ended, as did the carefree life with the Lodes family. Our school class got a new teacher, named Herr Popp, who had apparently set himself the task of bringing me up to scratch. He enjoyed coming up very close when talking to me: "Now, Wagnerchen, let's just hear what you've been learning." This sentence was the prelude to his interrogations, which always ended in my having nothing left to say. With a malicious grin he would slowly curl the fingers of his right hand into a fist, then belabor the back of my head with it in short, rhythmic blows. "The Wagnerian musical skull sounds hollow yet again," he would say, before finally pulling the hair over my right temple and, to the delight of my classmates, gleefully entering a six in his notebook. Another favorite pastime of Herr Popp's was to recount his experiences as a soldier in the Second World War. "If we Germans had only had a bit more time, we would have been certain of the Final Victory. But the whole world was against us," he would moan.

After one of Popp's attacks I would have severe pains in my head. When I complained at home about his treatment of me, my father called me a crybaby, but he did send my mother to talk to the man, and from then on Popp reminded me only once a week that I had a hollow Wagnerian musical skull.

During this time my father was away from home more often than usual for the festival, and with his production of *Tristan und Isolde* in the summer of 1957 he was scarcely approachable at all. He no longer gave me any introductory information on the works he was directing, so I read the contents of the program instead, understanding little of the story, but gripped by the *Tristan* music as never before. I attended every orchestral rehearsal and performance, under Wolfgang Sawallisch, that I could. Two famous Wagnerian singers, Birgit Nilsson and Wolfgang Windgassen, gave unforgettable performances as Isolde and Tristan.

My grandmother only had time for my father's productions and campaigned against Wieland's work. She constantly tried to play my father off against my uncle, and so the tensions in the family continued to increase. I was not exposed to this strain for long, though: my grades were bad yet again that summer, and because of an allegedly weak heart owing to growth problems, I was sent off to the Schliersee to stay with an elderly couple named Zankl. There were no playmates, but at least I was free of Herr Popp.

In September I came back to the Graser school. My new classmates welcomed me by chanting: "Wagner, Sitzenbleiber, Zeitvertreiber [Wagner, loser, time-waster]!" Their antipathy was coupled with a growing pressure to do well as I now had to prepare myself for the forthcoming entrance examination for the Humanistisches Gymnasium, the classical secondary school. My grandfather, my uncle, and my father had all attended this school, and I was constantly reminded of their example. Frau Moritz, a teacher who appreciated my situation and encouraged me, provided a little relief. It also says much for Frau Moritz that she was obviously uneasy when we had to sing all three verses of the German national anthem. The first verse describes geographic borders that no longer existed for Germany after 1945 and proclaims, "Germany, Germany above all nations": "Deutschland über Alles." The second verse is equally chauvinistic, while the third is about unity, justice, and freedom for the German fatherland. Since 1952, only the last verse has been officially sanctioned in Germany.

Winifred, my grandmother, had returned to the Siegfried Wagner House in 1957, after the Americans had left. I visited her now and again and usually found her in the anteroom to the dining room on the ground floor, sitting at her desk. She would be chain-smoking her unfiltered North States, writing letters or gazing through the open window out to Wahnfried Park. That way she could keep a check on who came in and out. During one of my visits I told her of Frau Moritz's reservations about the first verse of the national anthem. She lost her temper and railed against the school, where they were now apparently starting to tell the children a distorted version of German history.

In July 1958 I found out that I had passed the entrance exam for the Humanistisches Gymnasium, although at first I couldn't quite believe it. Buoyed up by my unexpected success, I sat in on the rehearsals of Wieland's first *Lohengrin* on the Festspielhügel. Just as his *Meistersinger* had, my uncle's new production enthralled me. Whenever I could I watched him at work. When Father noticed my enthusiasm, he forbade me to spend so much time in the Festspielhaus. But that had little effect on me. I would say I was going to the cinema or swimming and instead creep into the Festspielhaus via my secret routes. Wieland understood my situation but didn't comment on it. Once my father suddenly appeared during a lighting rehearsal. He had somehow found out that I hadn't gone swimming, and angrily he asked my uncle if he had seen me. Wieland had spied me shortly before, on the lighting bridge, but he played dumb. Scarcely had my father disappeared in fury when he winked at me with a grin and murmured: "The coast's clear."

This was not our only conspiracy. One day I crept secretly into Wahnfried Park again, waited until Wieland came out of the villa, and then told him how fantastic I thought his *Lohengrin* was. Such naiveté from the other family camp surprised my uncle. He went back into the villa and returned very soon with an envelope, which he pressed into my hand. I didn't dare open it in his presence. When he got into his car I asked him for his autograph. "But I'm your uncle," he replied, astonished. "But we can't ever talk to one another, so at least I'll have something from you," I explained. When I got home, I opened the envelope and found a twenty-mark note in it. I had hoped for a more personal present, but I was still pleased. With the money I bought my first record, a Louis Armstrong LP—"nigger music," as my father and grandmother would say.

After my first exam success I was looking forward to secondary school. But my optimism was soon quelled. I became ill again, and private tutors had to visit me in Bayreuth and Berchtesgaden. It wasn't until April 1959 that I was able to attend the gymnasium.

In the autumn of that year my father started preparations for his first production of *The Ring*, which he intended to put on in the coming season. My mother, as usual, had to give all of her time to my father's great Wagnerian undertaking. My father became more and more of a stranger to me: our holidays together in Braunwald in the Swiss Alps were mainly for our exhausted parents to recover.

On our return from one holiday our enormous schnauzer, Froh, died after a painful death drawn out over months. He had been my companion for twelve years, and I had loved him very much. My father had no sympathy for my tears.

As the 1960 festival approached, my sister and I were once again sent off to Berchtesgaden, this time to the elegant Hotel Geiger. By this time I viewed the festival solely as a threat to domestic peace. A visit to the ruins of Hitler's Berghof on the Obersalzberg left me feeling very oppressed. When I told my father about it, he replied with a positive observation on the architecture of Hitler's Alpine home.

The competition between my father and my uncle lay like a

shadow over my parents' marriage. I became, at the age of thirteen, the mediator of their many disputes. Confronted by the problems of adults, my childhood ended. I found the intrigues of the hostile camps sickening, and yet I was being pulled into them more and more. I tried to be loyal to my father, but his productions excited me far less than Uncle Wieland's.

In the summer of 1961 I opposed my father openly for the first time, protesting against his constant reprimanding of my mother. It ended in a beating for me and an almighty row between my parents. And the conflict had a sequel. My father threatened that he would put me into the strictest school in Germany, to finally make a man of me, little wimp that I was. I answered back defiantly: "Go on then, do it." Promptly a chauffeur delivered me to the boarding school in Stein, near Traunstein. The drive was agony for me, as I was very worried about my mother; she was scared of being alone with my father and cried as I left her. I felt guilty for leaving her to deal with the dueling Wagner brothers and all of my father's demands. She had referred again and again to the festival as "suicidal." Yet in spite of all the family strain, life in the boarding school proved to be far from punishment. I now reaped the benefits of the Bayreuth training, for I was ahead of my new classmates and found myself in the unaccustomed position of being one of the best in the class. Instead of studying diligently, I did everything I was not supposed to do: I smoked, secretly visited girls at night, drank beer, annoyed the teachers, and preferred going swimming to attending class. My only worry was having to go back to Bayreuth.

One day I was surprised by the news that my cousin Wummi was joining the Stein boarding school as well. The everlasting family battle had proved incapable of weakening my affection for Wummi, much to the annoyance of my father, who had kept on running Wummi down. We had many things in common: he too had grown up practically parentless, had changed schools and tutors frequently, and had acquired the reputation in Bayreuth of being stupid and lazy. I hadn't seen him for a long time and was keen to meet him again. He just said, "Hallo, Gottfriedla," and immediately the feeling of belonging together was reawakened. At that time we were convinced that we would one day take over our quarreling fathers' "shop." Despite our shared childhood experiences and dreams of returning together to run the festival as adults, we hardly spoke about our parents and Bayreuth, finding these subjects awkward and painful. But I did confess to him how much I admired his father's work. Wummi was always generous to me and treated me affectionately, like a younger brother. It was a pleasant time, but it ended abruptly—in fact, as soon as my father learned that Wummi was there. Immediately I was brought back to Bayreuth, although I continued to meet Wummi secretly.

My sudden departure from Stein did have one advantage, however, in that I was able to enjoy Wieland's *Tannhäuser* rehearsals. There was a commotion in the Festspielhaus: the beautiful young black singer Grace Bumbry was portraying Venus, and Maurice Béjart created a provocatively erotic choreography for the *Tannhäuser* bacchanale in the Venusberg scene in Act One. The Wagnerian old guard were horrified and declared: "Thank God she's not singing Elisabeth—that's all we'd have needed, a negress singing a Wagner heroine in Bayreuth!"

But that wasn't the only reason for the uproar. Wieland had joined up with the left, verbally supporting East Germany's politics and taking advantage of a West German media whose leftist sympathies were increasing. In the end, Wieland was an opportunistic bystander: leftist politics were good for promoting his image, but certainly he would have hated to live in the GDR. The anticommunist hysteria affected the Society of Friends of Bayreuth too; there was even talk of war. Quite beside herself, my grandmother raged publicly: "How on earth could Wieland join up with those left-wing Jews Bloch and Schadewaldt, of all things? And then Bumbry on top of everything else! Bayreuth is turning into a whorehouse." My father said nothing. At the time I had only vague ideas of what "left," "Jew," and "Negro" meant, but as a secret Wielandian I was angry at my grandmother's intrigue and my father's silence.

After so much freedom in Stein and the excitements on the Festspielhügel, going back to the Bayreuth gymnasium became torture. When a ruptured appendix had me bedbound, my schoolmates accused me of shirking. I was often ill after that and became once again the outsider in my class, especially as my best friend at the time, Tyll Schönemann, had moved to Munich. I developed an aversion to the opinions enforced by bully tactics in my class, and was unwilling to approve of certain teachers just because the majority demanded it. One of the most popular teachers was named Herr Och. On one occasion before Christmas he decided to tell us about his experiences as a soldier in Russia. Sparing us no detail, he raved about the courage of the Nazi army. I dared to criticize Och in front of other classmates, for which they gave me a thorough beating one day.

Though instructed in school by a man who used Christmas as a time to glorify his bloody wartime service to the Nazis, I was fortunately also the student of a more righteous Christian man. In the spring of 1962, after a year's preparatory instruction, I was confirmed by the witty Reverend Flotow. In his positive, kind way he opened my eyes to the splendors of the Bible as a history book, and I owe an awakening of my interest in ethical questions to him. My interest in Christianity became yet another departure from my family's philosophy. My family hardly ever discussed religion outside of the home, but when they did, it was to talk about "stupid priests" and "the bloody church." If pressed to say something positive about religion to the public or their guests, my parents would mention Albert Schweitzer, a man who had had contacts with my grandfather Siegfried. Not even Schweitzer was acceptable to my grandmother, however, who expressed her antagonism toward Christianity more and moe openly. My father called us "pious heathens," in Goethe's sense of the phrase. Meanwhile, I was a religious child, always interested in philosophical questions, and quickly frustrated by my parents' hypocritical religious posturing. In the end, I think, they found religion in the cult of Wagnerian mythology.

In the summer of 1962 Wieland staged an epoch-making new production of *Tristan und Isolde.* The set was strongly influenced by the English sculptor Henry Moore, with a lighting design clearer and more penetrating than ever before. This production in particular illustrated just how wide the artistic gulf was between Wieland and Wolfgang, and my admiration for the creative work of my uncle reached a new pinnacle. Not so my school career, unfortunately: in 1962 I had to repeat the forth level at the gymnasium.

The summer of 1963 was devoted to the 150th anniversary of Richard Wagner. The slogan was "A life for the theater," and Wagner was yet again presented apolitically as a "European genius of the theater"—something of an absurdity, as Wieland had already moved further to the left through his contacts with the Marxist philosopher Ernst Bloch, which provoked some very sarcastic comments during rehearsals. He continued to criticize the Christian Democratic party (CDU) and the Christian Socialist Union (CSU), although this did not prevent him paying court to the ultraconservative Friends of Bayreuth and accepting their financing. The more Wieland played the armchair socialist, the more conservative my father acted. It was only logical that my grandmother regarded him as the true heir of the Wagnerian legacy.

Wieland's second *Meistersinger* production, in 1963, was marked by elements of the Shakespearean stage, comprising a basic set that remained the same throughout, with only minor changes. This concept coincided, of course, with several anti-illusionist elements of the Brechtian stage, such as clearly visible scene changes and mobile screens. There was something else too. In 1960 the very young Anja Silja had made her debut in Bayreuth as Senta in *Der fliegende Holländer*. For Wieland she embodied the ideal of the modern singer-actor. For him she meant, as he so wonderfully and provocatively put it, the end of the "bourgeois singing cow." So it was no surprise that he cast her as Eva in *Meistersinger*—and soon fell in love with her. Whether he got divorced for that reason is something one can only speculate about, since in November 1966 he died suddenly at the age of forty-nine. My father moralized heavily against Anja, who had loosened up the internal climate of the Bayreuth Festival with her loud Berlin accent, sharp remarks, and noisy behavior.

As usual, we were sent away before the festival, but this autumn two important turning points took place in my life. First, my sister, having now finished secondary school, was sent to a domestic science college for young ladies, freeing me from her constant supervision, so I spent much of my time with a warmhearted and cultured Bayreuth family named Grossmann, who together with Gunda had kept an eye on me for years. I used my new freedom most of all, when Father and Mother were on holiday, to hold parties on and over the Festspielhaus stage, which was empty outside the season. I waited for the weekends, when nobody was working in the administration building, and using Father's master key I let my party guests in through the office area, up to a giddy height over the flies into a large room over the circle, which we turned into a dance hall. From there Elvis Presley's "Jailhouse Rock" boomed out so loudly that passersby alerted the police to the noise in the "Woogna Deooda"—"Wagner theater" as tendered in the Upper Franconian dialect. Grandpa Lodes turned up with the police, we hid, and scarcely was the place "fuzz free" when we rocked on.

The beginning of my friendship with Eckart Grebner and Reiner Heller also dates from this time. Together we kept an eye out for pretty girls and played at dares, one of which was to smear red paint over Arno Breker's post-Nazi Richard Wagner bust, which had stood in the Festival Park since 1955. I looked on with relish while the fire brigade cleaned up the menacing monster. My school grades went rapidly downhill.

The other turning point of autumn 1963—one that was to have a long-lasting effect—occurred when my parents were on holiday, recovering from their Bayreuth Festival exertions. I took the chance to explore a wooden shed next to the garage, where Father's heavy BMW motorcycle and sidecar were housed. In the sidecar, in two cardboard boxes, I found a large number of round, aluminum cans of various sizes. They were so rusted that I could not open them with my bare hands, so I secretly conveyed them to my room, got rid of the rust, and prized them open carefully with a screwdriver. In each can there was a reel of film. I took out one of the larger reels and inspected it with a magnifying glass What I discovered left me stunned. I saw my aunts, Uncle Wieland, and my grandmother, Winifred, together with Hitler, who was dressed in an elegant double-breasted suit, laughing as they strolled in Wahnfried Park. Happy Führer, happy Wagner children, happy Grandmother Winifred! Then pictures of the Führer in the Festspielhaus. All arms were outstretched in a "Heil Hitler" salute: Wagner's art and the Führer's power. Strutting members of the Master Race and laughing victors, in premature celebration of the Final Victory. "Uncle Wolf" and the Wagners belonged together—such was the message behind the film. And my father had been the cameraman throughout.

He and Wieland, like the rest of the adult world, suddenly became sinister to me. I remembered pictures of Buchenwald from the cinema newsreels I had seen in 1956, and it became clear to me that I had to keep the films and prevent my father hiding them again or even destroying them, so I hid them away in my wardrobe, covered the empty cans with dirt again, and put them back in the two cardboard boxes in the sidecar. I decided not to tell my parents anything about my find but to question them persistently about Hitler.

The first opportunity presented itself during the winter holidays in Arosa, in Switzerland, in December of that year, on one of the long walks with my parents and my sister. I didn't want to put my father on the defensive, as that would have brought the conversation to an abrupt end. So I emphasized, against my convictions, that I was interested more or less for purely historical reasons in the connection between my family and the Führer. I asked Father what impression Hitler had made on him as a human being. He made no secret of the fact that Uncle Wolf had fascinated him, and described his meetings with him with restrained affection. Later he told me proudly again and again of how the Führer had visited him in the Charité hospital in Berlin, where the famous surgeon Ernst Ferdinand Sauerbruch himself had treated Father after he had been wounded in the Polish campaign. "Your uncle was exempted from war service by Hitler—I alone had to serve the Fatherland," he added, and in detail and with enthusiasm he talked of community service and military training, where a unique camaraderie had developed. He recounted how the only friend in his life, Emil, had been killed in a village by "crafty Polacks" as the "brave German army" had conquered Poland.

And Hitler, again and again! After the National Socialists'
seizure of power a "Führer annex" had been specially built onto
the Siegfried Wagner House, and inside the annex was built the
"Führer fireplace." After a performance of *Götterdämmerung* in
the Festspielhaus, my uncle and Father accepted Hitler's invitation
to a lengthy nighttime discussion at the "Führer fireplace" on the
future of German art in the spirit of Richard Wagner, as an expression of the renewal of the world through National Socialism. I had
some difficulty in understanding my father's torrent of words, but
didn't interrupt for fear of provoking him to break off, and he continued his story. "We were sitting around the fireplace, and Hitler
sketched out for us his cultural visions of the future. 'Once we have
rid the world of the Bolshevik-Jewish conspirators, then you,
Wieland, will run the theater of the West and you, Wolfgang, the
theater of the East.'"

Quietly I asked Father whom he meant by the "Bolshevik-Jewish
conspirators." My interruption annoyed him, and I was worried he
might end the conversation; but instead he launched into German
history. It had all started with the "shameful Versailles treaty,"
which was then followed by mass unemployment in the chaotic
Weimar Republic with the incompetent left and the "bloody liberals." And so he came to the "great achievements of Hitler up to
1939." I wanted to know about this in detail, and Father did not let
me down, answering: "Hitler cured unemployment and restored
worldwide respect for the German economy. He freed our people
from a moral crisis and united all decent forces. We Wagners have
him to thank for the idealistic rescue of the Bayreuth Festival."

"But what about the Jews, Father?"

He replied: "There's a lot of talk about that, and there are a lot
of malicious lies told about us Germans by left-wing intellectuals
about how many and so on. But that was the only real mistake
Hitler made. If he had won over the Jews to his side, we would have
won the war. After the war things would not have got as bad as the
Allies' propaganda machine makes out."

We continued side by side in silence for the rest of the walk, until
my mother started talking about Christmas presents.

It was after our return to Bayreuth in January 1964 that I met Maria Kröll, my first great love. In her were combined the qualities of joie de vivre, mental alertness, and femininity that I found so fascinating, and she wrested me from my isolation in the golden Festspielhaus cage. Because of her I drove regularly to Creussen, thirteen kilometers south of Bayreuth, where she was living with her parents and her younger sister, Dorle, who was in my class. Her father, Professor Joachim Kröll, was extraordinarily gifted in many fields. He taught German, history, and geography at the German Gymnasium and was popular with his pupils, having a quite unconventional manner and teaching methods. Maria's mother, Ursula, was a kindly, intelligent, and cultured woman.

Maria helped me to be more self-confident, and I owe to her parents—active liberal socialists—some essential influences for my intellectual development. The Krölls were keen readers of books on every conceivable subject. I quickly felt at home with these friendly and open people, and woke from my provincial Festspielhügel sleep. Joachim Kröll, the first person to explain German Jewish history to me, also stimulated me to read Heinrich Böll, Günter Grass, and other committed writers. I was full of enthusiasm for my new reading matter.

After such influence I found my parental home, festival business, and the audience unbearable. My father could not fail to notice that I was becoming critical and that my interest in German history and politics was growing, not least because I found myself continuing at home the discussions I'd had at the Krölls'. For example, I applauded the existence of two German states at a time when my father regarded Franz Josef Strauss as the only decent politician: he reacted to my remarks with fury.

The discussion on the GDR's right to exist ended, like many previous discussions, with my father forbidding any further word on the subject, and cursing Joachim Kröll as a "dirty leftie" who was having a bad influence on me. Furious, I stormed out of the dining room, slamming the door behind me. My father tried to catch me up on the stairs, but I was faster than he was, ran to my room, and locked the door behind me. Hammering on the door, he ordered me to open it. I had no such intention. "The only answer you've got is giving me a hiding!" I shouted at him. Then I climbed down a rope ladder from the first floor into the garden and sped off on my moped, cigarette in mouth, to Maria in Creussen.

My father couldn't come to terms with my new attitude and, unbeknownst to me, visited Joachim Kröll to demand that the relationship between Maria and me be broken off. He also wanted to put a stop to Professor Kröll's influence upon my politics. In my father's extremist view, Professor Kröll's liberal influence was responsible for my love affair with Maria, which my father prudishly condemned. Maria later described the clash between our fathers. Fortunately, Professor Kröll was not impressed by my father's views on love or politics and defended Maria and me.

After this episode I threatened to disappear for good if my father interfered in my life or beat me ever again. In fact, one year before this I had disappeared during the night because of another unhappy love affair, and that occasion had become the subject of Bayreuth scandal. This time my father thought up an alternative means of punishing me for my rebellion. At the end of April 1965, against my will, I was taken once again to Stein, to separate me from Maria and her family. My cousin Wummi had passed his *Abitur*—A levels—in Stein, and the new headmaster, Olf Ziegler, was the son of a friend of my grandmother's; thus my father thought the school would be a suitable place for me again.

The pain of parting from the Krölls and in particular from Maria was enormous. And adapting to a life with a lot of people in a small space was difficult. But gradually I made friends with some of my fellow pupils who, like me, turned their backs on the rest of the student body, which comprised the arrogant sons and daughters of "good" and not-so-"good" homes. Most of them came from "economic miracle" families, and their parents either had no time for them, or were divorced, or knew their spoiled offspring were bone idle, ungifted, and would probably never have gotten their *Abitur* in a normal school. Two descendants of the Bismarck family behaved with particular arrogance. Constant quarreling with such insufferable showoffs strengthened my urge to read left-wing literature. A classmate, Henry Hohenemser, helped me to come to terms with my family history, and drew my attention to forms of open and concealed anti-Semitism. It was an important time for me. I started reading the works of Ernst Bloch, Sigmund Freud, Theodor Adorno, Hannah Arendt, Max Horkheimer, and Bruno Bettelheim.

In the 1965 summer vacation I sat in on rehearsals of Wieland's new *Ring*. Although I found the vision of the atomic mushroom at the end of *Götterdämmerung* effective, its style contradicted that of the set, which was oriented toward the world of Henry Moore, and Richard Wagner's music, which certainly does not end in nothingness.

The contrast between the sponsors, the Friends of Bayreuth, and festival guests such as Ernst Bloch and Hans Mayer, the distinguished literary historian, became even clearer to me. And even my uncle's halo started to fade. Wieland hardly knew where to draw the line in his relations with his colleagues. Once during a rehearsal he clouted the electrician of the Festspielhaus, his former playmate, on the head, in front of everybody, because he allegedly or actually had not meticulously carried out Wieland's imperious demands. This, coupled with other events, led me to believe that Wieland had not really overcome his own past, tacking back and forth between

Krupp and Siemens on the one hand and Bloch and Mayer on the other. In my eyes he became more and more opportunistic, leaning to the left because he vaguely realized that the balance of power in the culture business was tending in that direction.

I returned to the Stein boarding school after the summer vacation and absorbed myself in the early writings of Karl Marx, in particular his essay "On the Jewish Question," in which he argues that for Jews to attain political emancipation in the liberal state, they must first attain human emancipation, liberating themselves from the bonds of their essentially materialist religion. Later, when I brought up my reading matter in a discussion with my father, he resorted as usual to a monologue, starting off with the 1935 race laws, which the Jews had themselves to blame for, as they had been "the worst racists in history." I ventured to counter this by saying that you couldn't confuse the Nuremberg race laws with Orthodox Jewish traditions. Angrily my father retorted that Jews had themselves made an essential contribution to the Nuremberg race laws: "Marx himself was an anti-Semite and wanted to emancipate society from Judaism." "But scarcely the Final Solution," I answered. That ended the discussion.

In the 1966 local elections in Bayreuth, when the neo-Nazis won three of the forty-two city council seats, my grandmother's hopes for a "Final Victory" were reawakened. Aunt Friedelind was furious when my grandmother slowly started to emerge again as First Lady and received as guests political friends such as Edda Göring and Ilse Hess; the then NPD chairman, Adolf von Thadden; Gerdy Troost, the wife of the Nazi architect and Hitler friend Paul Ludwig Troost; the British fascist leader Oswald Mosley; the Nazi film director Karl Ritter (related to the Wagners); and the racist author and former senator for culture under the Reich Hans Severus Ziegler. At her receptions one could "finally" talk openly about the Führer again, having been forced to refer to him in code as "USA." Rightly, in a *Spiegel* interview in December 1967, Friedelind criticized the return of "fascist demons."

In July 1966, shortly before the festival season, Wieland was admitted to the hospital in Kulmbach and was later transferred to the

University Clinic in Munich. My father did not inform me of my
uncle's state of health, but like others I suspected that the matter
was serious. Now open warfare broke out between the Wieland and
Wolfgang camps, the latter believing their man's hour had come. In
the Wieland camp the first cracks appeared. Some toyed with the
idea of changing sides, and my father enjoyed a sudden syco-
phancy. Quite unexpectedly he was now the sole director of the festival, at least for that year. Even I was now greeted with friendly
words by people who had ignored me until then. The Wolfgangs
were in, the Wielands were out, and I found the new situation just
as repugnant as the old one. Bayreuth, the Festspielhügel, the family, and the whole shebang just made me feel sick. I toyed with the
idea of leaving Germany. But how, without money and without a
profession?

On 17 October, while I was watching the film *The Spy Who
Came in from the Cold*, I was informed that my uncle was dying. I
hitchhiked to Munich, and there my father embraced me for the
first and last time in his life. Not a word was spoken. Mother informed me of Wieland's death with tears in her eyes.

I shall never forget the funeral ceremony. Held in the Festspielhaus on 21 October 1966, it was a demonstration of superlative
hypocrisy. Grandmother Winifred burst into tears—for her poor
Wolfgang, "Wolf," who would now have to bear the responsibility
for the Bayreuth Festival all on his own. Meanwhile, high society
suddenly discovered its love for Wieland. The only bright spot was
Ernst Bloch's address.

Flashlights popped and cameras whirred as the long procession
moved off to the cemetery, and almost immediately, the power relations began vying for position. My father, my grandmother, and
my sister, Eva, held the best cards.

During the following winter holidays with my family in Arosa,
the discussion came around to an open letter written by Günter
Grass, the Polish-born author of Germany's postwar conscience, in
which he warned against the formation of a grand coalition—"that
bad marriage"—in Bonn, "which will see the youth of our country
entrenched into left and right positions." My father was horrified

by my "lurch to the left" and attributed it, not without reason to my reading matter of the time—Bertrand Russell, Erich Fromm, Karl Jaspers. He complained bitterly about my ingratitude for all the sacrifices he had made for my education in a boarding school such as Stein. Were it not for my mother, I would have packed my bags; but it was Christmas, after all.

I also refrained from telling him about my grandmother's reaction to my choice of Christmas present. I had asked her to give me Bloch's book *The Principle of Hope.* She replied: "I'm not giving you any of that left-wing Jewish trash." I answered that from now on she could strike me off her Christmas-present list: her Nazi attitude was incompatible with my principles. I was to get a few more paybacks for that comment.

3

The Will to Power I

In 1967 my father began to alter beyond recognition. While the festival had always been the central focus of family life, it now became an obsession for him. He began by eliminating the Wielandians, except for those who vowed allegiance to him. As a consequence, Wieland's productions were overshadowed by those of my father. Realizing that the pressure of sole responsibility for the festival and the stress of the final battle on the Festspielhügel were threatening to damage our relationship even further, he allowed me to attend the school in Stein as a day pupil.

During this time my friendship began with Dietrich Hahn, and that friendship continues until this day. He is a man with an unusual literary gift, who is interested in contemporary art, painting, and who originally had wanted to be an actor. Grandson of the famous radiochemist and Nobel Prize–winner Otto Hahn, he had suffered greatly from losing both parents in a traffic accident, after which he was fostered by the Kalkhoff-Roses, a family of industrialists who supported Helmut Kohl. He felt ill at ease in their home, and vacations were always something of a problem for him. I sometimes invited him to Bayreuth. Having worked in the theater for only a short time he, like me, was soon disgusted by its superficiality and hierarchy.

He then started, as a journalist specializing in the history of science, working through his grandfather's considerable posthumous works and making these universally available. What particularly drew us together was an interest in humanitarian activities and German-Jewish history. Both of us now view our boarding-school time in Stein without any rosy glow.

It was while we were both day pupils that another life opened up for me. Forbidden reading matter was followed by forbidden activities: namely, disrupting NPD meetings in Upper Bavaria with my friends Norbert and Henry. Norbert and I carefully planned our escape routes before turning up at neo-Nazi meetings disguised as Charlie Chaplin's Great Dictator. Merely walking through the beerhalls in our costumes was enough to goad the mob, at which point we would run off like hunted hares and leap into Henry's ancient VW Beetle, waiting for us with the engine running.

At that time I was no longer capable of integration in the Stein school, despite a regime that was almost liberal by Bavarian standards, and so I left. The chorus master of the Bayreuth Festival, Wilhelm Pitz, interceded for me in June with Charles Spencer, the chairman of the renowned New Philharmonia Chorus in London. It was to be a stay that was to steer my life in a decisive direction.

The Spencer family gave me a warm welcome. I took full advantage of what was offered in concerts and opera that season and attended a language school daily to improve my English. I was thrilled to be living right near the Beatles' studio. Charles Spencer, a successful choir manager and businessman, was a keen music-lover and a discerning Wagnerian, and we often conversed jokingly in Wagner quotations.

This idyll was abruptly broken off by a political event of world importance: the Six-Day War between Israel and the Arab countries in June 1967. More violently than ever before I was confronted by Jewish history. Anxiously we sat in front of the television. Day and night we passionately discussed the events, during which I discovered that Charles's parents had been Viennese Jews. In 1938, after the Anschluss of Austria to Hitler's Germany, they fell victim to the Nazi terror. Charles and his sister escaped. Charles's daughter Diana told me further shocking details while we were looking at family photos. There I was, a child of criminals, living like a son in a family that had suffered terribly under Nazi barbarism. Charles noticed my embarrassment and shame. I confessed how oppressive I found the Bayreuth legacy with its anti-Semitism and told him about my Grandmother's fanatical racism. He said: "Only after the generation of the perpetrators will there perhaps be hope for a new beginning between Jews and Germans. But that will not prevent the possibility of friendships between individual Germans and Jews. Don't feel guilty, but learn from your family's mistakes." This wise advice from my "elective relation" was to be a motto for life.

Charles had an exemplary influence on me. Despite tragedy, he lived without enmity and hatred, and with quiet modesty he helped people in need as he went about his daily life. During my stay I watched a television program with contributions from many countries, including a report from Germany on the opening of the 1967 festival with *Lohengrin* in my father's new staging. I felt remote from everything connected with Bayreuth and Wagner, and was relieved when, after the usual boring excerpts from the Bayreuth stage, there came a Beatles song. During a telephone call, I told my mother that I did not intend to return to Germany for some time: she understood, and Charles supported me when I decided to live in France for a while.

But before that I did visit Bayreuth briefly. With amazement I noted how my father was acting as the man holding the reins, and my sister, who had just finished training as a kindergarten teacher, was playing the lady boss. My father only tolerated yes men around him, and any form of criticism, especially of his *Lohengrin* production, made him aggressive—tacitly, Wieland's epoch-making *Lohengrin* of 1958 was the yardstick. Contrary to my convictions, I did not voice an opinion on the new Festspielhügel dictatorship for fear of damaging my relationship with my father even further. Grandmother Winifred and the chorus of right-wing old Wagnerians rejoiced at the beginning of a new era. I was glad when I could finally leave for Paris.

I was overcome by Paris just as I had been by London. Overnight I changed from an Englishman into a Frenchman. I would have loved to deny my German roots, but I gave myself away by my accent, of which I was often reminded with a certain arrogance. Much of my time I spent on language courses at the Sorbonne and the Alliance Française, although I didn't actually learn much there, as I spoke mostly in English with my fellow students. In the sixth arrondissement, where I lived near the jardin du Luxembourg, I often went walking, visiting museums and, at night, the lively and disreputable Les Halles. My aunt Blandine de Prévaux, a great-granddaughter of Franz Liszt, took touching care of her *cousin allemand.* She lived in an elegant apartment on the Seine, with portraits of her great-grandfather, the future father-in-law of Richard Wagner, hanging on the walls. I knew hardly anything about the Austro-Hungarian composer, piano virtuoso, and promoter of Wagner's music. My father rated him just as low as Uncle Wieland.

Aunt Blandine told me that the Nazis had murdered her husband, a resistance fighter. She did so without reproach. After that our talks became open, and we overcame the generation gap between the barely twenty-year-old nephew and the seventy-three-year-old aunt. I owe to her not only initial critical introductions to Liszt's work and biography, but also the stimulus to learn something of French painting and literature. She mentioned her cousin Winifred only in passing, but made fun of her lack of education in subtle hints.

In the middle of July Blandine's daughter Daniela invited me to Lessey in Normandy, where she lived in a castle. There I got to know her daughter, also called Blandine, my age, who fascinated me with her open opposition to the world of her parents. After a brief exchange of civilities we recognized at once that in all essential matters we had similar views and that in the few points we didn't agree on we found the difference an enrichment. Cousin Blandine told me a lot about her contact with the film director Jean-Luc Godard, of *Breathless* fame, and about the radical democratic circles she frequented. For whole nights we discussed how our depraved world order could be changed. She argued passionately, fought social injustice, had courage, and formulated her sociopolitical ideas in an admirably creative yet concrete way. This close intellectual relationship, which still continues today, has only peripherally to do with Wagner and Liszt. How musty the Wagner cult on the Festspielhügel seemed compared with all this! But once again it got me in its grip as school beckoned. I avoided conflict with my father, knowing his insecurity. He was still far from comfortable with his role as sole ruler and often suffered from severe criticism by the media.

In the autumn of 1967 I had to repeat twelfth grade because of my long absence. I wanted to get school over with now as quickly as possible, and in a bearable way. I assured the headmaster at Stein that I would keep up an acceptable standard of achievement if, in exchange, he agreed to allow me to organize my presence in the classroom "more freely." That meant, among other things, that I went to Prague and Budapest with Henry Hohenemser, where we sent postcards to the teachers whose classes we had cut. But the excursions were not just tourist jaunts. When we crossed the heavily guarded border between East and West we felt the breath of world politics. The Vietnam War and the student unrest in West Berlin and Paris occupied our thoughts and dominated our discussions. At home I defended the students' positions, to the horror of my father and my sister as well, who was looking for her niche on the side of the establishment.

In the hot political summer of 1968 my father staged the premiere of his *Meistersinger* production, which, after Wieland's stagings of 1956 and 1963, I found unbearably conventional. My grandmother and the majority of the mostly uncultured bourgeois sponsors were thrilled that *Die Meistersinger von Nürnberg* was finally being staged again as it had been in the good old days. I restrained myself from commenting on my father's artistic achievement, but reacted passionately to any glorification of the Nazi past, after which my grandmother introduced me to her "terribly decent circles" with the phrase: "This is Gottfried, the friend of Bolsheviks and Jews." Then she would give a loud and manly laugh.

Before the opening of the festival a police contingent arrived, armed as if prepared to counter terrorists intending to blow up the

Festspielhaus and its first-night audience. In fact it was just a few harmless students protesting against the West German industrialists among the festival guests. When I saw the police using violence against the protesters, I swore at them as "pigs," and only the fact that I was the boss's son saved me from arrest.

After the premiere there was the usual reception in the Neues Schloss. Demonstrators had gathered there as well. Although I wasn't welcome at the reception, I sat down at Willy Brandt's table. At that time the only German politician I respected was Brandt, the Social Democratic party's chairman, who then was serving as the country's foreign minister and vice-chancellor of the coalition in Bonn. In an effort to boost their careers, Bayreuth Social Democratic bigwigs fawned over their chairman and grew nervous when some members of the ballet openly sympathized with the protesting students. Alarm grew when they started asking Brandt uncomfortable questions on contemporary world politics, on Vietnam and Rudi Dutschke, the leader of the Socialist German Student Federations (SDS). Brandt, on the other hand, remained unflappable: he invited the protesters to his table and debated with them, to the horror of the Bayreuth establishment and the invited guests, including sponsors, who, like my grandmother, referred among themselves to the Social Democratic head as a "socialist pig" or "Willy Weinbrand"—Willy Brandy. My father voiced no opinion on this. I took that as acquiescence.

Although I didn't want to go to Arosa that winter with the rest of the family for the Christmas holidays, I finally obliged for my mother's sake, since she missed me now that I was mostly at school. My father complained bitterly about my alleged communist worldview: he criticized my political opinions as infantile, and reminded me of the great sacrifices of his youth, the things he had had to do without during and after the war and his struggle to build up the festival. He said he had put a lot of money into my education and now had to put up with his own son demonstrating as a "parlor pinko" against the very people who financed the Bayreuth Festival and consequently his own life. My answer was heartfelt and uncontrolled: "You and your bloody ideals from the past! I'm talking here about the criminal war in Vietnam. It's about time you finally took part in a demo instead of serving as supplier of luxuries to an inhuman international bourgeoisie!"

At the beginning of 1969 I finally understood that the *Abitur* was my key to personal freedom, and began intensively studying for the final exams. I was particularly interested in German-Jewish authors of the Weimar Republic, so to the consternation of my German teacher, Herr Grutter, I chose Arnold Zweig's novel *Der Streit um den Sergeanten Grischa* as my essay topic. In the era of the Vietnam War, I was interested in the book's antiwar themes and Zweig's way of revealing the bourgeois capitalist society as the cause of the war. Zweig's example of protest was also pivotal in my personal journey away from my family's anti-Semitism. In the journal *Weltbühne* in 1930 Zweig wrote about his novel: "How, I ask, does one refute a system, a social order and the war, which is difficult to conceive as not being connected with it? By letting off steam with passionate counter-actions and producing caricatures? In my opinion one refutes a system by showing what its level best might perpetrate, how it forces the average decent person to act indecently. . . . We don't want to expose villains like our friend Schiller, but systems."[3] Just to provoke, I told first my grandmother and then my father of my decision. Grandmother was indignant: "Left-wing Jews—how can you do this to us?!" Father's reaction was once again eloquent silence.

Around this time I heard talk at family meetings of some planned "Festspielhaus Foundation charter." I wanted to know more about it. Father kept emphasizing that this was all in my interest as well and was for the sake of my future too. He mentioned one article of this charter that set down the rules for my succession if I could provide evidence of the appropriate qualifications. I found this vague information worrying, especially as I was wondering how I could attain my chosen profession once I had completed my *Abitur* and left secondary school. I wanted to work in the theater as an assistant director, but my father had quite different plans: he wanted me to study law so that one day I could join the festival business as manager.

Only my mother came to the *Abitur* graduation ceremony at Stein; my father claimed he was indispensable in the Festspiel-hügel. When I got back to Bayreuth, I found much had changed. The troop of yes men had grown bigger, and their servility, even to me, the boss's son, was disgusting. Opportunism ruled. And a lot of them had an eye out for signs of the times, picking up on long-lasting changes in the political and cultural climate. The 1968 re-volts had broken down many outdated structures. West Germany's socialist-liberal coalition under Willy Brandt was just around the corner; it was soon to prove courageously democratic, and more open to our Eastern neighbors. But already in the time of the grand coalition there had been clear signals that the mood of the country was altering. Times were changing, and gradually the ideological spectrum was shifting to the left in the cultural world too. If you didn't want to find yourself an outsider, you had to shift your ideas. In particular, the head of the press department of the festival, Her-bert Barth, tried in an adroit and cautious way to convince my fa-ther that a moderate move to the left was now necessary.

But my father was still dedicated to the old Bayreuth style. In 1969 he hired August Everding as the first non-Wagner to direct *Der fliegende Holländer* for the festival, knowing that Everding would do nothing innovative. Only the gossip was new. To my sur-prise, this monotonous production aroused enthusiasm among most Bayreuth sponsors and Wagner societies.

Meanwhile, my grandmother had lost any tact she once had. The American conductor Lorin Maazel had led operas in Bayreuth in 1968 and 1969 and had been hired for the 1970 season. At one of her receptions in the Siegfried Wagner House, Grandmother Winifred declared, to the amusement of her guests: "Although Maazel is a Jew, he does seem to be quite gifted. So in spite of everything Wolf will engage him again next year." I was sitting next to Maazel and his wife and wanted to die of shame. Maazel ap-peared not to have heard this remark, or perhaps he didn't want to hear it. In 1970 he cancelled because of illness.

The official press reports of the 1970 season were mixed. The media, especially in the artistic world, had moved too far left to

applaud Bayreuth's nearsightedness. My father was forced to recognize these changes in order to secure the festival—and himself—
financially.

In the autumn of 1969 I yielded to pressure from my father and
started law studies at the University of Munich. But I also used the
time to attend lectures in the humanities, which interested me very
much. In the semester break in October I visited my parents in
Bayreuth. At that time they were reading Albert Speer's memoirs.
Speer had been Hitler's architect; together with the Führer, he had
designed bombastic buildings which were to be constructed after
the Final Victory. During the war, Hitler had appointed him head
of war production, and it was in this capacity that Speer saw to it
that, among other things, Nazi Germany was able to prolong the
war and therefore the system of terror. Speer understood how to
construct a technically perfect exploitation of the masses, using a
complex bureaucracy as his tool. In the Nuremberg war crimes tri-
als he was sentenced to twenty years' imprisonment, which he
served in Berlin's Spandau prison, using the time to write his book
of self-justification. He died in 1981.

Father quite openly expressed his sympathy for Speer, who had
repeatedly voiced his admiration for Hitler. This provoked a fresh
quarrel between us, which continued throughout the winter holidays in Arosa. As always when we were not of the same opinion, I
was forced to hear how I was too immature to understand the tragic
and martyred history of Germany. The atmosphere worsened when
I applauded the change of government in Bonn: Brandt had become federal chancellor, which was unbearable for my father, who
consequently suspected left-wing plots everywhere.

As it was, Father was in a *Götterdämmerung* mood. The reviews
of his 1970 *Ring*, discussions on the future course of the festival
and on the projected foundation, had all worn him down. I advised
him to just drop the whole bloody festival and finally make a decent life for himself, without his band of toadies, and without playing the entertainer of German high society. My suggestion was not
destined to improve the atmosphere.

My sister found such discussions pointless. Quite coolly she started to get friendly with Everding and to safeguard her future in Bayreuth, was supported by Grandma Winifred. She was soon the darling of influential sponsors and industrialists and was of one mind with Father, regarding everything I suggested as worthless, and integrating herself fully into the festival business. From time to time she was allowed to play directorial assistant to Everding and Otto Schenk. By these means she discovered that the international opera business was destined to be her profession; and her future, the intendant's seat in Bayreuth. Anyone who did not stay on her good side had a difficult or a short life on the Festspielhügel until 1975. The maxim advocated by Wieland that "after Cosima and Winifred, never again a female dictatorship," no longer applied.

Father and Eva found my way of life quite unreasonable: a left-wing idealist, absorbed in contemporary philosophy, psychology, and politics—in other words, totally unworldly things that were a waste of time. Eva shared our grandmother's opinion that there was no place in the Festspielhügel for Marxist crackpots like me, a label I was never to lose. Even then she knew that it would earn her the applause of the Society of Friends of Bayreuth.

My father's 1970 Bayreuth *Ring,* which was only a technical improvement on his previous cycles, contributed nothing new and relied solely on previous productions. Men at Bayreuth who opposed my father were able to manipulate the media adroitly and show how unreceptive he was to criticism of any kind. The only people whom my father still tolerated on the Festspielhügel were those who submitted to his authoritarian rule, a leadership he presented to the outside world as liberal. Anyone who praised the artist Wolfgang Wagner earned privileges.

But the real masterstroke of Bayreuth power politics came with the discovery of a "left wing" Wagner, one the cultural media would embrace, just in time for the festival's centenary season. I noticed with some unease how the marketing of Bayreuth for the 1976 centenary celebrations had a left-wing image grafted on. The architects of this shift were Herbert Barth, the head of the press department; the writer and Wagner devotee Martin Gregor-Dellin, appointed together with Dietrich Mack as editor of Cosima Wagner's diaries;

Egon Voss, later the editor of the new Richard Wagner complete critical edition; Dorothea Glatt-Behr; and, later, also Oswald Georg Bauer, today general secretary of the Bavarian Academy of Fine Arts.

A typical example of this deliberate shift to the left was Dietrich Mack's essay "The Tragedy of Power," based on his conversations with my father about the interpretation of *The Ring*, in the *Rheingold* program from 1970. There I read to my amazement, among other things:

> Does this mean afterwards [at the end of *Götterdammerung*] an apotheosis, a salvation of the world, a certainty of salvation or does it mean an apocalypse, a total annihilation; an optimistic tragedy or total·tragedy [*Pantragismus*]? . . . [It is rather] not a handing on of the legacy, not a continuous transition from one generation to the next, but a radical break, tabula rasa, smoking ruins. So is it the apocalypse? Yes, but as example, not as end in itself; for two things have been added. People, who . . . have been demagogically abused with alcohol and drugs to become a dull and stupid mass, experience this inferno. They fall prey to lamentation and horror [sic]. Enlightenment must be brutal, the world must burn from one end to the other. One funeral pyre alone is not enough to achieve a cathartic effect. Knowledge of this terrible end must be attested to and the realization handed on, so that perhaps a way can be found out of this void."[4]

No trace of all these atrocities was to be seen on the stage, though. What Father meant by the break between generations, I only understood later: unconsciously he had woven his own family problem into his directorial concept.

Under these circumstances I had no intention of becoming Father's assistant, especially as Eva was making it clearer and clearer that my presence on the Festspielhügel was a nuisance. To avoid such tensions and intrigues, in the autumn of 1970 I moved to Mainz, where I finally began studying what interested me: musicology, psychology, and German literature. My father was against these new studies and could be placated only by my promising not to give up my law studies completely. He asked the musicologist Professor Gernot Gruber to keep a discreet eye on me and tried to find out from him whether I even had the prerequisites for this study. Gruber told me of my father's reservations, and relations between my father and myself were jeopardized once again.

In Mainz I took piano lessons in addition to my other studies. In the summer semester of 1971 I studied piano, counterpoint, and harmony in Graz, Austria, and then in the Festspielhaus with Maximilian Kojetinsky. I went about this thoroughly and astounded my father, who never had believed that I could pursue my self-chosen studies with such dedication.

The rumor arose that I would soon be taken on board in the festival business. Eva vehemently denied this. Rather defiantly, I declared that on the basis of my progress with Kojetinsky I would continue studying musicology. Gernot Gruber supported me in this resolve, and finally my father agreed to my giving up the loathsome law studies.

In the summer of 1971 I learned from Mother that one of Wieland's closest collaborators, Gerhard Helwig, had been fired. On 7 August 1971 Helwig handed over to my father all the documentation he possessed from the Wieland period. Father voiced doubts on the completeness of these documents. Such events increasingly aroused my interest in my family history and at the same time a mistrust of the official methods of dealing with family documents.

In the winter semester of 1971–72 I continued my studies at the university in Erlangen and started looking for openings as an assistant director. The university disappointed me; I found both the style and the content of the music classes too conservative. Students and teachers alike treated me like a museum piece who might prove useful for making a few contacts. The teaching of the psychology lecturers dealt solely with formal analyses. I felt equally uncomfortable in the theater studies department. Although I could get along with the heads, I found a lot of the students ideologically too fixated—stragglers of the 1968 generation. Anyone who was

not as "progressively Marxist" as they were—in other words, anyone who did not embrace their specific viewpoint—was quickly
branded a reactionary, no matter how sincerely Marxist the person
was. As Bertolt Brecht already fascinated me at that time, I attended a course on his theater work and so initially was ranked
among the progressive forces. When the student guardians of pure-
left doctrine found out who I was, though, they wouldn't believe my
interest in Brecht: how could the reactionary Wagner be compatible
with the progressive Brecht? So yet again I was relegated to being
an outsider. But I regarded Erlangen merely as a stopgap, a place
to get the necessary papers, and then to continue my nomadic life
elsewhere.

The urge to do practical theater work continued to grow, and in
the autumn of 1971 I had contacted Hans Peter Lehmann, chief director of the Nuremberg opera house. Lehmann had been one of
Wieland's assistant directors, and my father had appointed him to
preserve some of my uncle's still existent productions for the
Bayreuth Festival. However, he was somewhat torn: on the one
hand, he was very affectionately attached to Wieland's legacy; on
the other hand, he followed my father, who was in favor of modify-
ing Wieland's works—for example, by making the lighting brighter.
Either way, for Lehmann it was certainly of advantage to foster the
connection with Bayreuth.

I believed at the time that he was interested in my professional
development as an opera director. At first everything went as I
wanted it to, and in February 1972 I was finally able to begin my
first assistant directorship with Lehmann, in Wuppertal on his
Tannhäuser production. I threw myself into the work with great
enthusiasm: keeping the prompt book; looking after rehearsals
with the second cast; planning rehearsals; making arrangements
with soloists, chorus, orchestra, technicians, administration, and,
last but not least, the media. I realized how difficult it must have
been to have been Wieland Wagner's assistant. After his death the
shadow of his great example lay over any Wagner production.

After the premiere Lehmann attested in writing that I had done good work. Despite this, I didn't get any further engagement from him when I was in difficulties and looking for work.

It was not far from Erlangen to Bayreuth, and I visited my parents on weekends now and again. For the *Tannhäuser* of the 1972 festival my father had engaged the opera director Götz Friedrich, who had been Walter Felsenstein's assistant at the Komische Oper in East Berlin and had earned an excellent reputation. So there were no grounds for argument where content was concerned. I hoped that the Everding episode with the 1969 *Flying Dutchman* had been a one-time mistake and that my father would give up his own directing efforts. I wanted him instead to attract distinguished people from other houses to Bayreuth. Only in the case of Chéreau were my wishes partly fulfilled.

The peace between my father and me lasted only a short time. It ended when the talk turned to Willy Brandt's *Ostpolitik*, which would open West German politics and economy to greater cooperation with the East. I didn't see any alternative to this, whereas my father described the policy of détente as a sellout of German interests.

I also visited my grandmother during these weekends, mainly to learn more about her and her years with the Führer. Although she knew my "radical left" attitude, most of the time she answered my questions quite frankly, describing such things as Hitler's wonderful, bright, hypnotic eyes, his gentleness, his good manners, his charm, his love for Father and Wieland, his plans for the boys in the future of a "better Germany," his profound knowledge of Wagner's works, his love of nature and of mankind.

Here I interrupted the flow and asked her about love of mankind in the case of the Jews. She replied: "You still don't know the Jews. Just wait. One day you'll understand me, and Hitler will be seen differently in world history." Her reaction was reminiscent of Father's.

At first in these discussions I made the mistake of reacting to her monstrous statements. "How can you say things like that! Six million Jews don't seem to be enough for you to stop kidding yourself!" But she constantly defended herself with the same sentence: "That's just lies and slander from American Jews!"

What I had more or less uncritically accepted as a nine-year-old who didn't understand, I now, at twenty-five, wanted to know in detail. My grandmother's anti-Semitism was shockingly brutal. I asked her about the fate of Jewish singers who had performed in Bayreuth before the Nazi takeover and later had to emigrate or were murdered in concentration camps, such as Henriette Gottlieb, Ottilie Metzger-Lattermann, Margarethe Matzenauer, Hermann Weil, Alexander Kipnis, Eva Liebenberg, Friedrich Schorr, and Emanuel List. At such moments she found herself caught out in her lying and became particularly aggressive. "You can't understand that. That wasn't Hitler at all, it was Schleicher and the other criminals who betrayed National Socialism. I always tried to help the Jews who sang in Bayreuth!" she screamed. I countered: "So you and the family did know about Auschwitz!"

This ended the discussion. Anyway, she had not shrunk from a blatant distortion of the historical truth in order to maintain her view of history: General Kurt von Schleicher had been murdered by the Nazis in 1934, and so he could not have had anything to do with the Holocaust. My grandmother meant Julius Streicher, the founder of the inflammatory anti-Semitic paper *Der Stürmer*.

No longer satisfied with this type of information, I decided to change my tactics and, remaining calm, acted as though I were a historian without personal involvement. It worked. Grandmother answered my questions and, more important, instructed her confidante Gertrud Strobel, a militant anti-Semite, to give me historical material without my father's knowledge. Gertrud Strobel—who, amazingly, did not see through my intentions—now regarded me as the only thoroughly decent Wagner and provided me with a wealth of documents. This included all the *Bayreuther Blätter*, festival programs, and other documents from the period from 1850 to 1944. I was particularly fascinated by the correspondence among Hitler, my grandmother, Wieland, and Father. The more I read, the more horrified I became: I could never have suspected the scale of my family's involvement in the Nazi tyranny.

4

The Anti-Semitism of the Wagner Family, 1850–1945

The starting point for discussion on Richard Wagner's anti-Semitism is a long essay, published in 1850, entitled *The Jews in Music*. Predominantly ideological, it is based on Wagner's pathological idea of the Jews as the enemy. This is for him the negative keystone to the future political and artistic concept that lies at the basis of the idea of the festival and its realization in Bayreuth. In order to defame the imaginary Jewish enemy and develop his counterconcept, Wagner resorts in *The Jews in Music* to disgusting abuse:

> The Jew is repulsive. . . . He rules and will continue to rule as long as money remains the power before which all deeds and actions must needs pale into insignificance. . . . In ordinary life the Jew, who, as we know, has a God unto himself, strikes us first and foremost by his outward appearance which, no matter which European nationality he belongs to, has something about it which is foreign to that nationality and which we find insuperably unpleasant. . . . The Jew, incapable in himself of communicating artistically with us by means of his outward appearance or language, and least of all through his singing, has none the less come to dominate public taste in the most widely disseminated of modern artistic genres, music. . . . The Jew has never had an art of his own, and therefore never

led a life that was capable of sustaining art. . . . We are bound to describe the period of Judaism in modern music as one of total uncreativity and degenerate anti-progressiveness.[5]

After a denigration of Felix Mendelssohn, Wagner concludes his diatribe with an appeal that sounds like a heralding of what was to begin scarcely ninety years later: "Join unreservedly in this self-destructive and bloody battle, and we shall all be united and indivisible! But bear in mind that one thing alone can redeem you from the curse that weighs upon you, the redemption of Ahasuerus: Destruction!"

Wagner's outbursts against his "enemies" Felix Mendelssohn and Giacomo Meyerbeer, without whose efforts Wagner's stage works are unthinkable, display disgraceful aggressiveness. He owed to his onetime supporter Meyerbeer essential elements of the musical dramaturgy of his early works and to Mendelssohn a decisive influence on melody and instrumentation. In *The Jews in Music* Wagner willfully blurs essential foreign influences on his artistic development. Herein lies a central motive for his pathological anti-Semitism, which runs like a red thread through all the composer's writings up to 1882.

The Jews in Music is by no means the end, as was later asserted in Bayreuth, but the beginning of Wagner's anti-Semitism in the sense of a politico-cultural concept. He repeats the ideas of his first anti-Semitic pamphlet, scarcely altered, in his key work on the theory of art of 1851, *Opera and Drama*. Later Wagner relativized his revolutionary art theory in order not to distance himself too much from the taste of the bourgeoisie. But his anti-Semitism remained and was expressed in particular in the writings *On State and Religion* (1864), *What Is German?* (1865/78), *German Art and Politics* (1867), right up to the regeneration pieces (1879-81). "Regeneration" was, for Wagner, a strongly moral argument, based on racial evolutionary theory, for the restoration of the German Aryan race to its ancient state of heroism and purity—free from degenerative Jewish blood. Influenced by the fascist philosopher Arthur Gobineau, Wagner's anti-Semitism increased. At the end of the regeneration essay "Know Yourself" in *Religion and Art* (1881) Wagner formulated ideas that today read like a horrifying anticipation of Hitler's Final Solution, invoking a Germany free of Jews as the "great solution": "And the very stimulus of the present movement—conceivable among ourselves alone—might bring this great solution within reach of us Germans, rather than of any other nation, if only we would boldly take that 'know thyself' and apply it to the inmost quick of our existence. That we have nought to fear from ultimate knowledge, if we but conquer all false shame and quarry deep enough, we hope the anxious may have called from the above."[6]

Wagner's attitude toward the Jews kept changing, for obvious reasons. He even claimed to admire them if he considered it useful for carrying through his ideological-political and artistic goals. But from 1850 on, every enemy of his art, irrespective of birth, was "an artistic Jew."

The Jews in Music provoked strong protests and also influenced many later reviewers of Wagner's operas and writings. His anti-Semitic writings read like a constant exchange of attack and counterattack between himself and the music critics of his time. Here Wagner loses sight of the development of European Jewry in the second half of the nineteenth century and therefore increasingly too his sense of reality and humanity. So Wagner's art, in spite of all the brilliant innovations manifested in his first works staged in the Bayreuth Festspielhaus—*The Ring* and *Parsifal*—also became anti-Jewish, or antiart, and the Festspielhaus an anti-Jewish, anti-culture establishment, completely in tune with the "Report on the Festspielhaus in Bayreuth" of 1873. In it Wagner compares his German "new European theater, taste and morals . . . to a Parisian whore or a successful stock market speculator"—an allusion to Meyerbeer's operas. So he tacitly refers back to his essay *What Is German?* and the second edition of *The Jews in Music*, which appeared in 1869. The circle closes here that Wagner had already begun to forge in 1850: the idea of the festival was realized as the Bayreuth Festival, which very soon had a propaganda effect all over Germany. Added to this were the Wagner Societies springing up everywhere, that appeared in the German-nationalistic *Bayreuther Blätter*. From the beginning of the festival, then, anti-Semitism and

racism were among the ingredients of the Bayreuth opera undertaking, whether implicit or explicit. Wagner's anti-Semitism was
closely connected to this.

Some of Wagner's writings—in particular *Modern* of 1878, *Public and Popularity* of 1879, and the reprint of *What Is German?* of
1878—encouraged other anti-Semitic, chauvinistic authors in their
efforts to align German culture according to the standards of the
Bayreuth shrine. How much the thinking of the bourgeois Richard
Wagner influenced his art is shown in the stage works he realized at
his Bayreuth Festival from 1876 to 1882 as director and theater
impresario. Who is portrayed by Alberich and Mime, the dwarfish
exploiters, and Hagen in *The Ring*, Beckmesser in *Die Meistersinger*, and Klingsor and Kundry, the female Ahasuerus figure, in
Parsifal? If we look at Kundry's baptism in Act Three of *Parsifal* in
connection with the regeneration writings, we understand how serious Wagner was about the conversion of the Jews to Christianity
already demanded in *The Jews in Music*. The abovementioned
"great solution" of 1881, on the other hand, is realized on stage in
the dramaturgically superfluous and therefore ideologically eloquent death of Kundry at the end of *Parsifal*.

Just as Wagner admits different interpretations in his works of art,
so he seduces his followers in his regeneration writings to his new
Christianity—a philosophy he largely borrowed from the philoso-
phers Arthur Schopenhauer and Friedrich Nietzsche. The result is
a confused blend of anti-Semitism, antifeminism, and Buddhism.
To quote from Nietzsche's *Human, All Too Human* of 1878:

> In regard of knowledge of truths, the artist possesses a weaker
> morality than the thinker; he does not wish to be deprived of
> the glittering, profound interpretations of life and guards
> against simple and sober methods and results. He appears to
> be fighting on behalf of the greater dignity and significance of
> man; in reality he refuses to give up the presuppositions which
> are most efficacious for his art, that is to say the fantastic,
> mythical, uncertain, extreme, the sense for the symbolical, the
> over-estimation of the person, the belief in something miracu-

lous in genius: he thus considers the perpetuation of his mode
of creation more important than scientific devotion to the true
in any form, however plainly this may appear.[7]

Cosima—Liszt's daughter, Richard Wagner's second wife, and
director of the festival until 1907—was no less anti-Semitic than
her husband. Evidence of this is offered *inter alia* by an entry in
her diary of 18 December 1881, in which she records a conversation she had with Richard:

Then he tells me about a recent performance of [Lessing's]
Nathan [*der Weise*] at which, when the line asserting that
Christ was also a Jew was spoken, an Israelite in the audience
cried: "Bravo!" He reproaches Lessing for this piece of insi-
pidity and when I reply that the play seems to me to contain a
peculiarly German kind of humanity, he says: "But not a trace
of profundity." . . . One adds fuel to these fellows' arrogance
by having anything at all to do with them, and we, for example, do not talk of our feelings about those Jews in the theatre
in front of Rub[instein], 400 unbaptised and probably 500
baptised ones.[8]

The attitude of Richard and Cosima Wagner expressed in such
remarks was to have its effect far beyond their deaths. This quotation from Cosima's diaries sums up in a few sentences what was to
form the Bayreuth tradition until 1945. Take, for example, the
writings of Cosima's son-in-law, the English racial theoretician
Houston Stewart Chamberlain, one of Adolf Hitler's mentors. A
quotation from Chamberlain's 1895 biography of Richard Wagner
substantiates the enduring effect of Wagner's anti-Semitism:

At the beginning of [*The Jews in Music*] Wagner tells us that
his purpose is: "to explain the unconscious feeling which in
the people takes the form of a deep-rooted antipathy to the
Jewish nature, to express therefore in plain language something really existing, not at all by force of imagination to in-

fuse life into a thing unreal in itself." And how was this really existing thing to be removed? How was the baneful yawning abyss to be bridged over? Wagner points to the regeneration of the human race, and to the Jews he says: "Bear your share undauntedly in this work of redemption, gaining new birth by self-immolation; we shall then be one and undivided! But remember that there can only be release from the curse, which rests upon you: the release of Ahasuerus—destruction." What he means by destruction is evident from an earlier sentence: "to become men in common with us is, for the Jews, primarily the same thing as to cease to be Jews."[9]

A direct line runs from Chamberlain to Hitler, whom he revered from the very beginning. On 7 October 1923, Chamberlain wrote to the future Führer:

Dear Herr Hitler
. . . You are not at all, as you have been described to me, a fanatic, rather I would like to describe you as the direct opposite of a fanatic. The fanatic heats heads, you warm hearts. The fanatic wants to persuade, you want to convince, only convince—and that is why you are successful; yes, I would likewise define you as the opposite of a politician . . . for the axis of all politics is membership of a party, whereas in your case all parties disappear, consumed in the fire of love for the fatherland. . . . You have tasks requiring tremendous force before you, but in spite of your strength of will I do not consider you a man of force. You know Goethe's distinction between force and force! There is a force that originates from chaos and leads to chaos, and there is a force whose essence it is to form the cosmos, and of the latter he said: "Ruling, it takes on any shape—and even in the great it is not force." I mean it in this cosmos-building sense when I say I want you to be listed among the ranks of the uplifting, not the forceful men. . . . My belief in Germanness has not wavered for a moment, but my hopes—I admit it—had reached a low ebb. At a

stroke you have transformed the state of my soul. That Germany in the hour of its deepest need has borne a Hitler, that attests to its vitality; likewise the effects emanating from him; for these two things—personality and its effect—belong together. That the great Ludendorff openly allies himself with you and joins the movement emanating from you: what a splendid confirmation! I could calmly fall asleep and would not even need to wake up again. May God protect you![10]

In 1915 Richard Wagner's son, Siegfried, my grandfather, married Winifred Williams. She held Hitler in just as high esteem as her brother-in-law Chamberlain, as documented, for example, in her "Open Letter" of 14 November 1923 in the Bayreuth *Oberfrankische Zeitung*—that is, only a few days after Hitler's attempted putsch in Munich:

The whole of Bayreuth knows that we have a friendly relationship with Adolf Hitler. We happened to be in Munich in those momentous days and were the first ones to come back from there. Understandably, Hitler's followers turned to us for information from eye witnesses. . . . For years we have been following with the greatest inner sympathy and approval the uplifting work of Adolf Hitler, this German man who, filled with ardent love for his fatherland, is sacrificing his life for his idea of a purified, united, national greater Germany, who has set himself the hazardous task of opening the eyes of the working class to the enemy within and to Marxism and its consequences, who as no other has managed to bring people together in brotherly reconciliation, has been able to do away with the almost insuperable class hatred, who has restored to thousands upon thousands of despairing people the joyous hope of a reviving, dignified fatherland and a firm belief in it. His personality has made on us too, as anyone who comes into contact with him, a deep, moving impression, and we have understood how such a simple, physically delicate man is capable of exercising such power. This power is founded on the moral strength and purity of this man, who without ceasing stands up for an idea he has seen to be right, which he is trying with the fervour and humility of divine vocation to realise. Such a man, who is standing up so directly for good, must inspire, electrify people, animate them with selfless love and devotion for his person. I freely admit that we too are under the spell of this personality, that we too, who stood by him in happy days, will remain faithful to him now too in his hour of need.[11]

From 1907 to 1930 Siegfried Wagner ran the Bayreuth Festival. He too corresponded with Hitler. But Siegfried Wagner's anti-Semitism was not as extreme as his wife's or his mother's. On 6 June 1921, for example, still quite uninfluenced by the later pro-Hitler atmosphere in Bayreuth, he wrote to an anti-Semitic editor of the *Deutsche Zeitung* in Berlin: "Among the Jews we have very many faithful, honest and selfless supporters who have given us countless proofs of their friendship. You want us to close our doors to all these people, to rebuff them for the sole reason that they are Jews. Is that humane? Is that Christian? Is that German? No! . . . On our Festspielhügel we want to produce positive, not negative work. Whether a person is Chinese, Negro, American Indian or Jew is totally immaterial to us. But we could learn from the Jews how to stick together and help one another."[12]

This letter was used after the Nazi period as a pseudo-liberal alibi for the Bayreuth Festival in order to be able to present the period from 1907 to 1930 in the light of the pure art of Richard Wagner. The extant documents of the period from 1925 to Siegfried Wagner's death show, however, that even in the 1920s Richard Wagner's work was serving politico-cultural ends on the Festspielhügel. In his letter of Christmas 1923, only a few weeks after Hitler's failed November putsch in Munich, Siegfried wrote to Rosa Eidam:

We got to know that splendid man [Hitler] here in the summer at the German Rally and remain true to him even if it should mean our going to prison. We were never timeservers here in Wahnfried. The situation in Bavaria is appalling. The times of the Spanish Inquisition have returned. Perjury and betrayal are sanctified, and Jew and Jesuit are working hand in glove to exterminate Germanness! But perhaps Satan has miscalculated this time. Should the German cause really succumb, then I'll believe in Jehova, the god of revenge and hatred. My wife is fighting like a lioness for Hitler—first rate![13]

It is in the light of this that Hitler's letter to Siegfried of 5 May 1924 becomes clear too. Recalling his official visit to Bayreuth on the occasion of the Deutsche Tage rally on 30 September 1923, aimed at a future electoral victory, and regarding the Wagner family's open support of him, Hitler says: "I was filled with proud joy when I saw the people's victory in the very city in which, first through the Master [Richard Wagner] and then through Chamberlain, the spiritual sword was forged with which we are fighting today."[14] Comparing Richard Wagner's and Chamberlain's inflammatory anti-Semitic writings with Hitler's racist politico-cultural ravings in *Mein Kampf* leaves no doubt of their historical connection.

The fact that Siegfried Wagner, his wife, and his sisters took over the honorary presidency of the national Bavarian Federation of German Youth (BBdJ) on 1 August 1923 further enhances the historical connection. The BBdJ set as future objectives "to convey the ideas of Bayreuth, the artistic works and politico-cultural ideals of Richard Wagner, to the whole of the German people; to reveal the profound sense of the direct bond between the great German memoir [*Mein Kampf*] of Adolf Hitler and his cultural will and the work of Bayreuth."[15]

Closely connected with the national stock of ideas and the Bayreuth Festival was the Deutsche Festspiele in Weimar in July 1926, in which operas staged by Siegfried Wagner were performed and national poetry published, by, among others, Hans von Wolzogen, editor of the anti-Semitic and nationalist *Bayreuther Blätter* from 1878 to 1938. The Weimar festival was, like the Bayreuth Festival, an aggressive politico-cultural counterconcept to the avant-garde art of the Weimar Republic. With the founding of the National Socialist Society for German Culture in 1927 and the

Militant League for German Culture (Kampfbund für deutsche Kultur) in 1928 by Alfred Rosenberg, the semiofficial National Socialist philosopher and author of the propaganda work *The Myth of the Twentieth Century*; the leading Nazis Hans Frank, Baldur von Schirach, Wilhelm Frick, Hans Severus Ziegler, Hans Schemm, and Adolf Bartels, as well as others, were won over to the Bayreuth cause. As son of the Master and cultural inspiration for Hitler as much as through his wife Winifred's party membership since 1923—confirmed by the Canadian Wagner scholar Philip Wults—Siegfried Wagner could play outwardly the role of the nonpartisan artist, but enjoy all the advantages of the pre–National Socialist nationalist movement.

Shortly before his death in June 1930, Siegfried Wagner had invited Arturo Toscanini to Bayreuth. Toscanini was a man who throughout his life had doggedly seen only the artist in Wagner, and his two seasons in Bayreuth were cited repeatedly after 1945 as exonerative proof that Siegfried Wagner had opened up to other cultural trends. Quite how Siegfried Wagner would have survived in the Third Reich is pure speculation today; his homosexuality rendered him decadent in the eyes of Hitler and his propaganda minister, Joseph Goebbels.

After Siegfried Wagner, my grandmother Winifred ran the festival until 1944. Her belief in Hitler's Final Victory is evident from a contribution by her to the *Meistersinger* program of the wartime festival of 1943:

> If during the wartime festival in 1943 *Die Meistersinger von Nürnberg* is presented, then that has a deep and symbolic meaning. For this work shows us in the most impressive way the creative German man in his nationally conditioned will to create, to which the Master gave immortal form in the figure of the Nuremberg shoemaker and national poet Hans Sachs and which, in the present struggle of the Western cultural world against the destructive spirit of the plutocratic-bolshevist world conspiracy, gives our soldiers invincible fighting strength and a fanatical belief in the victory of our arms."[16]

_____

5

The Will to Power II

My investigation into my family's Nazi past was interrupted in February 1972 by my first stint as assistant director in Wuppertal. After my experiences
with *Tannhäuser* there, I was keen to see how Götz Friedrich would
direct that opera for the festival; so in April 1972, a few months before his debut in Bayreuth, I visited him in East Berlin. He explained his concept to me and I was thrilled. Afterward Friedrich
invited me to a performance of the Berliner Ensemble's *Coriolanus*,
which turned out to be disappointing: sterile in its production and
robotic acting.

I used the time after Berlin to continue conversations with my
grandmother and Gertrud Strobel. My father didn't like this at all.
Grandmother had faithfully reported to him my great interest in
Bayreuth's political past, my numerous questions and note taking.
Father was particularly on edge during these months regarding
anything to do with the festival, Hitler, and the Wagner family: he
wanted to carry through his Foundation charter and avoid any ir-
ritation that could prejudice this great undertaking. Consequently
I had to be even more careful in my investigations. Frau Strobel in-
formed me with horror of the left-wing musicologists of the
Thyssen Foundation, who were constantly pestering her concerning the great 1976 jubilee. I later learned she meant Egon Voss,
Dietrich Mack, and Michael Karbaum, of whom I was to have per-

sonal experience. The Thyssen Foundation supported these and other authors financially, and they were now working on the project of the festival's centenary.

In July 1972 the dress rehearsal for Götz Friedrich's *Tannhäuser* took place in Bayreuth. Friedrich had not raised my expectations in East Berlin in vain. I was fascinated in particular with how he handled the soloists and the chorus in Act Two. I expected an uproar at the premiere when the Wartburg guests, clothed in dinner jackets and evening dress, greeted the Landgraf with raised-arm "Heil Hitler!" salutes and later tried to evict Tannhäuser from the Wartburg Nazi-style. Grandmother Winifred put pressure on my father to prevent this production from being performed unaltered, but I urged my father to let Friedrich work in peace. It says much for my father that he exercised restraint.

As it happened, there was indeed a furor at the premiere, not in reaction to Act Two, but because of the epilogue, which I had found rather tame. The chorus, dressed in out-of-place leisure clothing, announced as a message for universal rejoicing that Tannhäuser was now redeemed. The majority of the audience misunderstood the final scene as a leftist "worker-and-peasant greeting" devised by the East German director, Friedrich. They screamed out their hatred as fanatically as their predecessors a few decades before had cheered the Führer. The cause of such hysterical aggression was clear: Friedrich had held up a mirror to the audience, and quite unconsciously, many of the ladies and gentlemen from the land of the "economic miracle" had recognized themselves in the Wartburg society. The fascistoid behavior acted out on stage by the singers was repeated after the premiere in real life in the auditorium.

I too got mixed up in one of these violent scenes as Friedrich came to take his bow in front of the curtain. A gentleman standing next to me, a member of the Society of Friends of Bayreuth, shouted: "Go back to your dirty Communists in the GDR, we don't need you here!" The members of the audience around us agreed enthusiastically. I asked the heckler his name, but he didn't want to tell me. "Who are you, anyway, to ask me my name here in the Festspielhaus?" he asked. Furious, I retorted: "You coward hiding here in a group! Have the courage of your convictions! Who are you?"

Scarcely had I said this when he grabbed me roughly by the neck. He evidently wanted to tear off my bow tie and would probably have beaten me up. Realizing that it might be to my advantage to introduce myself, I said: "My name is Gottfried Wagner. I am the son of the director of the festival, who fully backed this splendid production. You are still on the private property of my family, and I shall take you to court for disturbance of the peace and bodily harm. Now come to the police with me." I had hardly finished speaking when this friend of Wagner fled from the theater. My behavior was to have repercussions a few days later, when one of the audience wrote to my father to complain about my "left-wing radicalism."

There was more controversy after the premiere. Ewald Hilger, president of the Society of Friends of Bayreuth, together with his retinue, was outraged by Friedrich's production. Hilger, who had succeeded his father—an influential gentleman of West German society and a patron of Arno Breker, Hitler's favorite sculptor—to this office, advised the festival administration and on that evening lost control of himself, attacking my father for having engaged Friedrich. Father scarcely defended himself. As Hilger's attacks got cruder, my mother and I intervened. She jumped up, pointed to the door, and shouted so loudly that the whole room fell silent: "Now that's enough! Stop insulting my husband like that. The Friends of Bayreuth have no right to dictate their opinions to my husband and us." She continued to stand pointing her finger until Hilger, deeply offended, rushed from the room, not before threatening: "This will have consequences!" It had no consequences. Father and he were soon bosom friends again.

I was thrilled by Mother's action. But all around us the atmosphere was icy, a foretaste of what my mother and I were later to experience frequently. Even the "left-wing vanguard" around Herbert Barth, the press spokesman of the festival, cautiously withdrew. Only a handful of people came to say a few words of appreciation to Mother; my sister and my father remained awkwardly silent. But seldom had Mother and I been so close as we were on that evening. The next morning my father asked for more restraint. Such an opinion made me very concerned, as I was convinced that Mother and I were fighting for the right cause. All these lies—and later, too, the opportunistic changes in the *Tannhäuser* production—disgusted me.

My father found himself so much under fire that he started questioning the final scene of Act Three. That sparked off a violent quarrel between us, as I was against any change and sacrifice of artistic freedom, just because the sponsors had set their minds on not being able to live with Friedrich's production. I told Father of the incident in the auditorium and he seemed to want to reconsider his decision yet again. But he finally gave in, and the second performance had to make do without the alleged worker-and-peasant greeting. This lame compromise satisfied the Society of Friends of Bayreuth, but I felt it to be a cowardly concession.

The reaction of bourgeois society, especially of Franz Josef Strauss, who had publicly pronounced himself vehemently against Götz Friedrich's staging and was negotiating with my father on the Foundation charter, hurt my father and probably contributed to him distancing himself from Friedrich's final scene. The liberal and left-wing press, which at first had only applauded, now voiced some doubts as well. The new and old endings were passionately discussed. Bayreuth had overnight not only been retheatricalized [*retheatralisiert*], as Friedrich put it, but publicly repoliticized. The fronts between right, liberal, and left, blurred since 1951 by Wieland's apolitical, psychoanalytical stagings, became clear again.

The era of the "left-wing Richard Wagner" had now well and truly dawned. The fanatical majority of the premiere audience was made insecure by such public debate, and before expressing any further opinions they waited for the reviews of Joachim Kaiser and other well-known Wagner experts in order then to repeat the critics' remarks, even if these strongly diverged from the opinions they had held in the auditorium shortly before. It was imperative to remain "in." Many Wagner friends who were in a quandary about what to think went to my grandmother for comfort and advice. She declared: "I think the *Tannhäuser* of this Communist Friedrich repulsive as well, but think of my son—he can make mistakes too, and he's already started altering the worst scenes. Our Bayreuth is still our Bayreuth! It just makes Wolf's great artistic gifts even more obvious!" A short time later the same ladies and gentlemen who had found Winifred's judgment so wise were to be in close cahoots with "wicked" Friedrich. "Fine friends," commented Grandmother, disappointed.

Father continued to be publicly abused. At the annual meeting of the Society of Friends of Bayreuth the members objected to being limited to supporting the festival financially; they also wanted a say over the content as well. The attitude of the majority of the sponsors regarding the *Tannhäuser* premiere in July 1972 reminded me of Nietzsche's comments in the epilogue to his essay *The Case of Wagner:*

One pays heavily for being one of Wagner's disciples. Let us take the measure of this discipleship by considering its cultural effects. Whom did this movement bring to the fore? What did it breed and multiply?—Above all, the presumption of the layman, the art-idiot. That kind now organizes associations, wants its "taste" to prevail, wants to play the judge in *rebus musicis et musicantibus* [matters of music and musicians]. Secondly: an ever growing indifference against all severe, noble, conscientious training in the service of art; all this is to be replaced by faith in genius or, to speak plainly, by impudent dilettantism (—the formula for this is to be found in the *Meistersinger*). Thirdly and worst of all: *theatrocracy*— the nonsense of a faith in the *precedence* of the theater, in the right of the theater to *lord it* over the arts, over art.

But one should tell the Wagnerians a hundred times to their faces *what* the theater is: always only *beneath* art, always only something secondary, something made cruder, something twisted tendentiously, mendaciously, for the sake of the masses. Wagner, too, did not change anything in this respect. Bayreuth is a large-scale opera—and not even *good* opera.—

The theater is a form of demolatry [worship of the people] in matters of taste; the theater is a revolt of the masses, a plebiscite *against* good taste.—*This is precisely what is proved by the case of Wagner:* he won the crowd, he corrupted taste, he spoiled even our taste for opera![17]

In the winter semester 1972–73 in Erlangen I suddenly became popular in the theater studies department. The institute had organized a Richard Wagner Music Theater Seminar, and I had invited my lecturers and fellow students to the dress rehearsal of *Tannhäuser*. Wagner was mistakenly identified as a pioneer of socialism in 1848, analogous to the assessment of Wagner in East German musicology, with Werner Wolf in the forefront, although he could not quite manage without the old Wagnerian Gertrud Strobel in the Bayreuth archives department. Authors such as Ernst Bloch, Martin Gregor-Dellin, Hans Mayer, and Walter Jens were quite indiscriminately numbered among left-wing Wagner interpreters in the Erlangen seminars. At my instigation, the dramaturge of the Bayreuth Festival, and at that time a close adviser of my father's, Dietrich Mack, was invited.

On my fleeting visits to Bayreuth I was careful not to say anything about my researches into the Nazi past of our family, and I also still kept secret from my father my meetings with Gertrud Strobel. Claiming that I had to prepare for a Wagner seminar at the university, I now stepped up my investigations in the Siegfried Wagner House. I can still clearly remember hearing my father complaining during one of my visits that "the situation" with Gertrud Strobel could no longer be tolerated: she persisted in passing on material that concerned only the family and that especially now, so soon before the signing of the Foundation charter, should not be made public.

Cautiously, I asked Father what material he meant.

"All those private letters between Hitler and Grandmother, and other things that have nothing to do with politics and the family. If the lefties from the Thyssen Foundation get hold of them, there'll be hell to pay!"

I retorted calmly, albeit not very diplomatically: "Everything should come out in the open, otherwise there will never be a fresh beginning!" My unreasonable demands infuriated Father. I remained silent, afraid that he might possibly remember his films from the Nazi period, which I had hidden. In fact, for fear of being discovered I occasionally checked to see whether he had taken the empty film cans out of the sidecar.

In May 1973 I took a job as assistant director with Götz Friedrich in Amsterdam and now had to combine practical theater work and studies while making sure that my exam deadlines were not missed. I had been following everything that was happening in music theater with the greatest attention. Hence my trip in mid-April with Dietrich Mack, at the invitation of the city of Leipzig, to the premiere of a *Rheingold* directed by Joachim Herz and designed by Rudolf Heinrich. The staging was based on Bernard Shaw, who had interpreted *The Ring* in connection with the early capitalism of the nineteenth century: Alberich and Wotan were swindling bourgeois businessmen locked in a deadly competitive struggle for world domination. Having seen so much noncommittal abstraction in my father's stagings, I was thrilled by such a strong narrative and interpretation. Herz and Heinrich created a model staging on which many directors were later to base their own, including Patrice Chéreau in his 1976 *Ring*.

Leipzig, Richard Wagner's birthplace, was a great contrast to this epoch-making *Rheingold* staging. The bleakness of the gray daily routine and the omnipresence of the security police depressed me. I wanted to know more about life in the GDR, but real discussion on social or political questions never got going. Instead, people took refuge in hints or bitter jokes which I could not find funny. For example: "[Communist Party leader Erich] Honecker spoke in our theater. Then the set fell down and killed him." Scarcely had Rudolf Heinrich's father finished the last sentence when everyone else burst out laughing while I waited in vain for the punch line. I was compensated a little by finds in secondhand-book shops: I discovered wonderful first editions of books from the "bad old" feudal and bourgeois days. They were dirt cheap compared with prices at home. I bought not just valuable old tomes, such as the famous Gotha peerage guide of 1863, but also, just as cheaply, GDR literature on Brecht and Weill.

On the way back, Dietrich Mack and I discussed the GDR. Like many left-wingers of the time, he defended the social achievements of the system, which I on the other hand rejected as too high a price to pay for the loss of autonomy. When we reached the border my opinion was confirmed: with German thoroughness a GDR border guard searched my VW Beetle, and, of course, he found the Gotha.

"Why did you buy this book?" he asked.

I replied: "I'm interested in German history."

"Why are you interested in German history?"

"Because I'm a German." I almost started laughing, which annoyed the guard. In the end I got fed up and introduced myself, informed the good man of my invitation by the city of Leipzig, and said I was going to be making a report of this journey as a journalist. At this, the dour man in uniform turned into a thoroughly polite human being who let us pass through the border without further ado.

Scarcely had we reached the Bavarian side when the game started all over again, this time on behalf of the West Germans. The border guard discovered the GDR literature during his inspection and found it offensive. This time I cut the procedure short and repeated what I had told his GDR colleague. Here too I experienced a wonderful transformation within seconds. The border guard begged for festival tickets. He didn't get any.

After such trips I felt ill at ease with my German nationality, so I was glad when in May I was able to go to Amsterdam to work with Friedrich at the Théâtre Carré. The opera was *Aïda,* and Friedrich depicted Giuseppe Verdi's opera as a violent political thriller, in which love comes into mortal conflict with the state. Unfortunately, the compelling concept was realized on a rather kitschy set, so that I was enthusiastic only about the directing. I worked like a slave twelve hours a day: my feet fled from the sheer amount of rushing between stage and auditorium—a situation that Friedrich, who tended to be a bit of a tyrant, found quite in order.

I learned much from him about my chosen profession. His keen intellect was coupled with wide-ranging imagination; his directing of both principals and chorus was of great intensity; and his theoretical passion gave me ideas for my own theater work. But I subsequently refused invitations to work with him, as I didn't want to become the eternal student of one master.

Two events remain particularly memorable from that hectic period. Friedrich was used to behaving in an authoritarian way—a hangover from his background in the GDR—and dealt with the chorus like a German army sergeant would deal with his troops. One day a representative of the chorus came to Friedrich and me and said: "We are familiar with this tone from the time of the German occupation, and we are not prepared to put up with it." Friedrich dismissed this out of hand, and the atmosphere abruptly worsened. I urged him to give in, which he finally did.

The next day I had my first *Aïda* rehearsal on my own. My enviable task was to select twenty slave girls out of eighty auditionees—beautiful dark-skinned girls from the former Dutch colonies—and to rehearse with them the scene from Act Two in Amneris's apartments. So there I stood, poor fool, surrounded by all these splendid flower girls, feeling like Parsifal in Klingsor's magic garden. I would have loved to engage them all. After I made my decision I had to instruct the chosen beauties in their tasks in Amneris's chamber. They were only supposed to serve as decorative framework for Amneris, and if need be comb her hair, adorn her, wave palm fronds, or just lie seductively on cushions; but still, I insisted on frequent rehearsals with my slave girls.

As it happened, however, I fell in love with the conductor's sister. Edo de Waart had generously offered me accommodation in his spacious home, and it was here that I got to know Manja. She had a finely formed oval face and an irresistibly sunny smile. We floated hand in hand through nocturnal Amsterdam, visiting the notorious area around the railway station and all the important museums. She taught me, with a combination of charm and knowledge, everything one ought to know about Dutch history, in particular the German occupation in the last war, and about Dutch painting and music. A gifted viola player, she was by no means interested only in the world of the arts. After a visit to the Anne Frank House I felt ashamed to be German, but Manja brought me back to the present, saying in her attractive Dutch accent: "Our generation has to make it better!" She was right. It was difficult for me to say goodbye to her when the time came to return to Germany.

In summer of 1973 I informed my father that as a result of my studies in Erlangen, I intended to write my thesis on the contemporary music theater of Kurt Weill and Bertolt Brecht. Brecht and Weill were the most notable opponents of Wagner and his Bayreuth shrine, and when Father realized that my choice was not for purely musicological reasons, his comment was cutting: "Can't you think of anything better than this honky-tonk music?" I was furious: "'Pirate Jenny' is a thousand times preferable to the whole phony bourgeois Wagnerian redemption shit!" It would probably have been better if I had kept silent, as Father had one of his fits of blind temper and left the dining room. With a certain relish I also brought the ill tidings to my grandmother. She reacted calmly and bluntly, as I had expected her to: "So you're getting mixed up with the Jews, even with the left-wingers! That your father has to do it in these Jew-ridden times I can understand to a certain extent—but you? The wheel of history will turn for us again, I'm sure!" I interrupted her with: "Maybe Wieland was right after all—you still believe in the Final Victory!"

The only person to encourage me to stick with Brecht and Weill was my friend Eberhard Wagner, editor of the *East Franconian Dictionary* at the Bavarian Academy of Sciences, a committed dialect poet, playwright, and novelist, and today the second chairman of the Bayreuth Studio Theater. I had gotten to know him in Erlangen, and he always proved one of my few genuine friends in Bayreuth.

6

The Richard Wagner Foundation

In May 1973 the founding charter of the Richard Wagner Foundation of Bayreuth was signed. Representing the family were my grandmother, my aunts Friedelind and Verena, my father, and the children of Uncle Wieland. I was indignant at the time that I had not been informed of the content of the document before the signing and that I was not invited to be one of the signatories. Although I had insisted on learning more, I discovered the content of the founding charter only from a superficial account of it by Martin Gregor-Dellin in the *Meistersinger* program of the 1973 festival. It wasn't until four years later that I received the complete text of the foundation document from the Wieland children's lawyer. Of its fourteen paragraphs the second, sixth, and eighth concern me particularly. In paragraph 6 the foundation council is defined. According to this, the members' votes were distributed—before the deaths of my grandmother and Aunt Friedelind—as follows: Federal Republic of Germany, five votes; Free State of Bavaria, five votes; Wagner family, five votes; City of Bayreuth, two votes; Society of Friends of Bayreuth, one vote; Upper Franconia Foundation, two votes; Region of Upper Franconia, two votes; Bavarian Land Foundation, two votes.[18]

Paragraph 8 entrusted to this heterogeneous foundation council, which was only partially capable of making judgments in artistic and cultural matters, decisions on the artistic suitability of a potential successor as director of the festival. This would appear to satisfy certain minimum democratic requirements, were it not for the second and third clauses, which state:

> The Festspielhaus shall in principle be let to a member—if applicable, several members—of the Wagner family, or to another entrepreneur should a member—if applicable, several members—of the Wagner family run the festival. This shall not apply only if other, more suitable applicants come forward. With the majority of their votes in the foundation council the descendants of Richard Wagner may make proposals. As soon as it is determined that the contract with a festival entrepreneur has ended or will end, the foundation shall indicate to the representatives of the Wagner family in the foundation council the possibility of making a proposal. . . . Should the foundation council entertain doubts on whether or not a member of the Wagner family is better than, or just as qualified for, the position of festival entrepreneur as any other applicant, then the foundation council shall seek a decision of a three-person committee of experts. This committee shall consist of the intendants of opera houses from German-speaking regions, whereby the intendants shall be consulted in the order of the hereinafter named opera houses: Deutsche Oper Berlin, Bayerische Staatsoper Munich, Staatsoper Vienna, Staatsoper Hamburg, Staatsoper Stuttgart, Städtische Oper Frankfurt-am-Main, Städtische Oper Cologne. [19]

This also sounded sensible, but in practice it is difficult to realize. So it is not much more than a question of taste whether or to what extent a member of the family, or another applicant, is suitable to run the festival. Furthermore, in view of the historical development of the family, one cannot automatically assume that they will agree on one or more candidates. This should be sufficiently clear from what I have already related. It is also a question of how far the members of the two boards—the foundation council and, secondarily, the committee of experts—are able and willing to judge objectively. Nevertheless, the intendants in the committee had to at least consider the possible question of nonfamily applicants for the post of director of the festival.

Yet if all this—which sounds so sensible—is examined in toto, it becomes clear that it leaves the door wide open to despotism. Unwearyingly, my father has for years publicly written off every member of the family (excluding himself, of course) as unsuitable.

I consider paragraph 2 equally dubious. In it, in connection with the joint will and testament of Siegfried and Winifred Wagner of 8 March 1929, the following four points are named as being the purpose of the Foundation:

1. To preserve the artistic legacy of Richard Wagner in perpetuity for the public good;
2. To maintain the Bayreuth Festspielhaus in perpetuity for the public good and make it accessible and constantly subservient to the purposes for which its founder intended, that is, solely for the solemn performance of the works of Richard Wagner;
3. To promote Richard Wagner research;
4. To promote understanding of the works of Richard Wagner in particular among young people and the younger generation of artists.[20]

Richard Wagner's legacy should be understood basically not only in purely artistic terms but also as a politico-cultural legacy. Out of the tragic history of the Bayreuth festival a special responsibility has arisen in dealing with this legacy. But the present purpose of the foundation denies and represses the possibility of dealing in the future with questions such as Wagner-Hitler and its consequences in a critical and unbiased way. One could counter this by saying that the Wagner research mentioned in point 3 would guarantee this. However, since in point 1 only the "artistic legacy" is mentioned, the generosity of point 3 is hogwash. From the legal point of view there are certainly no objections to point 2, but it does indicate how little the compilers of the provisions have learned from history. For to focus the festival solely on Richard Wagner precludes any end to the Wagner cult, the horrifying consequences of which have already been shown in the past. In order to counteract a monoculture focused solely on Wagner, the existing concept of the festival should be broadened:

1. All Wagner's works, including his early operas, symphonies, chamber music, and Lieder, should be performed in the Festspielhaus, as they would make the various artistic influences on Wagner clear and capable of being materially experienced.
2. The works of those artists who had a particularly long-lasting effect on Wagner should be offered within the framework of the festival. This would bring about a considerable broadening of the artistic horizon.
3. All his life Richard Wagner emphasized the open, provisional nature of his concept of the festival. In this sense, contemporary representatives of all forms of art—with the emphasis changing from year to year—should receive a regular opportunity to present themselves to the public.

These three points would also lead to the long-overdue alteration in the structure of the audiences. Or, to put it another way, the festival would then, in the spirit of Richard Wagner, exist not only for the "upper ten thousand," but would have a broad, democratic effect in keeping with the modern world.

Such a program is rendered impossible, however, by paragraph 2, which makes me and my proposals, as a cosmopolitan interested in the multiplicity of human culture, sound like an unworldly Utopian. I could live with that if the Foundation charter did not, according to its own logic, force me into a dual role: on the one hand, I belong through membership in my family to the "circle of candidates" for the succession; on the other hand, I could conform to the demands of paragraph 2 of the articles only if I were prepared, in everything I do, to comply with the articles' monocultural claims. My personal involvement in the succession discussion is fictitious, yet it has nevertheless proved a serious obstacle to the development of my careers as a director and a music journalist. Apparently a Wagner should be able to be a trustee of Richard Wagner only if he keeps strictly to the Foundation charter. The dilemma I face is that by suggesting any changes, I lay myself open to charges of personal ambition, no matter how ludicrous those charges are within the context of my life.

7

The Will to Power III

In the autumn of 1973 I enrolled at the University of Vienna, where I had Professor Otmar Wessely as my doctoral supervisor and Professor Gernot Gruber to oversee my dissertation. They both helped me a great deal with my doctoral thesis on Weill and Brecht, and I was pleased to have escaped the intrigues of Bayreuth. The university library was rich in materials, both for my studies and for my research into the history of the Bayreuth festival during the Nazi period. I also spent a lot of time at the music publishing house Universal Edition, where my passionate interest in Weill and Brecht caused much headshaking. I was addressed in Austrian fashion as "Herr Doktor Wagner," which I found amusing. If the subject of Kurl Weill came up, again and again a covert anti-Semitism came to light. Many Viennese claimed they had had nothing to do with the Nazis—in their eyes the Germans had annexed Austria by force. So there was nothing to come to terms with. "But Herr Doktor, why go poking around in the past, and about Weill and all that? Wagner's music is much more wonderful!" was one of the many good suggestions proffered.

On holiday together in the winter of 1973, I wanted to talk to Father about paragraph 8 of the Foundation charter, which in my view acted as a muzzle. On a long walk, I explained to him my concerns: "Isn't it absurd to assume that our family would agree on a candidate from the family? And who decides on which criteria the better, more suitable candidate would meet? And what interests do the intendants from Munich, Vienna, Hamburg, Stuttgart, Frankfurt, or Cologne represent? Surely first of all their own—and they would surely a priori be against a Wagner family in conflict! Anyone from the family who wants to get in there must get on with everyone, including the politicians, industrialists, and members of the Society of Friends of Bayreuth. I don't understand that."

Father replied: "If you stand the test according to the Foundation charter, then you have a good chance of making the running."

It was also during these Christmas holidays that a quarrel erupted between my father and me over the inclusion of the Federal Republic and the GDR in the United Nations organization. I considered the universal recognition of the GDR as a sensible and logical continuation of Willy Brandt's and Hans-Dietrich Genscher's *Ostpolitik*. Father didn't: "That means the end of the unification of Germany—and not only that, it means the Communists will be rewarded for the division of Germany."

Early in 1974 my father and Peter Stein and Patrice Chéreau competed against one another to direct the new production of *The Ring* scheduled for 1976, the centenary of the Bayreuth Festival. Pierre Boulez had already agreed to be the conductor, but the negotiations with the directors made no progress. Father considered directing *The Ring* himself, although I advised him strongly against this, because it would have meant interrupting the beginnings of a trend toward modern, if not avant-garde, interpretations of Richard Wagner. Because of my knowledge of French I was occasionally called in to the negotiations. Whether Father dangled the tasty morsel of directing *The Ring* under Chéreau's nose or Stein's depended entirely on their remarks on the opera, and whether such remarks conformed with his own ideas, especially in relation to the so-called reception history and the subject of art and power from 1850 to 1945. Father wanted an ambiguous, apolitical interpretation. The process reminded me of a poker game with marked aces. Once, when I picked up Peter Stein at the Nuremberg airport, he said: "Your father's constant patronage reminds me of the old times." Chéreau finally won.

In July 1974, at the end of my summer semester, I returned to Bayreuth. But in the Festspielhaus I saw only *Tristan* under Carlos Kleiber's fascinating musical direction. August Everding's staging pleased the old Wagnerians and the circles around my grandmother. My sister knew about Everding's growing influence in the German opera and theater scene and waxed enthusiastic about him. I, on the other hand, talked to him about the weather; we had nothing else to say to one another. Though he tried to please everyone, Everding was especially favored by my grandmother, who shared his conservative attitudes. At that time Eva and my grandmother were taking on more duties in the Siegfried Wagner House as the unofficial representatives of the family and of Bayreuth. Ironically, their increasing prominence as conservative Wagnerian voices came at the same time that my father and his supporters were promoting a new left-wing image for the festival.

For several years I had been seeing a woman named Beatrix Kraus. My family had given her the cold shoulder from the first time they met her because of her refreshing lack of respect for the Wagner cult. She was equipped with a razor-sharp wit, social confidence, and the ability to defend herself with aplomb in the festival snakepit. On 1 August 1974 Beatrix and I were married. People from the Festspielhügel were not among our many guests. That day I unexpectedly introduced her as my wife to my astonished family. I moved with her to an apartment in the villa of the Feustel family on the outskirts of Bayreuth, surrounded by a beautiful garden.

After my marriage the next most important event in these months was Ernst Bloch's visit to our home. I collected him and his wife, Karola, from Tübingen. Bloch gave me some important tips for my doctoral thesis and provided me with contacts—for example, with the Austrian-American actress and singer Lotte Lenya, Weill's wife and muse. And it was because of him I got involved in a controversy with Bayreuth's Social Democratic mayor, Hans Walter Wild. I had suggested appointing Bloch an honorary citizen of the city of Bayreuth. Hitler had been granted honorary citizenship in 1933, and nobody objected that in 1974 a street was still named after the Nazi admirer and Wagner worshiper Chamberlain. In a letter dated 25 April 1974, the mayor wrote how he could see no grounds for my proposal and cited the names of other honorary citizens, among them my grandmother.

Bloch attracted me at that time mainly because of his passionate interest in all things cultural. I found his accounts of the Weimar Republic, and his time with Otto Klemperer at the Kroll Opera in Berlin, fascinating. Most of all I liked listening to him when he talked about the devil: he created images in my mind from the Old Testament that I shall never forget. When my father and Herbert Barth, together with the Macks, invited him and Karola to the centenary production of *The Ring* in 1976, he talked about Wagner as he understood him—in other words, about Wagner as revolutionary.

In that festival summer of 1974 our guests included the set designer Roland Aeschlimann and his wife, Andrea, and the literary scholar Hans Mayer, who brought with him a publisher's proposal for us to write a book together on the history of the Bayreuth Festival. At the time I regarded Mayer's interpretation of Wagner stimulating and also saw an opportunity of making myself financially independent of my father. So I agreed to the proposal and began work, filling in the gaps in my material on Wagner and the Festspielhügel.

In autumn 1974 I moved with Beatrix to Vienna to concentrate on my doctoral thesis and continue my research for the book with Hans Mayer. I was also able to gather further experience as an assistant director when Joachim Herz and Rudolf Heinrich invited me to work with them at the Staatsoper on a production of Mozart's *Die Zauberflöte*. Herz, another pupil of Walter Felsenstein's, taught me a lot of things, both theoretical and practical: and he made it clear to me what a great, if still underestimated, influence Meyerbeer had had on Richard Wagner's musical dramaturgy.

On a day-to-day level, working together was often difficult: Herz was always on edge and expected me to be prepared to work day and night. I went along with it, as the results said a lot for him. Equally stimulating for me in these weeks were talks with Heinrich, the brilliant set and costume designer, who with Felsenstein had brought world recognition to the Komische Oper in Berlin, a company that was known as the "Anti-Bayreuth." The assistants attached to the opera house, who were mostly close to the clique of the influential director Otto Schenk and the baritone Eberhard Wächter, found it disgusting that the Saxon Herz was daring to stage *Zauberflöte* in Vienna in a critical way. The whole thing nauseated me, and I prepared my first interview as journalist for the Vienna newspaper *Die Presse* in order, out of solidarity with Herz's exemplary staging, to create a platform for his conception.

At the beginning of December Roland Aeschlimann, Gernot Gruber, Eberhard Wagner, and I had a meeting with Father. We were supposed to discuss *Parsifal* with him on the basis of a set model by Aeschlimann, and we hoped to be able to give Father some ideas for his first staging of that opera, which was planned for 1975 and had to measure up to Wieland's 1951 production. In 1974 I had gotten Aeschlimann hired at the Festspielhaus, where he worked as lighting technician. He had worked out a set based on the work of the avant-garde set designer Adolphe Appia, who died in 1928, a set that Cosima Wagner had violently rejected at the time. We all supported Aeschlimann's model enthusiastically; but although my father acted interested, and paid noncommittal compliments, it amounted to a rejection. The set that he finally used reminded some critics, not without reason, of the architecture of Albert Speer, Hitler's favorite architect.

8

Winifred's Film

O n 20 January 1975 my sister wrote to tell me that the film
director Hans Jürgen Syberberg wanted my collaboration
on a film about our grandmother. The idea appealed to
me, and I accepted Syberberg's invitation to Vienna, where he was
presenting his film about Karl May. In a conversation after the premiere Syberberg informed me that Ernst Bloch, Hans Mayer, and
Walter Jens had also reacted positively to the idea of his new film.
He noted my interest in German-Jewish history and the work of
Kurt Weill with obvious attention and seemed impressed by my
courage in tackling taboo subjects, such as the involvement of my
own family in National Socialism. At this first meeting I noticed
that he didn't know much about this area or about my grandmother's role in it. I was not only to procure him an entrée to my
grandmother and my father, but also to place my knowledge at his
disposal. A prerequisite to my participating in the preparation,
shooting, and editing of the film was my passionate interest in dis-
closing the darkest epoch in the family history.

I informed Syberberg that I was also working on a TV documentary on the subject of the festival's centenary for the BBC with
Brian Large, but he drew up a contract that took this other project
into account and cleared important rights for me. I showed the contract to Father and he agreed to our beginning filming in April

1975. Beatrix and I used the time until then for further research, which was later to come in useful for the book with Hans Mayer.

It turned out to be the start of an obstacle course, however, as my father had no intention of handing over all the documents on the Wagner family and National Socialism that I found listed in the archive catalogue or that my grandmother had told me about. For example, there was the correspondence between Hitler and Winifred, Wieland, and Wolfgang Wagner from 1923 to 1944, which my grandmother had secretly removed from a special steel-lined cupboard and handed over to me for a short time to study. The letters were evidence of the great familiarity among the four of them and were full of declarations of belief in the Final Victory of the Third Reich. My father ignored inquiries about the letters involving himself and Wieland.

He was also irritated when I broached the subject of the presents from Hitler to my grandmother and the family, such as the gilt-edged copy of *Mein Kampf* with the dedication "From Wolf for Winnie" from 1925, and categorically refused to make such intimate family documents available for the Syberberg film. He watched over the preparations and the subsequent filming too with suspicion, not least in an attempt to prevent any of my grandmother's statements from damaging the festival's liberal-left image of the moment. I, on the other hand, wanted everything to come out into the open: it was only by exposing fully my family's involvement in National Socialism that it would be made to work through its guilt.

I showed Syberberg the films from the Nazi period that I had found in the BMW sidecar, and I stupidly gave him some to take back to Munich. He assured me that he would look after them and would not use them without my permission. That Syberberg, as he claimed, had already devised an artistic direction and concept for the film when he was in Bayreuth was difficult to believe. Two basic factors were missing: knowledge of the material and any understanding of my grandmother's character.

She took over right from the beginning. What emerged from the Siegfried Wagner House was a film by Winifred Wagner, featuring Winifred Wagner, with assistance from Syberberg. The moment shooting began, he fell under my grandmother's control. She saw her moment of truth and seized the opportunity ruthlessly. Syberberg flirted as if he were bowled over by the old woman. When he reported on the filming, he avoided the whole truth. He kept silent about the fact that during filming my grandmother turned to me when she was singing the praises of her "Wolf." I did not agree at all with her statements on Hitler, and it was difficult for me to suppress my anger while the cameras were rolling, especially as Syberberg had requested that I should not make any comment. So during breaks in filming I discussed Grandmother's crazed statements about the Führer with her. Syberberg wanted to just let Winifred talk, so he didn't get involved and was evidently relying on her giving herself away. Woe betide me whenever I lost my temper through frustration with Grandmother's version of events! Each time, Syberberg claimed he was being hindered in his art. And so Grandmother went down on record saying such things as, in connection with the "Jewish question": "We [Hitler and Winifred] never talked about these things—to be frank, I didn't feel competent enough. I'm a totally nonpolitical person, and I was extremely astonished that in the trial court [during denazification in 1947] I kept being accused of politics. I said politics didn't enter into it. Then they all laughed. They said, 'Of course you dealt in politics.' I didn't deal in politics."[21]

The members of the trial court were right, of course, to laugh; Grandmother was in reality a very politically active woman:

"At Christmas in 1923 I made a collection among the National Socialists here. They all brought their Christmas presents here, and I packed them all in boxes and sent them to the director of [Fort] Landsberg [where Hitler was imprisoned] . . . with the request to distribute them and so on. That was done. Well, and I had asked what he wanted, and he said, well, writing paper was something he urgently needed, and so I sent him masses of writing paper. Good God, now people are accusing me of having supplied the paper for *Mein Kampf*, aren't they? Sort of almost as though indirectly it's my fault *Mein Kampf* was written. Whatever you did, you were constantly attacked for it."[22]

My relationship with Syberberg became increasingly strained. At first I had seen the potential in his film of publicly clearing up the family past. But during filming I began to mistrust him because of his undistanced and uncritical way of putting questions and his slavish attitude to my grandmother. He noticed my creeping mistrust and tried with my sister's help to keep me happy. I stayed in Bayreuth until the end of filming.

In the summer semester of 1975 I met my cousin Nike Wagner again in Vienna, the second daughter of Uncle Wieland. After this we met regularly in Vienna and an intensive dialogue developed between us, far from Bayreuth and family intrigues. Syberberg's film about our grandmother was a key talking point, and through that we came to the role of our fathers in the Nazi period. The subject proved ticklish, as at that time Nike didn't want to talk about her father's privileged role during the Nazi period, whereas I saw my father and Wieland in such a light and spoke openly about it. Only at the beginning of the nineties was she to talk about the subject of Wagner, Hitler, anti-Semitism, and the Wagner family in Bayreuth from her point of view. We were agreed, though, that it was necessary to deal with Jewish artists, as we did in our theses—she with Karl Kraus, I with Kurt Weill. Wummi probably felt something similar; it was no accident that he was living with the daughter of one of the people who had tried to assassinate Hitler, Nona von Haeften.

I told Nike about my mistrust of Syberberg, which continued to grow, as Syberberg kept me only vaguely informed about the progress of the film, and then over the phone. At the beginning of June Father, Syberberg, and I met in Munich. Prior to this my father had had Winifred make out a power of attorney, according to which he could decide whether he accepted or rejected the film and how the material could be made further use of—for example, in books.

At the meeting Syberberg showed us a version of the beginning of the film, which my father passed. Immediately afterwards, in an interview on 9 June, Syberberg summarized our meeting from his point of view. On the same day, my father issued a statement in response to Syberberg's account. As he was gradually recognizing his own contradictory role, he had suggested "other solutions" for the legal position of the film, which his legal advisers had worked out for him, unbeknownst to me. On 10 June Syberberg produced a five-page protocol which seemed to sum up everything that had been agreed between him and my father and his lawyers. For my part, I completely lost track of the legal situation. At the time I had no idea that the version Syberberg had shown Father and me bore little resemblance to the finished product, and when I phoned him, he told me that Hans Mayer had seen excerpts from the film and was enthusiastic.

Then problems arose over my BBC project. Syberberg wanted to market my grandmother exclusively, which pleased the British TV team as little as it did me. I asked my father's lawyer to look over my contracts with Syberberg and with the BBC. Despite countless reminders, I never saw the contracts again. The following was decided: the British were allowed to film Grandmother driving through Bayreuth to the Festspielhügel in her old Volkswagen and posing silently in front of the Festspielhaus. Brian Large got permission to film the productions of *Meistersinger* and *Parsifal* in 1975 and the centenary *Ring* of Chéreau and Boulez. My situation did not look very favorable: I was ousted from the BBC project. Large now had his own Bayreuth connections.

At the end of June I visited Syberberg in Munich, accompanied by Nike and Beatrix, and was shown some insignificant excerpts. When I asked him to show us certain scenes with Hitler, he explained that this was impossible, as those scenes were being edited. My suspicions grew. By chance I noticed that in another room he was projecting my father's films—the ones I had found in the BMW sidecar—onto a screen that had a still camera standing in front of it. It turned out that Syberberg not only was taking stills from these films but already had had complete copies made. Furious, I demanded that he hand over both the originals and the copies. These weren't returned until the autumn, and I decided to store them with Beatrix's parents, where they remained until my father's lawyer demanded them back.

The situation had already become confrontational. The world premiere of *Winifred Wagner und die Geschichte Des Hauses Wahn-*

fried von 1914 bis 1945 was due to take place at the Cinémathèque Française in Paris. Syberberg had neither informed me about it nor invited me. Quite rightly, he feared a row if I discovered how he had assembled his film. It was my French cousins who told me, and Nike, Beatrix, and I rushed to Paris. The premiere was a nightmare: I found myself in the large auditorium in the middle of a swarm of sensation-hungry onlookers and journalists all keen finally to learn everything about Winifred's "affair" with "Wolf."

While the film was running I realized with horror that it didn't have much to do at all with the version Syberberg had shown me in Munich. It was in fact a different film, with new captions and cuts and in altered sequence, and conveyed quite a different content. My French relations understood at once what had happened. They remained the only ones in the family who did not attack me. After the premiere I sat in the Capitol restaurant with Syberberg, Nike, and Nikolaus Sombart and Wolf Donner from *Die Zeit*, and there Syberberg and I had our first dispute. I took him aside and asked him furiously how he could have lied to us. He immediately threatened me with lawyers. I was angry not only because he had broken our agreement and disregarded my right of veto on the use of the films, but also because he had failed to have a private viewing before this public premiere. Moreover, Syberberg had overlaid stills— partly taken from Father's films—with cynical remarks made by my grandmother which he had recorded without her knowledge during breaks in the filming. His project ultimately mythologized my grandmother as time's witness. Syberberg had contributed to the monumental myth about my grandmother's role during the Nazi period. As an actress, my grandmother appeared both convincing and demagogic. And so many observers of the film saw it as yet another piece of Nazi propaganda. The film also damaged my reputation. When I got back to Bayreuth I was deluged with criticism from all sides, as people identified me with the film. Jewish Wagnerians suspected me of being a Nazi sympathizer. Right-wing Wagnerians dubbed me a nest fouler. And the liberal left publicly disowned me, on the grounds that I had allegedly crossed over from the liberal Syberberg to the conservative Winifred. The Society of

Friends of Bayreuth and the representatives of Bayreuth decided to distance themselves, as the film had allegedly damaged the image of the city. Doubts were even cast on the honesty of my intentions in writing my doctoral thesis on Weill. The *Nordbayerischer Kurier* now carried this headline over an article about my grandmother's role in the film: "Monument to Personal Courage." There was no better way to render innocuous the fascist past of Hitler's friend Winifred Wagner.

In July 1975 an international press conference was held in the Festspielhaus restaurant. There could only be one subject, Winifred and Wolf, so my father asked me to stay away. He announced to the media that my grandmother had acknowledged that her remarks were made "without due consideration" and had consequently withdrawn them. He also said that he had for the time being forbidden her to enter the Festspielhaus. Regarding his own role in the Syberberg affair, he remained silent, and although he had been well aware of the conditions I had laid down prior to collaborating with Syberberg, and had initially approved them, he remarked that I had "collaborated on the film with youthful impetuosity" and was "horrified by the result." I later protested over such a public declaration of my incompetence, but it did nothing to help my cause.

Afterwards, I went purposefully to my grandmother. Opening the door, I saw with horror that on her desk, next to the picture of my father, was a photo of Hitler, with the dedication "From Wolf to his Winnie." When I asked her why she had put the photo out, she retorted furiously: "Wolf[gang] is treating me the same way Wieland did with all his talk about me still believing in the Final Victory! He was there at all the negotiations with Syberberg, after all. Now he's being celebrated as a left-wing resistance fighter." Of Hitler, Wieland, and my father she said bitterly: "They understood one another perfectly, even though he is now pretending they never had anything to do with him. In 1945 I sacrificed myself for the two of them."

At the end of the 1975 festival season I sent Hans Mayer, with whom I had been working for some time on the book *Richard Wagner in Bayreuth*, everything that I had collected on this subject in the last few years. It was a mountain of documents and pictures. Mayer had already been grappling with Wagner and the Bayreuth Festival for a long time, and he knew what it was all about. For that reason there was no dissent in the compilation of the documents and photos. He also worked in some text excerpts from the Syberberg film. It hardly needs saying that Syberberg was foaming at the mouth when he got word of this, as he had wanted to market my grandmother exclusively, in book as well as other forms. In a telephone call to my father's lawyer, Syberberg announced that he no longer considered himself bound by agreements he had made in June and requested that I did not make it known that I had withdrawn from the film. Should I do so, he threatened, he would issue statements that would damage me.

The German premiere of the Syberberg film took place in November 1975. My father asked Ewald Hilger, the chairman of the Society of Friends of Bayreuth, to be present, and it was Hilger who on 25 November informed me in writing what had happened. He had no objections to Frau Winifred's remarks, he wrote. The film was an honest and fascinating account of a life, and was also understood in this way by the public. If people hadn't wanted to hear about it, then they needn't have asked Frau Winifred about it. The excitement about the film Hilger considered unfounded, yet he had reservations on the publication of the interview in book form, because this would create a completely different impression. There was a difference between hearing Frau Winifred's "explosive statements" being spoken and reading them in print.

It was farcical. Hilger assumed an almost prototypical position for people of his turn of mind. He accepted without question that Grandmother was continuing to consider Hitler as a private individual, as though Auschwitz had never been, nor *Mein Kampf*, in which Hitler had already described his annihilation plans long before he put them into effect. What could be honorable about Winifred Wagner, even thirty years after the war, doggedly refusing to see the mass murderer in her "Wolf"?

This by no means concluded the Syberberg affair, however. During our last Christmas holidays together in Arosa in 1975, my father read me a reply from Ernst Bloch, in which the philosopher refused my father's request for a contribution to the "Jubilee" volume for the centenary celebrations of the festival. Bloch wrote that as a Jew and antifascist he was incapable of doing this: through Syberberg and Winifred Wagner, the old association between Wagner's music and the Nazis had reemerged, and any denazification by Wieland and Wolfgang Wagner had been disavowed.

I regretted Bloch's refusal. I was, and still am, of quite a different opinion with regard to the role of my father and Wieland. There can be no question that Bayreuth has been consistently denazified. Father tried to change Bloch's mind, visiting him secretly, as my mother informed me, but he did not succeed.

Syberberg later showed his true political colors and became a right-wing chauvinist, believing in the new great Germany after 1990—something I felt was always behind his left-wing pose in the 1970s.

9

The Festival Centenary

worked only one stint as assistant director in Bayreuth while my father was intendant. It was during the centenary *Ring* in 1976, directed by Patrice Chéreau, with François Regnault as dramaturge. I ought to have been happy when I was told at the beginning of 1976 that I was to be part of the *Ring* team, since it had been one of my childhood dreams to work on the Festspielhügel, after gaining my professional spurs outside Bayreuth. But my parents' imminent divorce was weighing on my mind, especially the circumstances. I was soon to learn that Dietrich Mack's wife was the co-respondent, which solved the riddle of Dietrich's sudden departure from the Festspielhügel in 1974.

My relationship with my father reached a new low, especially as he, in view of the change in his private life, wanted me out of the way. But I was not prepared to give up working with Chéreau and Boulez, quite apart from the fact that I didn't want to leave my mother in the lurch in this situation. Also, the book project with Hans Mayer could not go ahead without Father's support and consent, as he was the source of some additional material I wanted to provide for Mayer.

The meeting with the new *Ring* team on 21 February 1976 in the Festspielhaus left a great impression on me. Despite all the subsequent marketing statements issued to the contrary after the production had been judged a success by the media, my father had at the time by no means agreed with Chéreau and Regnault's concept. The atmosphere at that meeting was extremely tense, and thanks to my father's patriarchal German attitude the project nearly came to grief. The tussles between Father and Regnault continued until June 1976. In a letter to Regnault of 11 June that year, regarding Regnault's major written exposition of the 1976 *Ring*, entitled "Richard Wagner's Theatrical Mission," Father wrote that the theses he presented were so misleading, half-baked, and false that in the final analysis it was obvious he hadn't the faintest idea what *The Ring* was about.

I knew of his disparaged text, of course. François, very upset, had given it to me to read and asked for my opinion. The brilliant analysis of key scenes, and of the leading characters, fascinated me, as did his profound knowledge of different cultures and mythologies. I also found his interpretation of German theater traditions from the classical and Romantic periods convincing. In a letter dated 20 June 1976, François ended his reply to Father's destructive judgment with the remark that in Bayreuth it seemed one had to capitulate before the power of the "all-knowing genius."

This meant that the hour had come for a new house dramaturg: Oswald Bauer, who later headed the press department remained a close adviser to my father until 1986. Bauer shared Father's opinion of Regnault's contribution in every detail. Where I was concerned, he watched my every step in the Festspielhaus and faithfully reported everything back to his esteemed boss. No detail was omitted, however ludicrous. For example, he reported "upstairs" that I had made some photocopies in preparation for an interview with the *Nürnberger Nachrichten*. From then on, Father forbade me to use the copying machine in the Festspielhaus, as he suspected evil intentions behind my interview.

But another affair hit me much harder. I had collected material on the subject of Richard Wagner in Bayreuth to give Hans Mayer for inclusion in his book. Meanwhile during this period, the music historian Michael Karbaum had been collecting similar documents on the same subject as part of his work under the aegis of the Thyssen Foundation. As my father, on the basis of family membership and his position as director of the festival, already had copyright privileges, Karbaum had to submit his material to him before using it. But my father passed it on to me to supplement what I had collected myself, with the remark that he had made this material available to Karbaum from family documents and assumed that I would pass it on to Mayer. Apparently, my father considered Karbaum and the Thyssen research far too left-wing and wanted to encourage a more moderate interpretation by Mayer.

Karbaum, however, filed preceedings against Belser Verlag, Mayer's publisher, for using material from Karbaum's book without permission. Karbaum lost his case.

Looking back on it today, I would like to believe that Father simply had wanted to help me. Still, it would have been better had he told me the whole truth on handing over the Karbaum material. The incident earned me a reputation for being untrustworthy among German academic circles, even as an "intellectual property thief." It even caused problems for me when I applied for a research grant for my Weill/Brecht studies from the German Society for the Advancement of Scientific Research in 1977; my application was finally rejected after more than a year. I further experienced how opinion had been whipped up against me in February 1976, when Dietrich Mack stopped in the foyer of the Stuttgart opera house to ask, cynically, whether the "Karbaum affair" wouldn't soon be blowing up in my face.

But the "Karbaum affair" would remain painful for me for many years. It was then I discovered that Mack's wife, Gudrun, was the immediate reason for my parents' divorce. This news affected me greatly, and I reacted against Mack's allusion to the "Karbaum affair" in a letter to him at the end of March 1976, protesting against such an attack on my reputation. In June Mack wrote me a fawning letter in which he tried to make amends. I rebuffed it in writing.

Later it came to light that Karbaum's historical interpretation differed considerably from Hans Mayer's, as Karbaum emphasized the significance of National Socialism in the history of the Bayreuth Festspiele. Of course, today I know that my father's misleading statements were intended to foil discussion on the subject of Bayreuth, Hitler, and the Wagner family, which Karbaum was so thoroughly investigating.

Back to April 1976: Beatrix and I had moved to Martinsreuth, near Bayreuth, in order to distance ourselves more from my father and the Siegfried Wagner House. The following month I started work as assistant director with Chéreau. I tried to support him wherever possible, as he faced a lot of resistance in the Festspiel-haus. My father urged me frequently, in view of the tense family situation, to give up the assistant directorship. From that time on, he wanted as little as possible to do with his first wife and their children. He even locked my sister out of the office, which was tantamount to giving her notice after nine years of collaboration. As I had no intention of leaving the team, he started harassing me. In a whole series of unpleasant letters he made threats and even gave notice of legal proceedings against me when I tried to help my mother in everyday matters. Consequently my time on the Fest-spielhügel turned into a nightmare. For instance, even when the official group photo of the *Ring* team was taken in front of the Königsbau of the Festspielhaus, my father insisted I leave, on the grounds that I did not belong to the team: the rest of the group maintained an embarrassed silence. The photographer, Siegfried Lauterwasser, a friend of my father's since youth, who had been very fond of me for decades, was horrified and pointedly photographed me separately with my musical mentor Maximilian Kojetinsky. In spite of all the strain, I carried on, rehearsing the alternative cast for the Chéreau *Ring*. Both Boulez and Chéreau understood my situation, and neither intended to suddenly ignore me the way the majority did in the Festspielhaus.

I look back with horror on the centenary celebrations which took place on 23 July 1976. *Richard Wagner and the Germans:* a program full of many lies about the composer and his heirs! The high point was a "people's party" after the third act of *Meistersinger* had been performed in my father's staging, under the baton of Karl Böhm. The choice of this particular act, in tandem with the party, meant that the celebrations were suffocated by Upper Franconian provincialism. Oswald Bauer was the organizer of this sorry spectacle.

Arriving at my father's reception in the Festspielhaus after the ceremony, without an admission ticket and, like my colleagues, in casual dress, I suddenly found myself in the hands of the police again. I shouted at the plainclothes officer: "I demand to speak to my lawyer! These are police-state methods!" One of the onlookers explained to the policeman that I was the boss's son, and at the word "boss" a bell rang in his brain and he let me go. Deferentially he said: "But why didn't you say who you were? Please go and get your invitation." As I hadn't received one, I couldn't very well do that, and knowing every nook and cranny of the Festspielhügel since my childhood, I decided to try to get into the hall by one of my secret routes. I had almost reached my goal when I was caught by two security officers, who started to lead me off. This scene was noticed by the publisher Klaus Piper, who was sitting at Martin Gregor-Dellin's table. He hurried to help me, took the policemen to task, and invited me to his table. I looked around at the piqued faces of the guests from the cream of affluent West German society, especially those of the Friends of Bayreuth, and discovered my father surrounded by his chorus of yes men. No, I could not stay here. I left the room as quickly as I could. I could easily have left Bayreuth altogether right then, but I had promised Chéreau and Boulez that I would continue rehearsing with the second *Ring* cast.

At the end of July I learned from the newspaper *Bild* that my father had married the former Frau Mack. Although I had had nothing to do with the matter, the tabloid press now descended on me too. My parents' divorce during the 1976 centenary celebrations, after thirty-three years of marriage, came as such a shock to my mother that she never fully recovered. In an attempt to find a new identity, she absorbed herself in writing an autobiography and worked through the copious entries in her diaries and her correspondence with my father since their engagement in 1942, complementing them with countless revealing comments, which often placed the official Bayreuth historiography in question. The conflict with National Socialism and the role of the Wagner family in it became one of her central themes, one that she addressed with great intensity.

It wasn't until 1978, after she had moved from Bayreuth to her native city of Wiesbaden, that my mother actually began constructing a life for herself according to her own ideas and needs. This painful process made me look more closely not only at the consequences of the Wagners' Nazi past, but also at my relationship with her. Because of her total identification with the Bayreuth Festival and Father, as had been expected of her, she had scarcely had the opportunity to do justice to her role as mother as well, which she often regretted. But since my father's first *Ring* production in Bayreuth in 1960, she had looked more and more to me for advice and comfort, as Father was totally bound up in his role as a director in competition with his more successful brother, Wieland. The consequent discord between the two families worsened my mother's situation. And after Wieland's death in 1966, the heavy load of social duties that went with her position as wife of the sole head of the festival increased the burden of her life on the Festspielhügel. Father, Grandmother, and Eva, absorbed in being representatives of the new era, offered her no support.

My family's pursuit of the will to power in the years from 1966 to 1975 isolated my mother more and more from the outside world. Naturally she was aware of this and tried to do something about it, but unfortunately she was unsuccessful—she was no match for the other family members. Not surprisingly, it was during these years that she began to wonder what might have happened had she not given up her successful career as a ballerina at the Oper Unter den Linden in Berlin in 1942. She even started questioning her career in the theater and regretting that she had not become a nurse. After her divorce at the age of fifty-seven, however, she was forced to realize that it was now too late to embark on a new career, and so she concentrated—almost by way of compensation—on looking into National Socialism and Jewish history.

Several sensation-hungry journalists, especially those from *Bild*, took advantage of Mother's lack of experience to concoct one of the usual Wagner scandal stories. In fact, they distorted her statements so outrageously that I had to take legal action. With her gradual liberation from the Bayreuth past, helped by her brother and his family, Mother's interest grew and that included in my eventual Italian family, especially in her grandson Eugenio. I was happy about this. It corresponds with our belief in harmony and peace and the search for a meaning to life. On my desk is a picture of her as a four-year-old, playing the part of Madama Butterfly's child "Trouble" in Puccini's opera in a 1923 performance in Wiesbaden. Her beautiful, delicate, childlike smile still shines through her features today and reveals what was always the real aim of her life: the theater and its world.

10

In Search of Myself

At the end of July 1976, at an international press conference, my father presented the newly published diaries of Cosima Wagner, edited by Martin Gregor-Dellin and Dietrich Mack. Shortly afterwards I packed my bags. The only thing that made my departure difficult was leaving Gunda, my foster aunt since my childhood. She broke down in tears.

First Beatrix and I went to the Chiemsee to visit her parents. There we decided to continue on to Ireland to recover from the Bayreuth lunacy. During a stopover we visited Charles and Germaine Spencer in London. They received us warmly, and Charles encouraged me to lead a life free of Bayreuth. In Ireland we were overwhelmed by the beauty of the countryside, although I could not really enjoy it: I was still too deeply distressed by my experiences.

Fortunately there were at least some glimmers of hope, professionally. I was negotiating with the opera house in Bonn for a production of *Fidelio* in the spring of 1977. There was also a generous offer from Lys Symonette in New York to work in the Kurt Weill archives on the publication of Weill's written works.

Dieter Rexroth, head of the Hindemith Institute in Frankfurt am Main and notable for his brilliant conceptual ideas on Beethoven, had made discreet contact with the opera in Bonn in 1975. I also requested that Roland Aeschlimann be involved in the production.

Rexroth and I kept our negotiations secret, as I feared that my father and his circle would obstruct any engagements for me. The influence of Bayreuth in the opera world should not be underestimated: the then-intendant of the Bonn opera house, Joachim Heyse, informed me of Bayreuth's attempts to manipulate opinion. On hearing that the contract had been signed, my father said to Heyse during a meeting of intendants: "You've landed yourself in a real mess there! *Fidelio* in Bonn in the Beethoven centenary year as his first production—can he really pull that off?" Doubt about my ability expressed by my own father spread like wildfire among agents, theater administrators, and the media, many of whom were already closely connected with Bayreuth. For agents and intendants it was more important to keep in with the Festspielhügel than to find engagements for me. It was now known in opera circles that my father looked unfavorably on those who gave me work.

Since the autumn of 1976 I had been living in the same apartment on the Wartburgplatz in Munich, where I'd also resided in August 1974. For me there were primarily two concerns: first, securing my mother's livelihood; and second, preparing myself for the *Rigorosumo*, the final oral examinations, in Vienna, after my doctoral thesis had been accepted in May 1976.

My father meanwhile had stopped my monthly allowance. One of my guardian angels at the time, the hotel owner Peter Kremslehner, knew of my precarious situation and generously took me in as a guest in his Regina Hotel in Vienna.

In December 1976 I passed my oral examinations in musicology, German literature, and philosophy. Only my mother, Beatrix, and a few Viennese friends came to the graduation party. Wummi called up and told me that he had informed Father of my success. The latter's sole comment was: "He copied it all anyway!"

In April 1977 I started my work in Bonn. Dieter Rexroth had merged the first and third versions of *Fidelio* to form a revolutionary interpretation. Now his concept had to be translated onto the stage. This theoretical exercise was explained in an extensive, provocative program including texts by Ursula Krechel, August

Stramm, Ernst Toller, Kurt Schwitters, Peter-Paul Zahl, Rainer Kunze, Paul Celan, Marie Luise Kaschnitz, and Norbert Friedrich.

At the curtain call I experienced my first clash with a predominantly conservative public, although the young members of the audience applauded my updated production.

The press reaction was varied. The tone for the German media was set by Josef Herbort in *Die Zeit* on 3 June 1977 under the headline "No Competition from Junior: Wagner Great-Grandson Gottfried Makes His Debut as Director with *Fidelio.*" His pertinent negative criticism was only mildly irritating, but I deeply resented his further assertions:

When Wolfgang Wagner was asked a year ago about whether he would soon hand over a festival production or even the running of the Bayreuth Festival to a younger member of the family, the shrewd Franconian answered diplomatically that he still did not see a suitable contender among the next generation. Now that Wieland's son, Wolf-Siegfried, has dabbled with *Tristan* and *Die Meistersinger,* reducing Wagner to the one-dimensional, and Wolfgang's son, Gottfried, has staged his vision of Beethoven's opera as nondramatic, the Bayreuth Festival boss can sleep peacefully again. In fact, he faces no competition from either of the Master's great-grandsons. And if the rumor going round the *Fidelio* premiere in Bonn is true, that Wolfgang Wagner warned his fellow intendants against his son, one may make of the family quarrel between the guardians of the Nibelung gold what one will. Fundamentally, though, the father is right.[23]

Herbort's piece had the desired effect: it was a long time before I found further employment in a German opera house, and even today reviews of my productions contain Herbort's prejudice and insinuation.

The Bonn critic Hans G. Schürmann was the only one who did not share the opinion of his German colleagues. The farther away from Bayreuth, the fairer opinions became. For example, the respected critic Roy Koch wrote in *The New York Times* at the end of May:

> Here, in Beethoven's birthplace, where every note of the Master's scores is regarded as sacred, a starkly contemporary production of his only opera, *Fidelio,* is bound to raise controversy—all the more so when the producer is making his professional debut, and specially when that producer is the great-grandson of Richard Wagner.
>
> Though visibly shaken by the few loud boos mixed with the enthusiastic applause at the end of the premiere Thursday night, thirty-year-old Gottfried Wagner stuck out the unmistakable Wagner chin, and his blue eyes flashed defiance at his detractors as he left the stage after several curtain calls.
>
> "I hadn't realized I would be so affected by the violent reaction," he said after the performance, "but the booing as well as the applause convinced me that we have achieved a genuine dialogue with our audience—and that's what we set out to do." . . . Gottfried Wagner is regarded by many observers here as a force among the new generation of opera producers.[24]

Even then I could see that I would be better able to develop professionally outside Germany.

Meeting Bettina Fehr again in Bonn was comforting too: I had been introduced to her for the first time only the year before in Bayreuth. She helped me through this and subsequent crises and soon became my second mother. Since then she has taken an interest in all the essential professional and private events of my life. Her selfless involvement in matters of public concern has been an example to me for two decades. For example, for a long time she worked as honorary manager of the Bonn Society for Christian-Jewish Cooperation, of which she has been a member since 1954. Her involvement in German-Jewish dialogue—a common interest of ours—stems from having a Jewish maternal grandfather, through whom she is a distant relation of Heinrich Heine. Classified in the insane system of the Nuremberg race laws of 1935 as "half-caste, second grade," she—the daughter of the respectable middle-class Christian doctor Arthur Lankes—was not allowed to study and became a bookseller, a profession allowed to her by the Nazis. After the war, through her marriage to Götz Fehr, the long-time director of Inter Nationes, she was able to ally people all over the world to her cause. One of our topics of conversation, apart from the German-Jewish one, is Bayreuth and my relationship with my father, whom she knows. It should come as no surprise that Bettina, despite her daily exertions for people in need and looking after her large family, has also been active since 1992 in the Olga Havel Foundation for the Handicapped. Advising her to take it easy is a waste of breath.

Fortunately in this difficult time Lotte Lenya and Lys Symonette renewed their offer to me of joining the Kurt Weill Foundation. But before I traveled to New York in the autumn I had a difficult errand in Bayreuth. My mother was determined to stay there and had moved in with my grandmother, of all people. Beatrix and I turned up at Grandmother's eightieth birthday, where we, and Mother, were shunned by the high-society guests. I had never heard so many feigned compliments paid to my grandmother. The Syberberg film had, if anything, strengthened her position with her right-wing admirers. The old-guard members of the Wagner Societies and the Society of Friends of Bayreuth toasted Hitler's "Winnie" while my grandmother gushed about the Führer's favorite sculptor, Arno Breker, who had just finished a bust of her. While she and her cronies wallowed in the good old times, my efforts to liberate my mother from this Nazi nest came to nothing.

Before my journey to New York there was an episode as short as it was curious. In August Wummi, Nike, and I were interviewed by Klaus Figge for a program called *Aspekte* on the German television channel ZDF. The media immediately reported that the fourth generation of Wagners was standing at Bayreuth's gates ready to seize power. This was in spite of the fact that I had clearly described how I wanted to make my way outside Bayreuth. My father wasn't at all happy with this. The interviewer had realized that my father, without being able to cite any specific reasons, had written off the whole of this fourth generation as incompetent. In order to bolster his displeasure with some muscle, at the end of August 1977, in a letter to the head of programming (now intendant) of ZDF, Dieter Stolte, Father described the interviewer's research as inaccurate and warned against any repetition of such procedures, as this would ultimately also affect the interests of the ZDF. The letter must have worked: the channel was later frequently allowed to televise Bayreuth productions.

In September I returned to Bonn to oversee rehearsals for further performances of my *Fidelio* production. The damning judgment of the German press had had a negative effect on the atmosphere among the production team and in the theater. But despite all the forebodings, the revival was a success with the section of the public that I most wanted to reach: young people, who normally never went to the opera.

Meanwhile, I continued to worry about my mother, who had suffered severe mental and emotional strain since the divorce. I frequently encountered the neurologist and psychiatrist Johannes Meyer-Lindenberg, who lived in Bonn and whom I had met through Bettina Fehr at the premiere party for *Fidelio*. She told him about my difficult family situation, and he offered to stand by my mother, who was in a particularly bad state at the time. Eva and I gratefully accepted this. One of our central topics of conversation, however, was the conflict with Father. Johannes had, through his own experience, a great sensitivity for difficult family situations. His father came from a Jewish family and his aristocratic mother from a Christian background. Hence, his parents were forced to flee the Nazis and go to Colombia, where Johannes was born in 1938. After the Second World War his father was West German ambassador in Rome and Madrid, and Johannes came to Bonn as a student.

He immediately understood my rebellion against my family's Nazi past and saw that my ethical and politico-cultural positions were incompatible with those of my father. Seeing how much I was affected by the situation, he offered to mediate between my father and me. From the autumn of 1977 until his painfully early death in 1991 at the age of only fifty-three, Johannes did all he could, through meetings and numerous telephone calls, to convince Father of the need to talk with me.

Bettina Fehr kindly looked after me again in Bonn. Once she invited me to accompany her to a reception at the Israeli embassy, where she introduced me not only to the ambassador but also to Heinrich Böll, who said: "So you're the Wagner who got up people's noses here in the sacred city of Bonn with your *Fidelio!*" I answered rather despondently: "People have been annoyed at me for that—just look at what was in *Die Zeit* at the end of May." When I told him what Herbort had written, Böll laughed and replied: "Gottfried Wagner, what you dared to do there was perfectly right. Don't be upset by people like Herbort, who swim with the tide. You have to learn to free yourself internally from the opinion of opportunists, otherwise you'll go to the dogs in the German cultural jungle. Just stop believing that *Die Zeit* has a monopoly on truth and honesty." I told Böll about the first time I had read his book *Wanderer, kommst du nach Spa* and how my father did not rate his work highly. Böll was hardly surprised: "Your father certainly won't change now, try as he might to give that impression to the press." He was right about that too.

While in Bonn, I applied to the German Society for the Advancement of Scientific Research for a grant. After months of delays, I learned that objections to my proposal had come from members of the board who had political grudges against my father. Now, with no money, no enthusiasm, and no energy for an endless and expensive lawsuit against the Bayreuth mire, it was time for me to leave Germany and try my luck in America.

11

On the Trail of Kurt Weill

In November Beatrix and I finally flew to New York. The leaden fatigue soon lifted once we landed in the murky yellow poison of exhaust gases at John F. Kennedy Airport. The customs officials had a style of their own. Coming from Germany, I found it a refreshing change to be greeted by a friendly African-American official with: "What do you want here, Gottfried?" I didn't exactly know myself. Rather embarrassed, I replied: "I'm here for fun!" The official grinned, slammed his stamp on my passport, and said: "So have fun, Gottfried!" In a terribly hot, crowded, and stinking bus we drove to Manhattan. We went first to the house of Beatrix's Aunt Gabriele, in Riverdale on the Hudson River, opposite the Toscanini house. Subsequently, Francis de Vegvar and his wife, Kitty, other relations of Beatrix's, invited us to their beautiful penthouse; they were to be among my most faithful friends in difficult times in the U.S.A.

The penthouse overlooked Central Park and the seemingly endless Fifth Avenue, running uptown to downtown—a view that almost made me forget my bitter experiences in Germany. But stark contrast to Beatrix's relatives' luxury lifestyle was not slow in coming: only a few blocks farther uptown, I witnessed the indescribable squalor of Harlem.

During this time I presented Lotte Lenya (who always wanted to be called plain Lenya) with the book version of my doctoral thesis, for which she had written an introduction. When she accepted the book she said, with emotion: "Finally Weill's name is in first place, and then Brecht's! It was always the other way round—you are the first one to recognize that Weill is the equal of Brecht." I answered, no less moved: "Weill's music is what makes the collaborations with Brecht immortal, because what will remain of Brecht will certainly not be his ideology, but his accurate knowledge of human contradictions and his wonderfully clear, poetic language!" Lenya shared my opinion. With great enthusiasm she started talking of her work with Brecht in the years from 1927 to 1933. "Brecht," she said, laughing, "always said to me, 'You are epic theater!'"

Of course I wanted to know more about Weill. The "Jewish seminarian" of 1927, as her "serious little Kurt" was called in those days, was certainly not looking for the intellectual, emancipated woman in Lenya, but the seductive Lulu, with whom he enjoyed all the attractions of the Venusberg. Eagerly I listened to Lenya's stories of the nights in Berlin until March 1933. Often during a boozing spree, the team would think up the names of people and cities to use in their works: Brecht would wildly spin a globe and Weill would stop it with his index finger. Once the finger landed on a place called Benares—hence "The Benares Song." "It's absurd what all these pseudo-intellectuals cobble together nowadays about the origins of works by Weill and Brecht and what ideological nonsense they pile onto Kurt," said Lenya heatedly. She would alternate, from one moment to the next, between talking about her past to wanting to know everything about me. "There's not so much to tell," I answered. "And you can image why I wrote my doctoral thesis on Weill and Brecht." "Did you run into a lot of difficulties?" she asked anxiously. "Certainly far fewer than Weill and you did!"

We fell silent and looked solemnly at one another. Then she burst out laughing and told one of her Wagner stories from the time she worked as a stage extra in Zurich: "In the third act of *Parsifal*, as a servant of the Grail, I and three others had to carry the coffin with the dead Titurel a long way from the center rear of the stage, right down to the footlights. We were marching very solemnly, and even more solemnly I had to unveil the wax head of the dead Titurel, which was covered by a velvet cloth. But unfortunately for me, I pulled the cloth too hard, and Titurel's head flew off and rolled down into the orchestra pit. The audience roared with laughter, the curtain came down, and I was sacked."

Lenya became more and more merry. She still had the charm of a girl, and I saw clearly how easily one could have fallen in love with this woman forty years ago. The evening ended with our singing excerpts from *Lohengrin:* she sang Elsa's Dream, in her rather smoky, brittle voice, but with clean intonation and exact rhythm. She knew every note and every word by heart, although she couldn't read music. I parodied the swan knight from the Grail Redemption Company, Inc. We were helpless with laughter and completely forgot our surroundings.

In the coming weeks I was to learn to my horror how indiscriminate Lenya was in her choice of friends, many of whom exploited her shamelessly. Lys was no match for Lenya's false friends. On my second meeting with Lenya I didn't manage to clear up all the questions connected with my work, so I started looking for another job.

During various meetings with theater agents I was once again sharply reminded of my origins and of Bayreuth. The agents were well informed about my rebellions against family tradition—the long arm of the Festspielhügel had made sure of that.

My life was further complicated by living in Riverdale. Everything important happened in Manhattan, and to get there I had to take the bus, which went through Harlem. I shall never forget the faces of these neglected young black people, distorted by hatred. As soon as they saw the bus coming they would run toward it, swearing at the passengers, sometimes even banging on the sides. The polite, mostly black, drivers tried to get through Harlem without stopping; accused of being "whitey's friends" for simply doing their job. If a traffic light turned to red, the driver would open his window to try to repel the onslaughts of black kids with choice words, but they just answered with obscenities. No melting pot, I thought at such times. Many of these mostly unemployed young people hated us just because we came from the rich Jewish Riverdale area, a social division that triggered off an evil explosion of class and race hatred. I increasingly doubted whether New York was really so wonderful, and the clean, beautiful Riverdale neighborhood took on more the image of an ivory tower.

During this period I also met Gert von Gontard, one of the most influential sponsors of New York operas and the Bayreuth Festival, in the Metropolitan Club. He was an eager and knowledgeable friend of art, theater, and music, and I was only ever to hear good things about him. A member of the Budweiser brewery dynasty, which offered him ample means to pursue his love of opera, he was by no means a mere snob; rather, as the offspring of a bourgeois family, he obeyed the aristocratic motto of noblesse oblige. He once had supported Max Reinhardt when the great director had to flee to New York to escape the Nazis. I described to him my unpromising professional prospects and explained my opinion of the festival, of which he had no good opinion, either. Although he could be described more as a conservative, he supported my criticism of the German cultural establishment, especially of Bayreuth, with fatherly sympathy.

I was pleasantly surprised when my sister asked me to be a witness at her wedding in southern France. With fewer illusions about a professional future in New York, I flew to Munich in December 1977 and journeyed on from there. Despite my time in New York being short, and only partially successful, I now felt ill at ease in Germany. The weeks there had had a salutary effect on me, however, and I began to view things in Germany with greater detachment. Job or no, I was determined to return to America as soon as possible. What August Everding, who was becoming more and more powerful in the German theater scene, or any other theater bigwigs, might say, was immaterial to me now. Even the fact that the German media ignored my book on Weill and Brecht didn't bother me much. America became for me a challenge. I wanted to seek my fortune there, build up a life of my own.

How I enjoyed the vastness and beauty of southern France after the confinement of Germany and the wildness of the New York jungle! Although it soon became clear to me that Eva was being more affectionate only because Father had rejected her, the friendly and open nature of my brother-in-law, Yves Pasquier, worked wonders. In the end Eva and I tried to talk honestly to one another, without the constant feeling of distrust or rivalry for the post of festival chief. I said to her: "The brutal way our father has frozen us out of Bayreuth can still turn out to have its advantages. Let's use them!"

This proposal was ultimately to prove a great illusion, but in those days in southern France the divisive shadow of Bayreuth could not come between us. The wedding and the Christmas festivities that followed were of such a cheerfulness and warmth that I became painfully aware of what we had never had as children: the feeling of belonging to a family, of security. Out of politeness, my new relations did not ask about Bayreuth, and so the atmosphere was scarcely clouded at all by bitter memories.

In January 1978 Beatrix and I flew back to New York. I now began systematically occupying myself with Weill's works after his escape from Nazi Germany and devised some initial suggestions on how they could be promoted in Germany. I also received a first lesson in how to behave to get a job from Betty Smith, a well-known New York agent, who was the publicist of Lauritz Melchior, and is president of the Melchior Foundation in New York. Betty presented me with twenty questions typically asked in job interviews with agents, theater directors, and publishers. I answered them all wrong, because I spoke the truth. Betty was horrified. For example, asked how I viewed the Bayreuth family tradition, I answered: "Why do you think I'm here? Because I don't want to have anything to do with the whole Bayreuth business!" Laughing at first, then seriously, Betty said: "Do you wanna get a job or not? Your capital is also to be a Wagner. Use it in the right way!"

Of course she was right. I had to learn how to handle my past and to present the relationship with my family in Bayreuth without doing myself a disservice or losing my identity. I began painlessly to de-Germanize myself and aimed at becoming a "liberal American." I began to frequent the doors of literary agents, which is how I met Eliot Ravetz, who worked for the influential Scott Meredith agency on Third Avenue. I soon enjoyed a warm friendship with Eliot, although unfortunately it ended. The agency wanted to make my revolt against the family heritage the focus of advertising for my book. I, on the other hand, had no intention of being touted as the uncouth, hotheaded revolutionary. Eliot had to obey his boss, and we parted company amicably. I was sorry, because I could really talk to him openly about Germans and Jews of our generation, and he helped me overcome my superficial philo-Semitism. I shall never forget Eliot's simple words on one of our drives from Manhattan to Riverdale: "Here in New York, where there are more Jews than in Israel, you'll meet a lot of unpleasant Jews who'll make you feel really anti-Semitic. Stop thinking we Jews are better than other people, especially here in New York. We aren't."

On one visit to the Metropolitan Opera I met Milcom and Yveta Graff, who were underwriters of the company. They had attached a condition to their sponsorship: that the money be invested in Czech music, since Yveta came from Prague. The Graffs lived in one of the luxurious apartments on Park Avenue. As Betty Smith had predicted, the entry ticket to the Graffs' home and consequently to New York society was my name. People were extremely curious about everything concerning Wagner and Bayreuth. Talk was by no means confined to Richard Wagner and his works; I was also questioned about my father's style of management and my relationship with him. Again and again came the question of whether I would follow him as head of the festival. Despite my hosts' charm and generosity I found this kind of conversation unpleasant. Most of the very conservative questioners were interested more in the private world of the Wagner family than in my views on culture and art. But with Betty's advice in mind—"Do you wanna get a job or not?"—I endeavored to answer politely and noncommittally. But when I was asked why I had written my doctoral dissertation on Weill and Brecht of all people, I had had enough of evasions. I spoke bluntly about Hitler, Bayreuth, and the Jews and passionately confessed that the book was the consequence of a disastrous marriage between politics and culture in Bayreuth. Mrs. Graff, who as a child had gone through the horrors of the German occupation with her family, showed sympathy for my commitment. But she remained an exception. The majority of the art patrons present, some of whom were members of the archconservative Wagner Circle and Bayreuth pilgrims, maintained a polite silence. This seemed to be their way of saying that they were more than skeptical regarding what I then, together with psychoanalysts Alexander and Margarete Mitscherlich, described as "mourning work." Their motto was: "What you can't alter is no longer a worthwhile topic of conversation." My impression was not improved when some of them assured me in private how courageous they found my attitude.

After a few moments of silence those present broached the subject of whether Wagner had been a Jew. If there had been any truth to this assertion, it would have been tantamount to a vindication, in view of my great-grandfather's well-known anti-Semitic attacks and the traditional family line culminating in Winifred Wagner. I was familiar with the speculations made by Ernest Newman in his biography of Wagner. In Bayreuth, support for and denial of such theories changed as frequently as the weather, according to which seemed more appropriate at the time. I pointed out that it was by no means clear whether Ludwig Heinrich Christian Geyer had been a Jew or that he was Richard's biological father. All that was provable was that Geyer was Richard Wagner's adoptive father. I had no proof for my denial of the claim and could only promise to go in search of the answer.

I finally succeeded a few weeks later in New York. The Leo Baeck Institute had kindly looked up for me genealogical documents on Geyer, which proved that he was not a Jew. Several weeks after that I met Milcom and Yveta Graff once again at the Met, during a performance of Debussy's *Pelléas et Mélisande.* I told them of the results of my research. Yveta was a little surprised and commented that for her only Wagner's music mattered anyway and not his ideology—an opinion I could not share in view of my knowledge of Bayreuth's history.

That evening will always remain in my memory, although for quite another reason. After seeing the moth-eaten production, which I had dressed up for as an invited guest, I missed the last bus back to Riverdale. To make matters worse, there was a fierce snowstorm that day in New York. As a taxi would have been too expensive, I decided to go home by subway. I somehow took the wrong line and ended up in Harlem. I noticed my mistake only when I was standing in the middle of a snowstorm on 154th Street. Faces peered at me from all sides. A black man sitting next to me on the subway had warned me to avoid the area: "Hey, mister, what are you doing here? Take care you get out of here! And take a yellow cab. The other taxis can be dangerous." Looking around, I saw silent people clothed in dirty rags, warming themselves around fires they had made in oil drums. Seeing such an elegantly dressed white man, they looked scornful and suspicious. My heart stopped, and I frantically looked for a yellow cab. It wasn't until over an hour later, and a number of dubious offers, that I finally found one. Before asking for any address, the somewhat surprised driver wanted to know if I had any money. When I then told him I came from Riverdale, he said aggressively: "That's the rich Jews' district, and we've got a snowstorm. So you can pay double." I offered him twenty dollars, but he demanded forty—"or you can walk there in the snow." The thought of walking twelve kilometers to Riverdale through this district and in this weather overcame all my resistance and I agreed.

Thus began a second adventure. The driver raced like a madman through shortcuts and over enormous potholes. I was flung from one side of the cab to the other, and several times my head collided with the windows. I implored him to drive more slowly, but that just made him even more daring, and he started skidding his Ford over the snow-covered, uneven streets. The weather was so bad I couldn't recognize where we were and already had visions of myself as a corpse in the Hudson River. Suddenly the driver slammed on the brakes and demanded his forty dollars. White as a sheet, I had hardly handed it over when he got out and tore my door open. With a broad smile that stood out particularly in the snowstorm, he shouted: "Hey, man, you better learn something about black Harlem!" I got out: he slammed his door and disappeared like a phantom. I took heed of this experience from March 1978 on all subsequent journeys into Manhattan and elsewhere. It was certainly another illustration of the obscene gulf between rich and poor in that city. That night I doubted whether my life in elegant Riverdale as a private researcher into Weill's history and as a frequent guest of New York society really had that much meaning.

But I had little time for social conscience. My financial situation was becoming critical, and Lenya was further delaying the promised contract. She had a fear of being poor, which made it difficult for her to commit to paying wages, although she was otherwise very generous. This fear was probably also the reason that Lys and I, on our visits to the beautiful Weill House on the river in New City, New Jersey, had to take our own lunch, although it did not stop Lenya inviting us to a restaurant afterwards. None of this bothered me much: I was happy to be in the Weill House.

The composer had financed the house with money he had received for his work in Hollywood. I was particularly impressed by his attic workroom with its spartan furnishings: simply a desk and a chair. Here he had written some of his major works, such as *Lost in the Stars.*

Lenya suggested that I write a biography of Weill, especially as it looked as though David Drew would never finish his book. Unfortunately she didn't tell me that the journalist Ronald Sander was already working on a similar project, and with her approval.

Another month passed before I explained to Lenya that I would have to return to Germany if she couldn't give me a contract. She realized I was serious. Lys had told her that I was already busy with Weill's work in America and had developed ideas on how best to promote it. Furthermore, an interview with me was about to appear in *The New York Times*, which would help publicize the Weill Foundation. This time it worked. Finally I had a contract in my hand, which ensured a modest living. It at least meant that I wouldn't have to depend on the loan that Gert von Gontard had generously offered me.

It was through Gert that I met John White, an unusual witness of Austrian-Jewish history, at a splendid lunch in the Metropolitan Club. As a former Viennese Jew, he had fled the Nazis to the United States and after an adventurous life had become the successful managing director of the New York City Opera. With great empathy, he immediately grasped my situation: "The great-grandson of the anti-Semite Wagner is working on the left-wing Jew Weill—that won't make you very popular in Germany! And I won't even ask you about your family. You follow your Aunt Friedelind's anti-Nazi attitude!" He had gotten straight to the heart of the matter, and I replied: "I do respect my aunt's attitude to National Socialism, but I don't share her uncritical attitude toward Richard Wagner's anti-Semitism. Unlike her, I can see an ideological line running directly from Wagner's article *The Jews in Music* to Hitler." When he noticed how important a conversation with him about National Socialism was for me, he invited me to his office, where he made some interesting points relevant to my work on Weill and gave me the results from contemporary research into National Socialism. He also recommended some standard works, such as Eugen Kogon's *The Theory and Practice of Hell.*

My meeting a few days later with Eric Werner, a distinguished music historian, went quite differently. I was familiar with his important works on Mendelssohn. Politely but warily, he inquired why I was occupying myself so intensively with Weill. Although Werner thought him interesting, he did not consider him important. Scarcely had I revealed my interest in German-Jewish history than he started to deliver a lecture on Wagner's anti-Semitism that was as knowledgeable as it was filled with strong aversion. Nor did he just refer to *The Jews in Music,* he also commented in detail on Cosima's numerous anti-Semitic remarks in her diaries, which had just been published in New York. I understood his horror at the anti-Semitic cult in Bayreuth and was not offended when he expressed loathing for Wagner and the Bayreuth "cretinism" as Nietzsche put it.

More difficult to accept was his condemnation of Germans in general, which included my generation and myself, of course. In fact he considered me part of the anti-Semitic tradition of my family, an opinion I was quick to refute. I described to him those decisive moments in my life as I confronted National Socialism, and he finally understood why I had written my doctoral thesis on Weill.

But his fundamental opinion remained unaltered. The meeting left me feeling like an ugly little German, a Nazi-Wagner, who could do no better than change his name as quickly as possible. Werner's bitterness and hatred strongly affected me, and I felt quite distraught when I left: dismayed by such a lack of interest in even talking to those who, like me, were suffering under the burden of their parents' Nazi past. I later discovered that he had suffered a particularly harrowing Jewish fate, although he never spoke of it in detail. That softened my judgment.

At the end of February 1978, I gave my first big interview in the United States. It took place thanks to Betty Smith, who had negotiated a conversation with Donal Henahan of *The New York Times*. As I had no experience at all with the American media, Betty prepared me for it with practiced patience. We went through my life in a game of questions and answers. As usual I answered her twenty questions on Bayreuth critically and had nothing good to say of Wagner and the German cultural scene. She was horrified: "You haven't learned a thing since our last talk. Just realize how important a successful interview with *The New York Times* could be for you!" So we went through the questions again and worked out a more diplomatic, but still tenable, version of the answers.

Betty's advice was spot on. Donal Henahan asked the questions she had expected, and my answers aroused his rather reserved but objective interest. In May 1978 the paper published an accurate account of what I had said regarding my production of *Fidelio*, music theater in the twentieth century, and Kurt Weill. Finally, I was able to read an article on me and my work that contained scarcely one word on the Wagner family and Bayreuth. This interview was the first of several with other important American newspapers, although none of them helped to improve my precarious financial situation.

One day I went to visit Lys in her apartment on West Seventy-third Street. By chance I noticed downstairs on the list by the doorbells a name written in English ornamental lettering which triggered a quite particular memory. It said: "Dr. Wolf, Kapellmeister." "Kapellmeister Wolf" was the alias Hitler had jokingly given himself. Until 1935, whenever he traveled between Berlin and Munich, Hitler would always make a stopover at the Hotel Bube in Bad Berneck, just outside Bayreuth; from there he would ring up his Winnie, announcing himself jovially as "Kapellmeister Wolf," whereupon Grandmother would dash by car to pick up her Führer and take him back to Villa Wahnfried.

I was cheeky enough simply to ring the bell to find out who this Kapellmeister Wolf on Seventy-third Street could be. The door opened and a distinguished, friendly-looking gentleman appeared, who asked with a strong German accent: "What can I do for you?" I didn't dare present him with the Hitler story out of the blue, so instead asked in German, not very originally: "Are you Kapellmeister Wolf?" He smiled and said he was. He opened his door wide and I spied a beautiful old Steinway grand that almost filled the small room. When I looked more closely, I saw there were a lot of yellowing photos standing on it. I don't know why, but to Kapellmeister Wolf's amusement I started looking at the photos and discovered to my excitement a photo from 1927 showing some people on the steps of the Baden-Baden Kurkonzertsaal. I read, "18 July 1927, Baden-Baden," and couldn't believe my eyes.

I burst out excitedly: "That was the day of the premiere of the *Mahagonny* Singspiel!"

Wolf was amused. "Yes—just look closely."

I recognized Kurt Weill, Bertolt Brecht, Lotte Lenya, Otto Klemperer, and Paul Hindemith.

"That's me on the left," said Wolf with modest pride.

"What, you were at the premiere?" I asked.

"Yes. But you seem very interested in Weill. Are you a descendant of his?"

In all the excitement I had forgotten to introduce myself. I laughed and said: "Excuse me. My name is Wagner."

"As in Richard?"

I nodded, and he started to study my profile. Then he beamed: "A Wagner in my home!" and we shook hands with mock solemnity.

With growing sympathy we continued our discussion, during

which I learned that he had led the rehearsals not only on the Singspiel *Mahagonny*, but also on the musical *The Eternal Road*, based on the novel by Franz Werfel, with music by Weill, which had its unsuccessful premiere in New York in 1937, directed by Max Reinhardt. We talked about the many good conductors of the Weimar years, and I named my favorites: Otto Klemperer and Bruno Walter. "Walter was my uncle," said Wolf. We roared with laughter. But the lighthearted mood came to an end when he told me his life story, which included persecution by the Nazis because of his Judaism, and emigration. Thanks to his lively and multi-faceted stories, for a while I was able, as though in a time machine, to journey back to the Berlin of the twenties. We parted like old friends.

It was only during our second meeting in his apartment a short time later that I hesitantly told Kapellmeister Wolf the association with his nameplate. He found my story bizarre and said magnanimously: "There are two sides to everything. Hitler brought us together here." I shall never forget Kapellmeister Wolf: he helped me to see myself not as a lousy German and, even worse, a lousy Wagner in New York—an attitude adopted by so many German Jews, who were by no means prepared to talk to the children of Nazi delinquencies.

Lys Symonette had a demanding job at the Curtis Institute in Philadelphia, one of America's leading conservatories, and gave up a lot of time to help Lenya, who left her all of Weill's mail to sort through. On top of that she looked after her husband and son like a true Jewish mama, as I teased her. In spite of all her commitments we met regularly in her one-room apartment, where there was always such a stimulating atmosphere, among the music scores and the historical photographs from Germany and the United States. The room was transformed into a glittering music theater when Lys started introducing me step by step to Weill's work in the period after his collaborations with Brecht. As soon as Lys started playing Weill, she was transformed, released from the cares of her taxing everyday life.

Lys helped me and encouraged me, although she had only modest means available. We often despaired at the state of the Weill archive and were hindered in our work by the fact that Lenya could not decide whether to transform the bequest into a professional center for Weill research. But such concerns disappeared when Lys started telling me about her time with Weill on Broadway, sat down at her Steinway grand for a swing session, and introduced me to American syncopation, jazz, and the wide variety of Weill's scores. It became clear to me how many prejudices there still were against Weill and his work, even in North America. During one of our Weill meetings—"with love for our Kurt"—I noticed a black-and-white photo of a conservatively dressed gentleman with a fine face, his melancholy eyes framed by round spectacles. "He looks like Victor," I blurted out, naming her son. Lys smiled and answered: "That's my father." And she started telling me about her dramatic flight from the Nazis via Italy to New York.

There was also a connection between a cousin of her father's, Emil Holzinger, and the Wagner family. He was a well-known member of the Jewish community in Bayreuth. After the First World War, when the general financial crisis reached even the festival, my grandfather asked Holzinger to urge the rich Jews of Bayreuth to support the festival financially. He advised Holzinger not to take Richard Wagner's anti-Semitism too seriously, which in view of his anti-Semitic writings and their effects even within the Wagner family was not very convincing. I maintained an embarrassed silence throughout the tale. Her parents, who came from a Jewish family in Mainz, had left the Jewish community, and so Lys had not been brought up in the Jewish faith. All the members of the family managed to emigrate from Nazi Germany in time. Lys is also a distant relation of the liberal German-Jewish playwright Carl Zuckmayer (1896–1977), a fact of which she is proud.

How paltry my problems seemed in comparison with the fate of so many others! And my father's lamentations, always bemoaning the "sacrifices" he had had to make in the difficult wartime years and after 1945: what did he know? And what did the onetime Hitler protégé *want* to know anyway about the suffering of the Jewish victims—the same suffering that Lys never complained about? When she noticed in her fine, sensitive way that her life story was moving me, she smiled and said: "I must confess to you that when I heard that you, a Wagner from that Bayreuth family, had written your doctoral thesis on Weill, I thought you must be meshugge. Other than your aunt Friedelind, all the other Wagners before you had probably been Nazis and anti-Semites."

Our friendship strengthened after this conversation. In the knowledge that we had become spiritually elective relations, we had a lot of fun when, as "free-thinking atheists" eating kosher chicken soup and garlic bagels, we blended the "September Song" and the *Tristan* Prelude or parodied the waltz of the Flower Maidens from *Parsifal*, and Lys attacked the keys with gusto to create the "Hollywood Wagner orchestra sound." She confessed to me with mock bashfulness, her lively eyes twinkling: "My family and I are Wagnerians! Can you forgive me? In spite of everything?" I blessed her solemnly and pronounced: "In the name of the Richard, the Kurt, and the Holy Ghost, may you and your family be forgiven for the mortal sin of being Wagnerians."

Lys is always there when I need her. That's something I can say of many friends, when I think of all the traps I've fallen into in my life and how I only emerged thanks to people like her.

Finally, my itinerary was ready to follow the trail of Weill in North America. I flew to Los Angeles. After a cold three months in New York, Beverly Hills seemed quite unreal, with its summery weather, its palm trees, the sterile cleanliness of its ostentatious mansions, and its snobs with their permanent impersonal smiles. This American artificiality became more bearable when I was able to spend a few days with the widow of Ernst Josef Aufricht on North Canyon Drive. Aufricht had been the distinguished director of the Theater am Schiffbauerdamm in Berlin during the Weimar period and until 1933 had staged the premieres of works by Brecht and Weill, Ernst Toller, Robert Musil, Paul Kornfeld, Georg Kaiser, Ödön von Horvath, Jean Cocteau, Karl Kraus, and Marieluise Fleisser. I had read Aufricht's autobiography of 1966, *Erzähle, damit du dein Recht erweist*, in New York in preparation for the meeting with Margot Aufricht and Paul Vambery, who had been Aufricht's dramaturg in Berlin. I found the book interesting not only for its description of how Brecht and Weill collaborated on *Die Dreigroschenoper* but also for the shocking account of Aufricht's flight from the Nazis to North America.

My passionate interest in her husband's work pleased Margot Aufricht, and she knew a lot about it. She spoke German to me, to show that she didn't think of all Germans in the same light—certainly not my generation—and she answered my questions quickly, accurately, and with great kindness. She described Brecht's family, their craving for money and power, in terms that reminded me of Bayreuth, which I pointed out to her, to her amusement. Her warm words made Weill, whose gentle and modest character I already had learned of through Lys and Lenya, more and more likable and easier for me to understand. I thought again and again during these talks how much generosity it must take for her to talk in an unprejudiced way with the grandson of Winifred Wagner, whose friend Adolf Hitler had driven the Aufricht family out of Germany. When we were talking of the Bayreuth Nazi and the new Bayreuth, she said kindly: "Your family with its view of German history has bequeathed a legacy to you which you will carry for the whole of your life."

During one of my visits I was surprised to find a beautifully decorated, candlelit table, with coffee and cake. It was 13 April—my thirty-first birthday. She gave me one of the last copies of her husband's book, with an affectionate dedication; it is one of my most treasured possessions. I was so moved I couldn't hold back my tears: the gesture was made all the more meaningful as I hadn't had any kind of birthday greetings from my family. At such moments I identified strongly with the German Jews of my grandparents' and parents' generation, and my anger at my family had grown to such a degree that after the four days in Margot Aufricht's house I toyed with the idea of becoming an American citizen and changing my name.

In mid-April, I visited Ira Gershwin, the lyricist and brother of George Gershwin. He had suffered a stroke only a few weeks before, but agreed to see me nevertheless in his luxury mansion in Beverly Hills. His staff, however, was obviously not enthusiastic

about my visit. Ira sat immobile in a wheelchair and had great difficulty communicating. We spoke briefly about his lyrics for the
1944 Hollywood film version of *Lady in the Dark* which looks critically at a woman's psychoanalysis. The little he was able to tell me
was revealing. On Weill he said: "You Europeans will never understand that the Volksoper was the model for the American musical,
as George and I showed in *Porgy and Bess* and Kurt and I tried to
do in the two works we did together. Kurt was a fine, soft-hearted
gentleman. Lenya never understood his character, but she felt the
greatness of his work." When I told Ira how much I liked *Porgy and
Bess*, he wheeled himself laboriously to his desk and pulled out a
double-LP album with all his well-known lyrics and gave it to me.
At the end of my visit he said: "Richard Wagner was a bastard but
a great composer!" Then he let one of his minders know that it was
time for me to go.

A year before, at Bettina Fehr's home in Bonn, I had met the
Germanist Cornelius Schnauber, the executor of Fritz Lang's estate
and a great expert on Jewish exile literature. On meeting him again
now, he invited me to his home. Among my fellow guests were
Ronald Schoenberg and his wife and Martha Feuchtwanger, whose
Bavarian origins were evident every time she opened her mouth,
even when she was speaking English. In spite of her great age she
had a very lively mind when she was talking about the work of her
husband, Lion, and about her life with him. She said: "Your work
on Weill is a pleasure for us emigrants. In this way we shan't be entirely forgotten either." What melancholy there was in her eyes
when she said these words!

The discussion I had with Judge Ronald Schoenberg, Arnold
Schoenberg's son from his second marriage, and his wife, the
daughter of the Austrian composer and Schoenberg pupil Eric
Zeisl, went quite differently. I wanted to know everything about his
father and his Jewishness, and Ronald, a Wagnerian, wanted to
hear everything about Richard Wagner, but nothing about his anti-
Semitism. We talked very pleasantly at cross purposes. He enthused about Bayreuth and was quite amazed that I had a different
opinion. Although he is ten years older than me, I identified with

his parents' generation of Jewish emigrants, whose children, born
in America, don't want to hear any more of their parents' stories
from the Nazi period and in defiant reaction sometimes act almost
pro-German. All attempts at finding a common subject for discussion came to nothing. When we said goodbye, we promised to try
afresh should we ever meet again. I said: "But please not Wagner!"—to which Ronald retorted: "And please not Schoenberg!"

During one of my meetings with Paul Vambery—who passed on
fascinating impressions of Weill and the Theater am Schiffbauerdamm—I got to know a close childhood friend of Weill's, Joseph
Joachim. Joachim has never gotten over his flight from Germany,
even assuming an English name, Jackson, in an attempt to sever
any obvious German ties. He was completely unaware of how German his manners were, however. Outbursts of hatred against
everything German were followed without pause by wild enthusiasm at the beauty of the German language. There we sat on Paul
Vambery's veranda with a view over Los Angeles and still we
couldn't get away from Germany. "Weill," said Vambery and Jackson, "was ruined by being kicked out by the Nazis."

The two asked me about my grandmother and the rest of the
family. It was difficult for me to answer without opening old wounds,
and I wanted to convey a discriminating picture of the generation
of the children of the perpetrators. So I spoke reservedly about
Bayreuth and the Germans. In so doing I gradually realized that I
had become an outsider. I only liked being with Germans who had
de-Germanized themselves abroad and tried to become cosmopolitan. Hitler, again and again, occupied center stage in my discussions—which were often interrupted by silence, to suppress tears.

How many uprooted people I met, with broken-off lives! Not all
emigrants were as successful as Weill. I learned much of Germany
through Vambery and Jackson.

On 20 April I flew via Chicago to Bloomington, Indiana—the
last stage rather hazardously in a single-motor propeller plane. In
Bloomington I hoped to meet another witness in time: Hans Busch,
who has since died. He was the son of Fritz Busch, who conducted
Die Meistersinger in Bayreuth in 1924 and had to leave Nazi Ger-

many because of his liberal views. He was subsequently one of the
founders of the Glyndebourne Festival in England, a sort of anti-
Bayreuth. He had worked together with Weill in 1923 and conducted the premiere of Weill's *Der Protagonist* in Dresden in 1926.

Hans Busch spoke openly about his loathing of the conductor
Karl Böhm, describing him as a "Nazi minion," who in 1933 had
ousted his father as a conductor at the Dresden opera house. My
grandmother disgusted him too. A lot of hurt resonated in his tales
of the brutal ejection of his family from Germany, and I felt
ashamed. But scarcely had he started to talk of his time with Weill
when his face became radiant, and he spoke warmly of the great
kindness and modesty of the composer.

Hans invited me to the dress rehearsal of John Eaton's opera
Danton and Robespierre, which after dedicated and thorough
preparation was having its premiere in Bloomington. While the rehearsal was in progress that evening, I briefly left the darkened auditorium. Pushing open one of the two swinging doors, I went
through and was about to let the door go when I noticed a small figure who called to me with an unmistakable German accent: "Attention, please!" I held the door back, and a little lady, whom in the
darkness I couldn't really see clearly, thanked me. I answered, "My
pleasure," and introduced myself.

The lady in the dark asked curiously: "Like Richard Wagner?"

I answered, rather amused: "Yes, but with mixed feelings. May I
know who I'm talking to here in the dark?"

A friendly, laughing voice said: "You may. My name is Busoni."

Upon which I asked, just as curiously: "Like Ferruccio?"

She said yes, and suggested we continue our conversation in the
light in the foyer.

So began one of my most important friendships: with Hannah
Busoni, the composer's daughter-in-law, who in the summer of
1978 took me into her apartment in her "Hansel and Gretel
House" behind Carnegie Hall, which was to remain my New York
base until 1994. Hannah helped me, in her discreetly generous
way, when I was up to my neck in trouble.

She told me a lot about Busoni; about her husband, the painter

Raffaele Busoni; about Weill and Lenya and the premiere of *Die Dreigroschenoper*, which she had attended as a girl in Berlin; and about her flight from Nazi Germany. Her maiden name was Apfel, and she was the daughter of a very respected Jewish lawyer in the Weimar Republic, who had fled to France in 1933. As Hannah's parents were divorced, she escaped with her mother to England.

Hannah had an extremely lively mind and a dry sense of humor, and she spoke such excellent German that her style of expression reminded me of my favorite German authors of the 1920s. She was gratefully affectionate toward New York, where she had survived by doing a whole variety of jobs, until the Federal Republic finally awarded her the pension of a German judge as "restitution," the Nazis having prevented her from finishing her law apprenticeship. Committed and selfless, she was now assisting young musicians and musicologists interested in her father-in-law, Ferruccio. It was through Hannah that I saw for the first time in America the other, better intellectual legacy of my family: that of Liszt, of whom Busoni had thought highly.

Anyone staying with Hannah might have thought he was living in the Berlin of the Weimar Republic. Many of her friends had a similar German-Jewish history, and all of them welcomed me, the grandson of Winifred Wagner, like a grandson of their own.

It was also at Hannah's that I met Paul Falkenberg. Until 1933 he had lived in Berlin as a prominent sound editor. He thought it exciting and plausible when I told him that Weill had appropriated Jewish sacred music in his songs with Brecht. One day when I was asking Hannah about her identity, she answered, "It's good to be Jewish," by which she meant the fated community of the persecuted German Jews, not the religious community.

Time stood still between us. Our goodbyes were always quick, as we assumed that I would soon once again come puffing and sweating up the steep stairs to the second floor. With my suitcases standing in front of her door, we would hug and she would set to cooking for her greedy guest. I put a stop to it in the end by taking her out for meals, but I will never forget Hannah's shining eyes when she opened her door. Hannah died in 1994.

After my trip to Bloomington, I stayed in Chicago for a few days with Peter Jonas, at that time artistic administrator of the Chicago Symphony Orchestra and before that personal assistant to Sir Georg Solti, whom I'd met as well. He had offered to help me in America with a letter of recommendation, and now fulfilled that promise.

At the end of April I returned to New York, where I moved into new lodgings in the Lincoln Towers on West End Avenue, which Lys had fixed up for me. Although the rather sparsely furnished apartment was on the thirteenth floor, I felt as though I were living in the middle of the street: day and night cars and trucks thundered to and fro, uptown and downtown. Beatrix had been in Munich while I traveled to and from Los Angeles, and now she rejoined me in New York. I started writing a synopsis for my biography of Weill, and together with Lys I studied all his works that had been written in America.

It was during this time that I first heard that Lenya had made materials for a Weill biography available to Ronald Sander as well. Eliot Ravetz, my agent at the time, wanted to sue her for this, as she had assured me exclusivity by contract. But I had no desire to take legal proceedings against Lenya: I was very fond of her despite all her weaknesses. Once Sander's biography of Weill was announced, my business relations with Ravetz and his agency deteriorated, and contacts with publishers became more difficult too. I learned what it means to try to do business in the jungle of New York publishers and agents. As always, Lys Symonette and Hannah Busoni stood by me with advice and practical help.

In this situation I noticed that I was still far from becoming Americanized. I could not come to like an existence in which all my energies were devoted solely to a better chance of survival.

Amid this crisis of identity and work, I met by chance in Greenwich Village one of my closest childhood friends, Eckart Grebner, a dentist in Munich. Eckart's mother had worked for many years in the Festspielhaus, so he knew what had been happening to me, even after we had lost contact with one another. If we spoke of the past in Bayreuth, then we did so with the awareness of two Germans who wanted in no way to be typically German.

When I talked with him then, I realized how much I still had in common with Germans such as him, and I felt facets of the German language and culture as a great enrichment in my homelessness. Eckart was, like me, fascinated at first by everything that was different from himself and loved every kind of cultural stimulus. He was extremely charming, and I loved listening to him, even though he couldn't always convince me of his "really new" art or ecological concerns. Unwittingly, he made me feel like an old man. Eckart never thought for a moment of his financial security or insurance for his old age. He registered every essential change in my development with curious sympathy and never made me feel I had to justify myself for the drastic changes of direction in my life. On the contrary, in his eyes nothing should stay as it is. And so he started, without self-denial or false politeness, to live with me in my new world beyond traditional morals. Out of interest, and out of aversion to prescribed Christianity, he immersed himself in Eastern cultures and meditation. He also looked into Judaism. In Eckart—with his inner unrest in the search of new facets of his own identity—I recognized something of myself too.

When Hannah Busoni went to a German health spa that summer, as she did every year, she invited Beatrix and me to move into her apartment near Carnegie Hall. We gratefully accepted the offer: it saved us paying expensive rent, and moreover the location was much better and quieter. We took every opportunity of going to concerts, operas and Broadway shows. I went mainly to the lesser known but much more lively venues that had arisen as alternatives to the New York establishment. The more avant-garde the production, the more curious I was.

An invitation from Schuyler Chapin and his wife, Betty, came like a bolt out of the blue. I had known Schuyler since his time as Leonard Bernstein's permanent adviser. He had been general manager of the Metropolitan Opera for several years and at the same time dean of performing arts at Columbia University. He is one of the least typical representatives of the New York establishment: always modest, discreetly helpful, and unselfish in his advice. Of a warmhearted spontaneity that ignores all social boundaries, he is a real liberal international gentleman. Betty came from the famous piano-manufacturing family Steinway and was just as modest as her husband. With them we celebrated Independence Day at their country house at Long Pond on Cape Cod, with its own lake and surrounded by beautiful forests. Such pleasure reconciled me to all the bad experiences with New York theatrical and literary agents.

In Schuyler's beautiful apartment on the corner of Sixty-sixth Street and Lexington Avenue I met Leonard Bernstein. I had first met him in 1977 during a rehearsal for my *Fidelio* in Bonn, and we had become friends. Lenny was always interested in learning about the Wagner family's inside stories, so seeing him in New York brought Bayreuth back to mind. He enthused about Wieland and fulminated against my father, whom he held to be a closet Nazi in spite of all his liberal-left airs. When I inquired how he had reached this opinion, he told me about a meeting with my father about a planned assignment conducting *Tristan* which eventually came to nothing. "As long as he is boss in Bayreuth, I won't conduct on the Festspielhügel," he declared angrily.

On the other hand, like many Jewish artists Bernstein had a lot of sympathy for Aunt Friedelind. "You seem to be continuing the tradition of your aunt with your work on Weill," he said kindly. I answered: "Friedelind still believes in Richard Wagner's innocence where anti-Semitism is concerned. I don't!"

It was obvious that this subject moved Bernstein. He became thoughtful and pondered aloud: "How is it that I as a Jew love the music of this repulsive anti-Semite, especially his *Tristan?*" I replied: "I have no right, as a great-grandson of Wagner, to say anything to you. But in *Tristan*, despite my aversion to the man Wagner, I can't see any anti-Semitism. And you should record it one day."

He did record *Tristan*, a few years later in Munich, and produced a video on his Wagner dilemma. In 1990 he gave me the still-incomplete film and asked for my opinion. I didn't think it very well done and told him so at our last meeting in April. Amused by my answer, he asked me to work with him on it. He died shortly afterwards, having helped me with my lecture tour on Wagner in Israel, in opposition to the machinations of Bayreuth.

—————

12

The Long Arm of Bayreuth

At the end of July 1978 Beatrix and I traveled back to Germany: my mother needed to move and I needed to make professional contacts. My fleeting visit to Bayreuth was clouded by the bad state of my mother's health. Finally, she agreed to leave Bayreuth, so together with Eva, Beatrix and I planned to set up a home for her in Wiesbaden.

I was worried about my professional future, and so I tried to pick up some commissions in Germany, in the theater or in the media. My efforts were all in vain. I had one unpleasant meeting at the end of September in Mannheim, where I applied for the job of dramaturg with Friedrich Meyer-Oertel, the head of opera production there.

After that initial meeting I had strong doubts as to whether I had a future in the German theater scene with its uptight, intellectual proceedings. It was a curious situation. I wrote about Lotte Lenya's eightieth birthday for the *Neue Zürcher Zeitung* and the Viennese *Die Presse* and couldn't wait to pack my bags again and get out of Germany.

This longing was increased even more when I collected my mother in Bayreuth, where she had been living with Grandmother Winifred. Grandma was once again the politician of yore. Although she had initially made out that she would support her former daughter-in-law and her grandchildren, she now had swung completely the other way, to my father's side. When, shortly before we

left, I asked her for an advance of forty-five hundred marks against
my inheritance, she answered with a cold smile: "You can get
money from your rich New York Jews or the Kurt Weill archive."
She was all enthusiasm now for my father's second wife and secretary, Gudrun, although she hadn't had a good word to say about
her in 1976. No wonder I felt less comfortable "at home" than ever
before. By mid-October 1978, with a cheap Pan Am ticket, I flew
back to New York.

Immediately after my return I put the final details to plans I had
made with Betty Smith for a Weill concert in honor of Lenya, to be
held at New York's Avery Fisher Hall. I had started to plan the concert with David Gilbert months before my visit to Germany. I had
met David in 1976, in Bayreuth, when he was Boulez's assistant,
and he had meanwhile become the permanent conductor of Con-
necticut's Greenwich Philharmonia Orchestra.

A trial run of the Weill concert was given on 12 November at
Avery Fisher Hall. Lenya attended—coiffured, made up, and dressed
like an aging Hollywood star. But our timing was unfortunate as far
as the media were concerned: on the day of the premiere the New
York press was on strike, and in America, what doesn't happen in
the media hasn't happened. So there was no improvement in my
job prospects.

I was now working with even greater intensity on the structure of
my Weill biography, while my new literary agent, Elsie Stern, was
looking for a publisher. Furthermore, the theater agent Germinal
Hilbert had promised me direction of a *Don Giovanni* in Marseille.
I would have been able to live carefree for several months on the
expected fee.

In this hectic period Beatrix and I moved twice, ending up as
lodgers of Marion McLaughlin in two small rooms in a house on the
corner of Seventy-first Street and Lexington Avenue. Our time
there was oppressive: our landlady liked to discuss her personal
problems with me, even at night, added to which some of the
neighbors didn't like us being there. Once for example, I was rung
up after midnight and sworn at in German by a quavering male
voice: "Dirty German swine, get out of our house—we don't want

any Nazis here. Clear out or we'll bump you off!" It literally took my breath away: I had never encountered such aggression before. I inhaled deeply and said: "We should get to know one another personally. I am German, yes, but I'm not a Nazi, and anyway, I was born in 1947." At that I heard a furious snorting, and the anonymous caller with the nervous male voice slammed down the receiver. This malicious game was to be repeated several times. It wore me down, not least because I couldn't get a good night's rest anymore. I later noticed that whenever I heard German being spoken on the elevator only moments before it stopped for me, silence fell as soon as I boarded. Now I suspected the kind of circle the caller came from. Obviously people with a German-Jewish history were living here. As I find any form of hatred offensive, I tried to dismiss these incidents quickly—but unsuccessfully.

In mid-June of 1978, at the Hampshire House on Central Park South, I had already met the man who wielded influence over the world opera market, Ronald Wilford. As an agent he commanded the highest fees for himself and his artists, although such exorbitant demands were jeopardizing the whole opera market and in particular the opera repertoire. Anyone wanting to make a career in opera took care not to criticize his business methods: no one wanted to land up on Wilford's blacklist. He seemed interested during our hour-long discussion and was distantly polite, like many of the powerful people in the opera business. Most of all he wanted to know how things stood between Father and me and whether, in spite of all the tensions (of which, apparently, Eva had informed him), I would be the successor. I understood: he was already networking for future business. When I answered him evasively, he cut short our conversation. But I hadn't come to exchange civilities with him, so I presented him with my CV, showed him interviews I had given, and supplemented this with other things that might be useful to an agent. He concentrated on the interview in *The New York Times* and declared he would give it to his best agent, Matthew Epstein, and ask him to see me. He then asked me to pass on his regards to my father. But after one hour I was as wise as before.

After eight months and many humiliating attempts, I finally got an appointment with Epstein in mid-February 1979. The words of a highly dramatic American singer who, shortly before, had not been exactly encouraging still rang in my ears: "Don't expect anything! You're neither gay nor Jewish, and people know your father is against you!"

We met in his New York office, and I quickly felt that he was making it hard for me to find any kind of basis for discussion with him. From the first moment to the last of our hour-long conversation—constantly interrupted by telephone calls—he made it clear that he was the boss and that my career now lay in his hands.

I felt as if he were interrogating me on my views on opera. When I spoke of Bertolt Brecht, Konstantin Stanislavsky, Vsevolod Meyerhold, Erwin Piscator, and other writers and directors, he said at once: "Unmarketable! You are only marketable as a Wagner, who produces Wagner and who is the future director of the festival. If you want to get into the business here in the U.S.A.—and that applies to Europe too—then you'll have to give up your left-wing ideas, because you won't get anywhere with him. Drop Weill too! You're entering an area there that doesn't belong to you."

I interrupted him and asked: "Why shouldn't I work on Weill? I've written a book on him, after all, that earned me my doctorate at the University of Vienna and the job with the Weill Foundation."

Epstein answered with a disparaging smile: "For a grandson of Winifred Wagner there's no place here for anything to do with Weill."

I had to stop myself telling Epstein that this was racism under a different name and answered guardedly: "I am a convinced liberal, even in the American sense of the word. Out of all the Jewish intellectuals I have met here in the United states, I have never heard anyone say I am unwelcome because of my work on Weill and because of my origins."

Epstein became rather embarrassed and said: "I know. Things have changed. We're also doing business with Bayreuth, although we know everything about Wagner and Hitler. But that doesn't mean we have forgotten that you come from the Nazi Wagner family."

I became more self-confident and retorted with some energy: "I find any form of discrimination and ideological fanaticism repulsive! A wide variety of opinions in art and life is part of my identity, and that has nothing to do with the character of my family in Bayreuth!"

Epstein was cool. "You'll never make a career for yourself like that!" he said. "Your only chance is to be a Wagner who makes Wagner, and to be in line with Bayreuth and your father."

I remained silent and wanted to leave. Epstein noticed and said: "I'll write you a recommendation, as no one knows you here in the United States, and introduce you as a Wagner who does Wagner and is right in line with his father and Bayreuth."

"No thanks! I'll try to make my way in life without making false statements against my convictions," I said, albeit unwisely.

Epstein was thunderstruck. "You'll never find a job here or anywhere else if you don't follow my advice. I only want to help you."

Disgusted, I left the office and hoped I would never be dependent on people like him. Sadly, that was to prove one of the many illusions I had with regard to agents.

Germinal Hilbert, meanwhile, who had offices in Paris and Munich and collaborated closely with my father, was now talking not only about Marseille, but also about Buenos Aires, where he held out the prospect of a *Lohengrin* for me. He said preliminary contracts already existed. I worked out detailed plans for both productions and asked Hilbert to conclude the contracts. But it now transpired that Hilbert could not even produce negotiation documentation. He had totally misled me. When I told the conductor Karl Böhm about this and considered bringing an action against him, Böhm said: "If you cross swords with Hilbert, you'll never set foot in any of the bigger opera houses in Europe again. Come to terms with Hilbert and your father and there'll be no lack of work."

But I had no intention of coming to terms with them, although I did not want to risk legal proceedings either, given my desperate financial situation. With the help of a lawyer, a compromise was reached.

13

Return to Germany

nable to earn enough money in the U.S.A., I flew back to Germany in February 1979 and started looking for work without an agent, writing to every theater in Germany and generally rushing from pillar to post. In mid-March an offer from the Kammeroper in Vienna seemed to be firm, and I began working with my friend Johannes Dreher on Johann Nepomuk Nestroy's *Tannhäuser* parody. In the sixties Johannes had been projection painter and artistic collaborator for my uncle and my father, but he remained a fatherly friend, one of the few from my Bayreuth past who did not swim with the tide.

Johannes had had a colorful life. As a pupil of the painter Otto Dix he had been on the Nazis' blacklist. They had persecuted him, and the torture to which he was subjected had left him with a permanent limp, but he had remained a nonconformist. He was a painter, and his set paintings were in demand in all the important opera houses of the world. He was always up to the latest developments in stage and lighting techniques, and the Bayreuth and Salzburg festivals owe him a lot. His modesty made him endearing, but didn't do him much good in the hostile opera jungle, which exploited him, much to my anger. With him I could talk about everything, and he followed, with amused approval, my ideas for ridding the theater, the opera business—in fact, the world in general—of corruption.

When we worked together he was sometimes as enthusiastic as a young man. Both sanguine types, we raged and screamed at one another if things didn't go as we had planned, afterwards hugging one another with the greatest affection. We were equally glad when things on the stage finally worked out as we had imagined.

I owe thanks to Johannes not only for essential knowledge of how one employs theatrical means, but also for the warning never to forget for whom one makes theater. For Nestroy's *Tannhäuser* parody I wrote a new prologue and read it aloud to the writer Hilde Spiel. She liked it, and so in April we started rehearsing. But after only two days Hans Gabor, director of the Kammeroper, had rehearsals stopped, without giving reasons, and refusing to discuss his surprising action. I was upset and confused—more so when the Kammeroper gave guest performances of the parody in mid-August 1980 at Bayreuth's Margravian Opera House. Someone in Bayreuth had evidently once again been pulling strings.

At the beginning of May 1979, my mother and sister's lawyer notified me that I could collect my furniture and other items from Bayreuth. I wanted to get the disagreeable business over with quickly, so I hired a small van and drove there at the end of the month with Beatrix's brother for moral support. As my father refused to see me, I turned to the caretaker, successor to the kindly Grandpa Lodes, who had always been a faithful servant of my father. Despite having known me for many years, he treated me like a stranger and in great haste unlocked a shed that had been named Rudelsheim, after one of the Bayreuth chorus masters. It was cold and dirty inside. The caretaker pointed into the corner where my things were stored, then stayed close by me to check every single piece I loaded into the van. I lost my temper and shouted at him to kindly clear off. That was precisely the language the caretaker understood. Deferentially he apologized and said he was only following Father's orders and had nothing at all against me personally. Angry, I recalled that Father has always surrounded himself with such people.

The caretaker finally got off my back and moved to stand between the door and the spot where my things were piled, and I set to sorting through everything. When I looked more closely I found that the furniture that I had lived with for many years was missing and that in its place Father had put a few shabby old wardrobes. I didn't want them, and gave the caretaker the job of telling my father so. Among the dirty pile I discovered my puppet theater and the sets I had made as an eight-year-old with the help of the set painter Otto Wiesner. Everything was falling to pieces and useless. But the puppets for the theater were in an old Bavarian chest and by some miracle had survived storage. Not so my diaries, which I had been keeping since the beginning of the sixties. Unfortunately, they were moldy and dirty, the pages stuck together and were unreadable. I had only one thought: get out of here, where they let memories of one's past disintegrate. One day I shall build my son his own puppet theater.

All I took as I left the shed were the puppets and a chair by the famous Viennese furniture maker Thonet. The chair had been used in Wieland's production of *Parsifal*, to carry Amfortas into the temple of the Grail. When I recognized the *"Parsifal* chair" I decided to take my own compensation and save it from the pile of junk.

How many memories came flooding back at the sight of that stage prop from Wieland's time: thoughts of George London and Thomas Stewart, who had sung Amfortas, and of the guest appearances of the Bayreuth Festival in Franco's Barcelona. Before I drove off, I told the caretaker that he was welcome to tell my father about the "theft." Then, in the almost empty van, we tore along the Siegfried-Wagner-Allee, past Breker's heroic Wagner bust in the Festspielpark, and then past Wahnfried on the Richard-Wagner-Strasse, without visiting my grandmother. I wanted only one thing: to get away as quickly as possible. Later I gave up my claim to all the furniture. It would have been too constant a reminder of Bayreuth.

Although I didn't want to give up America as the big alternative, I nevertheless still clung to the illusion of being able to build an existence for myself in the German theater and opera world, especially as my finances were at a very low ebb. And so in summer 1979 I accepted a job as assistant director at the Salzburg Festival, working on Dieter Dorn's production of Richard Strauss's *Ariadne auf Naxos*. Dieter is, in his personal relations outside the theater, a witty, sensitive man with brilliant ideas, and I greatly admire his directorial work. But as soon as he entered the Salzburg Kleines Festspielhaus, he changed into one of the most stereotypical of theatrocrats.

The Salzburg Festival, like the one in Bayreuth, is a collection of prominent or allegedly prominent figures who regard nothing as being more important than themselves—the acme of high society. These people were interested in me only insofar as I was part of Bayreuth gossip. They asked about the family quarrel and whether I would follow my father as boss of the festival. It was made clear to me that a Wagner without Bayreuth connections would not get a footing in Salzburg, either.

In Salzburg there was also the celebration of Karl Böhm's eighty-fifth birthday. Leonard Bernstein and his Jewish melody performed by Christa Ludwig as "Piccola Serenata," and the great Herbert von Karajan congratulating his friend Karl, greatly moved me. Everybody was moved in fact: the public no less than the fine gentlemen of the classical-music industry. The biographical gray areas of the musical heroes of the Nazi period were not mentioned: that had all been long forgotten.

In September 1979, after my weeks in Salzburg, I flew to Ankara to direct Carl Orff's *Carmina Burana*. When Johannes Dreher, who had negotiated this contract for me, and I arrived at our quarters, in what was at the time a rather unattractive Ankara, after a tiring flight and a wild drive, we felt quite ill. The sanitary installations were not functioning, and when we went out for a walk we saw that the city resembled a besieged fort. The ruling military junta feared an armed resistance.

During the first night we heard shots and then a bloodcurdling scream. I dashed to the window and saw two soldiers in the twilight beating a man to death with their rifle butts after they had shot and wounded him. It was the first time I had witnessed someone being murdered. I was angry but paralyzed by fear; my instinct was to fly back to Munich immediately. When I told the directors of the opera house the next morning of my traumatic experience, they retreated into aloof silence. That made me even more uneasy and strengthened my urge to get out.

I decided to stay on until the dress rehearsal, however, upon meeting with the opera house chorus and the ballet master Attila and his group. The majority of the chorus were young, open-minded conservatory graduates who were eager to learn. They agreed with my concept and wanted to play *Carmina Burana*, Orff's masterpiece and a celebration of transformative power, in Ankara in 1979. I discarded Orff's mythological elements, which were incomprehensible to them. They amused me in particular with their embarrassed giggles as we worked on the many erotic scenes. But prudery and embarrassment soon disappeared, and together we discovered the political statements contained in *Carmina Burana*, which, like *The Ring*, portrays a struggle between love and power. However, for some friends of the military junta the concept was unsettling: for "inexplicable" reasons the stage equipment wouldn't work and rehearsals were boycotted for days. After the dress rehearsal, I said goodbye to all those who had gone through the last weeks with Johannes and me.

What was particularly important for me in those days in Ankara, though, was the beginning of my friendship with Pulat Tacar and his wife, Selda. Pulat came from one of the few families who had a lot of influence in Turkey. He had been general consul in Munich and had enjoyed great esteem among the Turkish population there, earning the honorary name "Workers' Consul" because of his efforts on behalf of their interests. When we met in Ankara at the beginning of my rehearsals, he had our quarters transformed into a place fit for human habitation within a few hours, before disappearing on diplomatic affairs. Both then and later, when he turned up at the end of rehearsals, he opened my eyes to his country, its culture, and its people, to whom he felt bound in critical sympathy. He is extraordinarily cultured, speaks eight languages, and is passionate about art, philosophy, and world religions. It came as no surprise that he knew Richard Wagner's works well too. His wife, Selda, was Austrian and therefore had not found it easy integrating into the Turkish diplomatic corps. Both were superb hosts.

In October 1979 Johannes and I left before the premiere of *Carmina Burana* in protest against the obstructing of our work. It was difficult to say goodbye to Pulat and Selda and we felt sad on the plane to Munich. Years later, I proudly told my son the story of the Turkish carpet which is now lying at the side of his bed. Pulat had gotten it for me at an incredibly cheap price at a bazaar in Ankara. It represents my director's fee for *Carmina Burana.*

I had gotten a job as the evening director at the Frankfurt Opera House through the journalist Wolf Rosenberg, and began work on 1 November 1979. At that time the conductor and composer Michael Gielen was director of the opera house. I only saw him once, for a brief, impersonal conversation when he asked me whether I really needed the job so urgently, as it wouldn't bring anything other than the salary. I was surprised by this comment. I thought highly of Gielen as a conductor, and it was because of him that I had accepted the job.

In addition to my managing the evening performances, the deputy director Christof Bitter told me which parts of the repertoire needed freshening up and gave me *Carmen* in an old production by Jean-Pierre Ponnelle and another old warhorse, a production of Johann Strauss's *Die Fledermaus* from the sixties.

The conditions under which I worked were pathetic. There was no piano score of *Carmen,* only a useless video recording. The opera house officials were indifferent to this miserable situation, and it was made clear to me yet again that a Wagner who has crossed swords with Bayreuth finds no allies on the administration floor of German opera houses. Even in Frankfurt, people gave the impression of being left-wing and progressive—the vocabulary of 1968—but were authoritarian in their management of people. As we were the least influential people in the opera house, my colleagues and I suffered in the day-to-day tussle. Many depended on their jobs, although they found what they did pointless. To use the words of one of the more cynical people in the administration, we were "alienated wage-earners." People reveled in unworldly ideas for saving the workers and indeed all the oppressed of the earth, and understood theater as an instrument for overcoming social contradictions or as a platform for doctrines of salvation. This theater comprised incompatible elements: absurdly luxuriant program books filled with pseudo-leftist jargon but keeping one eye on the media and sponsors, deferential toward political power and contemptuous of the public. And the whole time their gaze was directed at the next free chair in German opera power-broker August Everding's intendants' merry-go-round.

When I saw Dorothea Glatt-Behr creeping around in the underground shafts of the opera house as ambassador from Bayreuth, I resolved again to have nothing to do with theater managers who confuse their stage universe with reality. The job was only a way to earn money, but it did help me to understand more clearly what was happening in the West German opera scene.

Once my work at Frankfurt was completed at the end of January 1980, I began work at Trier. I had chosen Busoni's *Turandot* as a parody of opera and his *Arlecchino* as a caustic settling of accounts with moralizing ideologies of every kind. As the performances were taking place in right-wing Trier, I had incorporated harsh anticlerical allusions, which were taken up by the chorus, the ensemble, and the excellent extras with great enthusiasm.

Our popularity among our colleagues grew, to the great annoyance of the administration, when I started reacting to the despotism of the administration in the interests of chorus and soloists. The intendant, Manfred Mützel, even tolerated the chorus master's absence for the dress rehearsal. So I drew media attention to the unbelievable working conditions in the Trier theater. Despite all the obstacles, the premiere was a success and the intendant endured our practices. Later Mützel blackened my name at a meeting of German intendants.

After my experiences in Trier I accepted an offer to work as dramaturge and director of the opera house in Wuppertal. Only later did I discover that the director of the opera, Friedrich Meyer-Oertel, and the general intendant, Hellmuth Matiasek, were interested in working with me simply because my name was Wagner and I therefore might, albeit in the distant future, play a role at Bayreuth. Moreover, when Richard Wagner's first opera, *Die Feen*, was performed in Wuppertal in February 1981, they thought it appropriate to pass me around the media like a museum piece. Meyer-Oertel also approved when I collected sixty thousand marks for the Wuppertal opera house from Wagner Societies and a private sponsor.

Richard Wagner in Munich, 1880.
Photographed by Joseph Albert.

Cosima Wagner in the 1890s.

Cosima and Richard Wagner in Vienna,
1872. Photographed by Fritz Luckhardt.

Left to right: Cosima, Siegfried, and Richard Wagner in Bayreuth, 1873. Photographed by Adolf von Gross.

Houston Stewart Chamberlain (1855–1927), the English racial theoretician and one of Adolf Hitler's mentors. He married Richard and Cosima Wagner's daughter Eva.

The Berlin Wagner monument, erected on 1 October 1903 by Professor Gustav Eberlein and presented to the public on 3 October 1903.

Thora Nissen Drexel, Gottfried's maternal grandmother (1891–1953).

View of Villa Wahnfried as seen from the back in the 1920s.

Siegfried Wagner and his wife, Winifred, on the grounds of Villa Wahnfried with their children. Left to right: Wolfgang, Siegfried, Verena, Winifred, Friedelind, and Wieland. The photograph was taken in 1924, the year the festival reopened after World War I.

Bust of Richard Wagner by Adolf
Hitler's favorite sculptor, Arno Breker.

Siegfried Wagner (right) with
Arturo Toscanini in June 1930
during the festival.

In the garden of the Festspielhaus, 1930: (standing) Alexander von Spring
and Heinz Tietjen (artistic director of the Bayreuth Festival from 1930–1944);
(seated) Wilhelm Furtwängler, Winifred Wagner, and Arturo Toscanini.

Winifred Wagner greeting Adolf Hitler at the front entrance of the Festspielhaus.

Adolf Hitler at the Festspielhügel in August 1938.

Winifred Wagner, Adolf Hitler, and Wieland Wagner ahead of Wolfgang Wagner and Hitler's guards on the villa grounds.

Verena Wagner, Adolf Hitler, and Friedelind Wagner at the Villa Wahnfried on 3 August 1938.

Adolf Hitler, Winifred Wagner, and some of her guests in the Siegfried Wagner House. An annex, called the Führer Anbau, was added in 1935 exclusively for Hitler.

Wolfgang Wagner. A photograph taken in September 1939, the week the Nazis invaded Poland.

Crowd gathering outside the Festspielhügel to see Adolf Hitler at the window of the Wagner family box.

Villa Wahnfried, badly damaged by the Royal Air Force in April 1945. On the right is Siegfried Wagner House, where Adolf Hitler lived in the 1930s. From 1947 onward, it was used as a base for U.S. counterespionage.

From left to right: Wieland, Verena, and Winifred Wagner, Heinz Tietjen, and Wolfgang and Friedelind Wagner at the Villa Wahnfried in the summer of 1934.

Gottfried's mother, Ellen Drexel (left), and her brother Gustav (right) at their confirmation in 1934, with their parents, Adolf and Thora. Gustav is Gottfried's only surviving uncle.

Ellen Drexel gave up a career in dance when she married Wolfgang Wagner.

Wieland and Wolfgang Wagner in Wahnfried Park, 1945.

Wolfgang Wagner (right) with Wilhelm Furtwängler (center) in 1951.

Conductor Herbert von Karajan (center), shown here in 1952, twice became a member of the Nazi party, in Germany and in Austria, then later created the Salzburg Festival, producing and conducting special performances of Richard Wagner's operas.

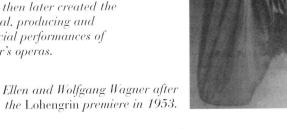

Ellen and Wolfgang Wagner after the Lohengrin *premiere in 1953.*

Gottfried at the age of four with his black Scottish terrier, Pupsi.

Gottfried (left) and Wolf-Siegfried (Wieland's son, nicknamed Wummi) with Hera, their Newfoundland, at the main entrance of Villa Wahnfried in 1953.

Gottfried posing with a papier-mâché swan, a prop used in his father's debut production of Lohengrin in 1953.

Friedelind, Winifred, and Verena Wagner in 1954, the year Friedelind returned to the festival for the first time after her escape from Nazi Germany.

Gottfried with his father and sister Eva at the Festival Theater in 1955.

Eva and Gottfried Wagner with their mother's friends in 1955.

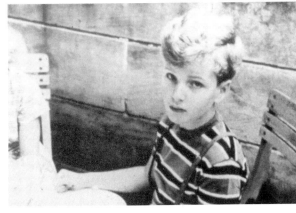

Gottfried at the age of nine in 1956, the same year he was confronted with a documentary on Nazi Germany and his family's past.

Wolfgang and Ellen Wagner at a Society of the Friends of Bayreuth dinner in 1956. Wieland Wagner is standing.

Winifred and Wolfgang at the stage entrance of the Festspielhaus in 1957.

Wieland and Winifred Wagner in the early 1960s.

Gottfried with Lotte Lenya in 1978.

A rehearsal of Arlecchino *by Ferrucio Busoni with the ensemble of the Trier Theater in 1978.*

Gottfried and his wife, Teresina, photographed in 1990 in Massada in front of the oldest synagogue in the world.

Gottfried with Ralph Giordano and Hanna Jordan, a famous German-Jewish set designer who lost part of his family in Theresienstadt.

Gottfried in Zurich in August 1992 with Herzl Shmueli, the well-known Israeli musicologist and Gottfried's host at Tel Aviv University.

Abraham Peck, the Post-Holocaust Dialogue Group cofounder, with Gottfried in Berlin, March 1994.

*Gottfried with Teresina, his son, Eugenio, and his mother-in-law,
Antionetta Malacrida, in 1997. Photographed by Fabio Tosca.*

But the mood changed when the media showed greater interest in my dramaturgical work on *Die Feen* than in the conventional staging of the director. In fact it triggered off some melodramatic scenes and petty jealousies. In a crowded canteen Meyer-Oertel made it clear to me, in a loud voice, that he was the opera director and I was only his employee. Matiasek regarded Wuppertal merely as a stopover point in his career, and his then assistant played the boss in his absence. So tensions were almost inevitable.

The only bright spots were new friendships. First I got to know and value the set designer Hanna Jordan. Our conversation revolved around matters we believed important: German-Jewish history, National Socialism, and its effects on the cultural and political climate in Germany. Hanna and her family had been victims of the Nuremberg race laws, and she reacted violently to any form of intolerance or discrimination. She is a trusty left-winger, a person who has suffered a lot and by no means always feels at ease in Germany, with its undigested past. Such feelings bind us in a special way. The fact that I am a Wagner amuses her, in particular as at the time she was living in the Wotanstrasse, of all places, in Wuppertal-Elberfeld. "Hanna of the Wotanstrasse": we still make jokes about it, as we do about Wagner, whom she considers important as a "theater animal," as I do. When we met again years later in Wuppertal, in 1992, at my lecture "The Case of Wagner in Israel and Germany," it was as though we had seen one another only yesterday.

On 5 March 1980 my grandmother died in the hospital in Überlingen. I had seen her for the last time three weeks earlier, a visit that will always remain in my memory because of the way she spoke with such disconcerting clarity about her approaching death. It was only Aunt Friedelind whose grief was genuine. The solemn burial on 10 March in Bayreuth was an embarrassment from beginning to end. My father had worked out a seating plan separating the family into the pro-Festspielhügel and anti-Festspielhügel contingents. A string quartet provided the only relief from interminable speeches in which my grandmother was acknowledged as the savior of Bayreuth. Not a word was said about the intimate friendship between Winnie and Wolf, and even Mayor Hans Walter

Wild distinguished himself by maintaining total silence on her National Socialist past.

And then there was the media circus, adroitly handled by the Bayreuth PR professionals. Among the onlookers were delegates of the NPD and old friends of my grandmother's from the Nazi period. I avoided their attempts at condolence. Free of his mother's presence, my father now exuded omnipresence as festival boss and did not consider it necessary to receive his own family or the guests. While the family feigned mourning to the outside world, they privately rejoiced that the domineering shadow had finally lifted, and got down to business: dividing up the inheritance.

Far more traumatic than the death of my grandmother was the breakup of my marriage to Beatrix. At Christmas 1980 Beatrix and I faced up to the fact that our weekend marriage between Munich and Wuppertal was ultimately unsustainable: among other things we disagreed about having children and on the paths our careers should take—especially mine, since I had no intention of returning to Bayreuth. She didn't want to move to Wuppertal, as the prospects for her career as a lawyer were better in Munich; and though I hoped to dissuade her from separation by offering to give up my job in Wuppertal, she wouldn't agree to that, either. As divorce proceedings began, so did one of the most difficult periods of my life. I took refuge in my work, and it soon became a drug for me.

After more than three years of trying, Johannes Meyer-Lindenberg finally succeeded in persuading Father to meet me face to face. So it was that in February 1981 we drove through a snowstorm to Bayreuth. The only place we could find to stay was the Hotel Goldener Anker, on the first floor, right next to room number 23, where Hitler had stayed in 1923 when he met my grandmother for the first time. To me this boded ill, but Johannes quickly talked me out of such superstition.

Father received us in the Festspielhaus out of consideration for his second wife, Gudrun, and my half-sister, Katherina. The conversation began superficially, with commentary on the weather. It was obvious that Father found the meeting awkward: he kept repeating that he had very little time and had a lot of other important things to do. But neither of us let himself get irritated. Johannes's tactical skills left me amazed. He told Father to stop his public attacks and derogatory remarks and to meet me regularly to air our views. However, when Johannes tried to arrange the next meeting, Father was reluctant to commit himself. Annoyed, Johannes insisted we meet in Wuppertal.

What we had achieved, though, was an agreement in principle to have regular conversations and for Father to no longer make negative remarks about me in public. Satisfied, Johannes left my father's office on the second floor of the Festspielhaus. As we parted, I tried to look my father in the eye, but he averted his gaze, and something told me he would not hold to the agreement.

In March 1981 my father and Gudrun attended a production of mine for the first and last time: Mozart's *Bastien und Bastienne.* For the administrative staff of the Wuppertal opera house, Wolfgang Wagner turning up was a great event. The performance took place in a school in Wuppertal-Ronsdorf under extremely modest conditions. There had been no publicity and the hall was half-empty, on which Gudrun commented: "In Bayreuth we are swamped with audiences. You seem to have quite the opposite problem." An embarrassed silence followed.

In April I met Johannes again and asked him to help me cope with my divorce. With some reluctance I took sedatives he prescribed and began treatment. I started talking. After I spoke for half an hour, Johannes declared with a kind smile: "You don't need psychoanalysis. You need your own family and the right professional environment—which you certainly don't have in Wuppertal with career-conscious types like Meyer-Oertel and Matiasek." The very next day I stopped taking the sedatives and, to the amazement of my boss, stopped living for the theater. After the premiere of my production of Berlioz's *Béatrice et Bénédict,* which to my great joy Aunt Friedelind attended, I flew to Paris to attend a Jewish wedding. I had a brief and refreshing flirtation with an enchanting Parisienne and slowly began to recover. I became aware of the pointlessness of my former life and realized things had to change.

14

Teresina

My new appetite for life had not been impaired by the appearance of my father plus his second wife. Things could only get better. I started by freeing myself from my self-imposed isolation and enjoying the generous society of my landlady, Dodo Koch, who accepted me into her household like a son and spoiled me. Dodo took a warmhearted interest in both my professional experiences and my private escapades. I lived in a small annex situated, like the main house, at the beginning of a forest path leading to the Gelpe valley amid beautiful countryside.

In the first week of July, Dodo started preparations for her seventieth birthday with the skill and attention to detail of a perfect hostess. Belonging to Wuppertal high society and greatly popular, she had invited many guests and meticulously planned the seating arrangements. Knowing of my divorce from Beatrix, she asked me in her pleasantly direct way: "And who should I invite as your lady partner at the table?"

I said defensively: "Better not have anybody!"

Dodo wouldn't give up and said jokingly: "Teresina Rossetti would be a charming partner!"

The comment slightly annoyed me. "Her of all people! I had such an awful argument with her a year ago over the Pope and his reactionary views. You can't do that to me."

Irritated, Dodo replied: "How silly you are not to see Teresina's human qualities just because of your excessive views on the Pope!" She had much affection and respect for Teresina, who had been a regular visitor since 1973, first as an au pair, then as a friend.

A few days before the birthday party Dodo and I were sitting in her drawing room talking about the party arrangements when the telephone rang. Dodo picked it up, listened, and answered: "Teresinchen, how nice that you've arrived! Get straight into a taxi and come here . . . No, wait—Dr. Wagner will pick you up at the station." I could hear Teresina's comments quite clearly, as I was sitting next to Dodo. She said firmly: "I'd rather take a taxi." But Dodo was firmly against it and insisted.

On the drive to the station I weighed whether I should direct the conversation immediately to the Pope or to the emancipation of women. Then when I saw her waiting in front of the station with her suitcase, tired from the long train journey from Milan, I refrained from all the little digs and greeted her in a friendly way: "Ciao, come sta?"

Surprised at my unusual friendliness, she answered with an irresistible smile: "Bene. Grazie per essere venuto a prendermi [Thank you for coming to collect me]."

From that moment on I preferred talking Italian with her. When we were sitting smiling in the car I couldn't resist asking her why she had insisted on the telephone on not being picked up by me. "I didn't want to start straightaway fighting with you about the Pope, as I can hardly imagine you have altered your opinions since our argument a year ago," she said with disarming hilarity.

"A lot has happened in my life since then," I said. "I've changed a lot, and I am more capable now of listening to you."

From that moment on until the time she left, we met up whenever we could, telling one another the story of our lives with an openness that only old friends are capable of—or people who have just fallen in love. We made it clear to one another from the first moment, based on our own bad experiences, what we thought meaningful and what was not. And yet the hurdles before us were anything but insignificant: my divorce proceedings, my difficult professional situation, the incurable illness of Teresina's father, the geographical distance, and our very different families. Amid all the plans we had for our future together, we completely forgot the Wuppertal world around us. With some satisfaction, Dodo immediately sensed that we had fallen in love. My change didn't escape the other guests either, and people whispered behind our backs: "How happy and open Gottfried Wagner has become, and how well this charming Italian woman suits him!"

When, on the evening of 12 July 1981, I watched the train on which Teresina was traveling back to Italy leave the station in Cologne, I knew that with her I had a chance of a meaningful and fulfilled life. Lots of things that had seemed insoluble to me lost their importance. I began to understand who I was. I became myself through Teresina's love.

After her departure I met Arno Adar, an Israeli set designer who was working at the Wuppertal opera house. We discussed how far the arts can influence politics. Arno doubted that the arts could influence politics at all. At once we were thrown into discussion on the dependency of art in totalitarian states like Nazi Germany and the Soviet Union. Only after that did Arno start talking about his experiences as an Austrian-Jewish emigrant. He told me of his flight from Austria and spoke exhaustively and fascinatingly about Israel, arousing my own curiosity about that country. I had finally found a new discussion partner during my Wuppertal period, which was otherwise not very stimulating.

I was impressed by Arno's skepticism toward my often too idealistic arguments, as well as by his reliability as a human being. He brought me closer to Erich Fromm, Hannah Arendt, and Viktor Frankl, authors I had known only superficially. He broadened my horizons and motivated me to investigate the subject of art and politics more profoundly.

I asked Arno if he would like to go with me to Bayreuth. "With you, yes," he said curtly.

We stayed with my mother who, against my advice, had recently moved back to Bayreuth from Wiesbaden. One afternoon we wanted to attend the dress rehearsal of *Tristan*, with Jean-Pierre

Ponnelle's conventional set and direction. When I went to pick up the tickets from my father's office, I wasn't allowed in. The porter, whom I had known for thirty years, clearly found the situation painful and apologized: "The boss's wife said you're not allowed into the Festspielhaus anymore. Frau Pitz will bring you the tickets." Arno was surprised and asked: "But this is the boss's son. Can't he go in?" At that moment Frau Pitz arrived. She wanted to avoid any lengthy and painful discussion and invited us into her office, which was crammed with flowers and presents—small tokens from those fortunate enough to attend dress rehearsals or performances. For the first time in my life I had to sign a receipt for tickets for myself and my guest. When I introduced Arno as a friend from Israel, my father's colleague reacted with exaggerated friendliness. "Herr Barenboim is an Israeli too," she declared enthusiastically, citing the conductor of *Tristan*. Evidently a new chapter in Bayreuth's tactical philo-Semitism had opened. When I asked whether we could see my father, she answered that she would first have to discuss that with his wife, Gudrun. "I'll tell you at the beginning of the first interval."

Without asking for permission I showed Arno the Festspielhaus. People returned my greetings either unenthusiastically or not at all. My presence was obviously undesirable. Arno quickly picked up on it, and I told him about my father. The story clearly moved him. When we went back into the auditorium after the first intermission, I was peered at as if I were a halfwit. Behind my back I heard, "He's back—he's made it up with his father," and similar stupid whisperings. Finally the curtain went up on Act Two, and in spite of myself I was enthralled yet again by Wagner's *Tristan* music. I completely forgot the coldness of my reception.

Arno was thrilled by the acoustics and the stage and said during the second interval: "Let's just go up and say hello to your father!" And so without a proper appointment I led Arno to my father's office. In front of his door his secretary intercepted us and requested in some excitement that first a time be agreed on. I answered drily: "I'm sure my father would receive Mr. Adar from Israel." At this we were allowed to see my father. Arno said in greeting, almost provocatively: "I would never have dreamt it—me sitting in the Bayreuth Festspielhaus!" My father misunderstood the remark, felt flattered, and answered: "We have a great tradition of Jewish conductors, and now Barenboim too." I restrained my comments. After two minutes the secretary burst in and reminded my father of an appointment—a familiar trick Father used when he wanted to get rid of troublesome guests. Generously, he allowed us to visit Daniel Barenboim during the remainder of the interval.

I didn't particularly want to join the queue of fans waiting in front of Barenboim's dressing room, but did so, mostly for Arno's sake. He spoke to Barenboim in modern Hebrew—quite new and unexpected sounds in the Grail temple. Arno introduced me to Barenboim as the son of the festival boss. I spoke of Aunt Friedelind, who had known him since he was eleven. The conductor remained diplomatically silent; he knew my aunt was persona non grata for my father.

The following day I met Meyer-Oertel and Maximilian Kojetinsky in the Siegfried Wagner House, in order to discuss the Dresden and Paris versions of *Tannhäuser.* Afterwards I showed Meyer-Oertel around the house. I noticed that several valuable family objects had already disappeared, although the final division of the inheritance had still not taken place. After visiting "the Führer's room," we came to my grandmother's bedroom, where we saw photos of my uncle Wieland in a Nazi helmet and my father as the Führer's soldier, standing on the bedside table just as they had years ago. Meyer-Oertel understood my horror and my wish to leave the house immediately.

It was then on the Festspielhügel that I understood why he had engaged me as his colleague: he had totally succumbed to Bayreuth-connection fever. Thank God Arno was nearby and had closely observed what had happened. We understood one another without saying a word.

After the dress rehearsal of my father's *Meistersinger* I set off for Italy, where the first meeting with Teresina's family awaited me. The first separation from Teresina had seemed like an eternity to me, although it had lasted only eleven days. Smirking, Arno hoped

I'd have a good time. "Italian families, like Jewish families, are run by women," were his parting words.

The twenty-fourth of July 1981 will always remain in my memory. On that day a new chapter in my life began: my integration into Teresina's family in Cerro Maggiore, near Milan. It was not without friction. Being from such a broken home, I did not find it easy to fit into the Rossettis'. Also, knowing Italy only as a tourist, I had to overcome a few prejudices. It made me realize just how questionable my social and cultural conditioning by Bayreuth had been. Added to this, my divorce had not yet gone through, and I didn't know how a Catholic family would react to this case history. And last but not least, my professional prospects were pretty thin.

Teresina assured me that the fact that I was German didn't bother her family. But nevertheless, the SS had had a base in Legnano, very near Cerro Maggiore, and had terrorized the population. With my heart pounding, we drove into Via Saffi, where Mamma Antonietta and Papa Antonio; Uncle Luigi and his wife, Maria; and Teresina's sister, Francesca, her husband, Enzo, and their little daughter, Silvia, were waiting for us. I was scrutinized by curious, expectant eyes, and they all concentrated totally on me. I was received as Teresina's fiancé. Teresina had advised me not to blurt out everything at once and mention my still pending divorce, as I had originally planned. I restrained myself, partly out of concern for her father's serious illness.

The *fidanzato* [fiancé] *Goffredo* was automatically assigned a place in the home—the idea of having the future son-in-law put up in a hotel would have seemed absurd to Teresina's family. In the living room the evening meal was waiting on a long beautifully decorated marble table. Mamma Antonietta gave unforgettable proof of her cooking skills, which immediately won me over to her. I earned a few points in her eyes too, when, much to the amusement of the whole table, I helped myself liberally to every dish. To my joy I was soon to learn that food was a valuable item in the culture of my new environment. There was a relaxed, jolly atmosphere at the table, such as I had never known before. But I was equally amazed by the intensity of discussions which the family was able to have. And I relished the fact that Richard Wagner was not the key topic of conversation. Uncle Luigi, Mamma Antonietta's brother and a onetime musician in the local band, turned after a few well-considered remarks on Wagner's orchestration to his favorite composers, Verdi and Puccini. Wagner was, to my relief, only one of the many music subjects.

The family was at its liveliest on the subject of mother and child. In Italy, children are the center of attention for female members of the family, and so the then nine-month-old Silvia soon became the main subject of discussion. It almost made me a little jealous when Mamma Antonietta, Francesca, or Teresina said to Silvia: "Fai un bel sorriso!" [Give us a nice smile!]

How unkindly in contrast my sister and I had been treated. Again and again, often with inner reluctance, I compared experiences from my past with the gift of my new family to live with a unique intensity in the here and now. Confused and happy, I started acclimatizing myself in Cerro Maggiore. The introductions to relations and the festivities each introduction entailed were endless. There was no question of any intimate time alone with Teresina. But when she looked at me with an understanding smile, I felt the warmth of the reception and gladly gave in to it.

Then at a stroke everything changed. At the beginning of August Teresina's father was admitted to the hospital in Legnano. There we learned that the bone cancer from which he was suffering would not give him much more time. From that moment on I witnessed what it can mean when a family is united through grief. There was no longer a moment when Papa Antonio was not being cared for by Mamma Antonietta, Teresina, and Francesca; his still-living four brothers, Ernesto, Franco, Angelo, and Luigi; and his sister, Giannina, with their respective spouses, children, and grandchildren. It was the first time I had been present when someone died. The silence was only interrupted by prayers in Papa Antonio's sickroom, by the shouts of the children in the corridor, or the nurses dashing to and fro. Seldom, but then with great convulsions, one of the relations burst into tears. Teresina's constant suffering moved me in a way I had never known before. Mamma Antonietta, who sought comfort in prayer during the hours in the hospital room when her husband was sleeping, held the family together. As always, she forgot herself and lived with superhuman strength for us. She remained silent and showed us with great, calm dignity how to overcome this sense of paralyzing helplessness, pain, sadness, and vain hope.

When Papa Antonio had moments free of pain, I could talk to him. His concern was only for Teresina, who was suffering too much to talk to him and needed all her energies not to break down constantly in tears. One night, when I was alone with Papa Antonio, we spoke frankly about my coming marriage to his daughter. In view of his imminent death I now felt responsible for Mamma Antonietta and Teresina and told him: "Don't worry, Papa, I'll be there for Teresina and Mamma."

At that moment I felt such a loss at my own fatherlessness: my father had never been there for me, while Papa Antonio, who had accepted me as a son, now lay dying. In my despair I rang my father, intending to ask him to come. But his secretary informed me: "Herr Wagner can't be contacted, he is in a meeting." I left my number with the secretary, along with a request for my father to ring back. He never did.

A notary from Legnano who was on the same floor in the hospital as Papa Antonio regularly wandered around the corridor of the intensive-care ward. I don't know how, but he had learned that I was a great-grandson of Richard Wagner. As he was a passionate Wagnerian, he wanted at all costs to get into conversation with me. So that night, softly, but quite audibly for me in the sickroom, he sang in the corridor with pure intonation the Grail Narrative from *Lohengrin*, in Italian. That even amused Papa Antonio, who, faintly smiling, said: "È matto, ma simpatico, il notaio!" [He's mad, but nice, the notary!] Papa Antonio knew some of Wagner's most popular pieces; we had listened to a recording of Toscanini's 1954 Wagner concert—his final performance—before he went to the hospital. "Tell him he's got to stop singing Wagner in the middle of the night or the others will get annoyed," he said.

I hurried out into the corridor and saw a scene Fellini couldn't have improved on. The notary and Heldentenor manqué stood there in operatic pose, with transfigured gaze, waiting for an imaginary Grail miracle. "Bravo, bravo!" I said, and shook his hand with melodramatic gratitude. The self-styled Lohengrin replied: "How does one as great-grandson of the great composer experience mankind?" I answered: "I'll tell you if you promise me to let people sleep now at three in the morning." He sighed and said ecstatically: "Che bello. A domani, maestro!" But I didn't have the time then and even less the inner calm to talk about Wagner. The notary understood and showed a delicate sympathy.

Only three nights later Papa Antonio died. I shall never forget Teresina's horror and shock when the coffin was sealed. His death touched me, too: for the first time I became painfully aware that our life must one day end. I began to respect just being alive.

Despair had caused a crisis in faith for Teresina. Who was this God who had let her father die in terrible pain from bone cancer at the age of fifty-nine? In this mood we went to a place that was to become a refuge for us: to Cannero, to the order of Augustinian Fathers of the Assumption, who lived over Lago Maggiore on a rock with a splendid view of the lake. Over these difficult days one of the priests, Father Giuliano, became an important helper and friend. No subject was excluded: Teresina's religious crisis; my indiscriminate aversion to Christianity, in particular to the Catholic Church; my divorce. I had to acknowledge, with some shame, what prejudices I had against priests as well.

Father Giuliano was a warmhearted, modest discussion partner with a lively vision of the Bible and Christianity and a wide-ranging culture. I realized that the Catholic Church does not merely consist of a repressive hierarchy but lives in worldwide spiritual dialogue with the other monotheistic religions and with atheists. Teresina's crisis of faith and the discussions with Father Giuliano strengthened my need to take another look into religious questions. I saw that I had made it too easy for myself when I criticized from the outside instead of helping to bring a little of the Sermon on the Mount into my own world.

Once back in Wuppertal, I made contact with a Franciscan

monk, Father Ising, who was anything but conventional. In a district of 128 different communities of faith and sects, he had turned his Catholic community into one of the liveliest and best-attended spiritual centers. He raged against the Pope, the ecclesiastical hierarchy, and corrupt priests and considered his co-Franciscan brother Leonardo Boff, the Brazilian liberation theologian, the German theologian Hans Küng, and other rebels in the Catholic Church to be true Christians. He spoke with such sensuality about men and women, marriage, and bringing up children that I couldn't believe my ears. On 31 October—Reformation Day, of all days—I decided to enter the Catholic Church.

For the event Mamma Antonietta went on her first flight, and Bettina Fehr also came as witness. Father Ising said to me after the ceremony: "The Christian Church is a heterogeneous universe. You will never subject yourself unconditionally to the church and its hierarchical ideology. But the church needs heretics like you, otherwise it would die, as it did in the Nazi period. Just don't give up your dialogue with the Jews. That is part of your life."

He was to be proved right.

15

The Monastery and the Bank

n the weeks immediately after my return from Italy, and conversations with Father Ising, my preoccupation with my life as dramaturge and director in the Wuppertal opera house seemed pointless. By the time Meyer-Oertel scrapped a production of *Mahagonny* that I had planned with Arno Adar, and which had been announced as my production for the coming season, I had already mentally served notice. I was simply waiting for the right moment to leave Wuppertal. I needed another job, and one came up quite by chance.

I had met the former director of the Deutsche Bank, Hans H. Asmus, at a premiere party in Wuppertal. Asmus is a keen friend of the arts and thinks highly of my theater work. Despite any objection on my part, he saw me as the future boss of Bayreuth and opined: "What you need is training and ordeal by fire in the Deutsche Bank! The German intendants have no idea about balancing the books. If you can read balance sheets and music scores, the world is your oyster!"

He had no sooner made the suggestion than the deed was done, and on 16 December 1981 I stood, dressed as a junior banker, in front of Adolf Sievers, one of the three personnel directors of the Deutsche Bank in Frankfurt am Main. The meeting had nothing to do with banking. Sievers was of a cheerful amiability and sensitive refinement and steered our one-hour talk in a direction that made me almost forget why I had made the appointment with him. Like me, he loved Mozart, and he understood interpretation to a degree that surprised even a professional in the classical-music scene like myself. For him the choice between Otto Klemperer or Bruno Walter was a question of conscience. When I finally reminded him of the reason why I had come, he asked, laughing: "What do you understand of the banking business?"

"Nothing," I answered. "And I never want to be a banker, only to learn how to handle money. And I need a job because, for various reasons, the Wuppertal theater doesn't interest me anymore."

Sievers retorted: "Seeing that you, as an exotic bird, will first have to prove yourself in our cage, I'll give you a half-year trial period. Where do you want to go?" With my imminent divorce in mind and a desire to live as close to Cerro Maggiore as possible, I suggested Munich.

The Christmas of 1981 was the first with my new family. It was also the first Christmas without Papa Antonio, and a pall of melancholy hung in the air, relieved only by my one-year-old niece, Silvia. As every year, the family went to midnight mass on Christmas Eve in the overcrowded main church of Cerro Maggiore, and over the following two days everyone met in Enzo and Francesca's house. Despite the sadness over the loss of Papa Antonio, people danced and sang, determined to give little Silvia a merry Christmas. This merriment, out of love and respect for the children, made me wistful, reminding me of the quarrelsome Christmases in my family, in which children were assigned the role of decorative extras.

It occurred to me that this was perhaps the fundamental difference between the Italian Catholic and the German Protestant family: the former was matriarchal, and the latter, patriarchal. In my Italian family, mother and child form an inviolable unit—the cult of Mary. Mamma Antonietta explained to me that respect for the child is a fundamental value that she had passed on to her daughters.

It was clear that after the death of my father-in-law, I was expected to support the family with all my strength. It was taken for granted that, as Teresina's future husband, I would be completely integrated into the family. What objection could anyone have to joining a family such as this, which stuck together in good times and bad and which accepted me as I was? Until that moment it was something I had never experienced.

Before long I had the opportunity of proving my loyalty to my new family, when I learned that Teresina and her mother would have to leave their home. It was the last thing we needed after the death of Papa Antonio: I was not yet divorced, a probationary trainee of the Deutsche Bank and still not yet officially finished at Wuppertal. But no matter, we went looking for an apartment. I finally signed a purchase contract on an apartment, despite my lack of assets. I was relying on the fact that Father would pay me my inheritance, which, for the moment, was only putting money into the lawyers' pockets.

The year 1982 began dramatically in every way. With the help of Father Ising I had found a room in the Franciscan monastery in the Annastrasse in Munich. My furniture wouldn't fit into the room, so I had to store it in Dodo Koch's garage in Wuppertal; it later ended up in a furniture warehouse in Bonn. In mid-January I ended my contract with the Wuppertal theater, to the horror of Aunt Friedelind and many of my friends. My last task in Wuppertal was to organize a matinee. With great inner detachment I saw what Meyer-Oertel had thought up for himself as director of *Tannhäuser*.

Relieved rather than regretful at leaving the German stage, I traveled to Munich at the end of January. After I had unloaded my car, Prelate Guardian invited me into his room, looked at me somewhat skeptically, and declared: "Brother Ising has told me you were working in Wuppertal as director and dramaturg. Now you want to work in the Deutsche Bank and live with us. Theater, church, bank: that sounds like a novel. But it is a monastery here. Please respect that!"

In return for a nominal rent, I was given a relatively large room on the first floor of the monastery, which looked down into the garden. It wasn't easy for me to share a bath and telephone with high-school children and students—they looked on me as a rather strange old man. But I knew that the coming months would only be a transitionary phase in my life.

First I had to visit the personnel office of the Deutsche Bank Bayern, in the Ungererstrasse. One of the heads of personnel explained to me that I was now number 42411 of the Deutsche Bank and no longer "Gottfried Wagner." When I mentioned my Munich address, it caused roars of laughter.

On 1 February 1982 I began working as trainee of the branch in the Schwanthalerstrasse. The director welcomed me warmly and made no attempt to hide his amazement at my former life. He assigned me a narrow place between the many desks behind the counter, and I was immediately let loose on humankind. As I hadn't even the slightest idea what I was supposed to be doing, I copied my new colleagues and played the part of the experienced banker to the customers. When I didn't know what to do—as was frequently the case at first—I would say with a friendly smile, "Excuse me, my colleague is more experienced in this matter," and turn for help to one of my colleagues, who with a certain amusement helped me out of often embarrassing situations.

At noon, walking from the branch to the main Deutsche Bank canteen on the Promenadenplatz, I was struck by three things along Schwanthalerstrasse: banks, brothels, and dubious export and import shops. The owners and employees of the latter enterprises formed the core of the clients I had to deal with in the first stage of my rather awkward training. They had no sympathy for my lack of knowledge and reminded me of it with a brutality I had never before experienced. I put up with it, thinking of Brecht's *Threepenny Opera*, but found that the reality had nothing to do with the world of theater. After working their night shift on the streets, prostitutes would come into the bank and sullenly tip their earnings out of their cleavages, growling at me when I didn't know immediately what I was supposed to do. It took some effort not to respond in kind.

When it finally got too much for me, I complained to my superior. In reply, the deputy branch manager gave me a lecture: "The fact that your name is Wagner, that you've studied musicology and philosophy and worked in the theater, is totally irrelevant. Here only one thing counts: that you stop costing us money and finally close some deals. With whom, why, or how doesn't interest us. And if you don't like it, there's the door! There's a long line of people outside it who would do your work without complaining."

I said nothing, simply giving him a withering look, for which he paid me back whenever he got the opportunity. He was a classic functionary: kowtowing to his superiors and trampling those beneath. As such, he was no different from most little bosses I've met. I soon worked out how I could avoid being affected by them, though: I pretended I knew the big bosses—and anyway, my academic title impressed them. Ultimately they even believed I was on the threshold of a long career, and held back.

The branch manager was, in his Bavarian stolidity, rather predictable. He taught me how to arrange credit loans and then expected immediate results. Every morning before the bank opened he asked his employees for the "racing lists"—their signed agreements. I did not fulfill expectations and saw with some horror how my colleagues targeted foreigners in particular, talking them into risky overdrafts and shamelessly exploiting their language difficulties.

I started working against these methods and became immune to the daily reproaches for not having concluded any deals. As scarcely any of my colleagues spoke foreign languages, I was often called in as interpreter for Turks, Italians, Yugoslavs, French, or Americans. I warned poor clients against signing long-term policies with the branch, especially if it was clear that they would be incapable of repaying their debt. Word of this got around among Turkish, Yugoslav, and Italian workers, and to the annoyance of my boss they came to me in droves. I had to see to them in a side room—foreigners without fat wallets were not welcome.

It happened that these groups brought me presents out of gratitude and invited me for meals after work. When this reached the ears of the deputy branch manager, he bellowed through the bank, to the amusement of clients and employees alike: "We are not a charity, Wagner!" and shunted me off to the cellar to sort savings leaflets. My protests were to no avail. The only comfort was that my time in the Schwanthalerstrasse would soon be over.

When I left the Schwanthalerstrasse branch at the end of April 1982, I felt I had been living on a different planet. From May, working in the Ungererstrasse in the heart of bank administration, I was initiated into the secrets and techniques of banking. As I was tolerated only as an observer, mostly reluctantly, people preferred it if I didn't disturb them with questions, which meant that I could finally pursue my own interests. To the amazement of my banking colleagues, I spent my time under the desk, reading the Jerusalem Bible Old Testament with growing enthusiasm, and the works of Shalom Ben Chorin, whose *Brother Jesus: The Nazarene from the Jewish Viewpoint* impressed me in particular, as did Pinchas Lapides's books on Bible translations. Back in the monastery, after my boring day at work, I would continue my reading of the Jewish Bible in the German translations of Moses Mendelssohn and Martin Buber and compare them with the New Testament. It made my isolation in Germany bearable and later my integration in Italy easier. It became clearer and clearer to me how inconceivable Christianity was without Judaism, and I grew more remote from Bayreuth, with its Wagnerian pseudoreligion.

In May I visited my sister, who was living with her husband in the elegant Schanbergstrasse in Munich. Both were working for Leo Kirch, the future media tycoon, who was already powerful. Eva didn't understand my professional and private direction, but unfortunately it never came to a frank discussion. The gulf between my spiritual development and my new family on the one hand and Eva's opera/film world on the other was unbridgeable.

After my bogus activity in the administration department I finally moved to the Bavarian headquarters of the Deutsche Bank on the Promenadenplatz. For two months I worked my way through the foreign department. There was no question of the much-quoted trainee principle of learning on the job. I was allowed to observe what the others did, and showed interest only because I hoped to get a place in the Milan branch of the Deutsche Bank or in an Italian bank.

The monotony at work, squabbles with lawyers over the divorce settlement, and the struggle for my inheritance were all left far behind, however, when I drove on weekends to visit Teresina in Cerro Maggiore or met friends in Munich. Unlike my colleagues at the bank, I had no desire to join the trendy set with their CSU party and BMW cars. I felt removed from the opera world too. It was more important to improve my Italian for my future with Teresina and attend marketing courses that might perhaps one day help me.

To the outside world I continued to feign great interest in the banking business, determined to prove that, contrary to all the predictions of friends and relations, I would stick it out in the Deutsche Bank. The first positive evaluations of my banking activities amused me. Adolf Sievers was the only one with whom I did not need to pretend, and he constantly encouraged me to keep going.

At the beginning of June I visited my sister to find that in May she had given birth to a son, Antoine, in the United States. My brother-in-law proudly showed me the baby's American passport with the name Antoine Wagner-Pasquier.

In August and September 1982 I was initiated into the deeper mysteries of capitalism in the property department of the Deutsche Bank. I also visited the Munich stock exchange. The stockbrokers, screaming hysterically and rushing around like hungry wolves, brought Brecht once more to mind: he saw no moral difference between bank robbery and bank business. But to be fair, in the Deutsche Bank in Munich there were superiors and colleagues who with great commitment provided me with essential insights into the banking business. They understood that my professional life would not end in a bank, and found me—the exotic—a welcome change in their day-to-day professional life.

I was bored to death in the property administration department too. My only comfort was the monthly check. In my free time I again explored Wagner's idea of religion in *Parsifal*—it now seemed dishonest to me.

I wanted at all costs to work in the theater again, so I went to see the musicologist and conductor Alberto Zedda, who was influential in Pesaro and in the left-wing cultural scene in Italy, and consulted the conductor Claudio Abbado. Both assured me they were convinced of my professional competence, but neither helped me in my search for a job.

Meanwhile the dispute over my inheritance entered a new phase. My father demanded that I hand back the rolls of film from the Nazi period, which were still being stored with Beatrix's parents. In January 1983 he had his lawyer's chauffeur collect the originals from me. After recovering the film in the spring, I sent the copies to my sister, making it clear to her how potentially explosive the material was that she was now guarding. Without a projector, I inspected the films once again by holding them up to the light: Hitler with the Wagner family in the Wahnfried garden and in the Festspielhaus; Father as a sturdy member of the Hitler Youth on the Bayreuth Sternplatz, his arm upraised. What unfortunate intimacy and foolish merriment! Then pictures from Nuremberg of the Nazi rallies with my grandmother and other family members, being cheered by fanatical masses. In the end, my father kept the originals and I kept a copy, which I later gave to my sister.

The divorce hearing took place before a Munich court and was remarkably unpleasant. Beatrix and I left the court building like two strangers—after a relationship of almost eleven years.

But now there was no turning back for Teresina and me. As I hadn't been married in church the first time round, there was nothing to prevent us having a classic Italian wedding. In the months up to the big day, 3 July 1983, I became aware of just how important the marriage ceremony was to my new family. After my atheist upbringing and the spiritual and ethical neglect in Bayreuth, the Catholic rites seemed very strange to me, as did the various important feast days and holidays. I envied Teresina and her family, especially Mamma Antonietta, their deeply rooted piety, which had and has nothing to do with bigotry or dependence on the Catholic Church. In time I learned to understand that what my new family possessed was a much more realistic philosophy of life than my pseudo-Protestant, idealistic, German worldview, which has nothing to do with human nature in all its inconsistencies. I realized that irrespective of all the dogma and the omnipresence of the

Catholic Church, in my new family a strongly pronounced individualism prevailed, which made any form of state and ecclesiastical tutelage impossible.

Fascinated, within my new family environment, I discovered my capacity to live in the moment, with all the sensuality of Mediterranean culture, reflecting by no means just Christianity, but also pre-Christian rites and myths. Much of what I had believed began to waver, and I started one of many, often painful, self-reevaluations.

In February 1983, well before the wedding, I had agreed in Munich to a disadvantageous settlement of my inheritance that left me with little money. I needed money to make a down payment on my future home with Teresina in Italy, but was willing to agree to those terms if it meant freeing myself from all future discussions with my father's second family. Bad though the settlement was for me, it nonetheless meant a further step in the direction of Italy.

It was also in February that the celebrations began for the centenary of Richard Wagner's death. Although I lay low in the bank, my Bayreuth past still came back to haunt me. I received idiotic offers from the media to appear as a great-grandson, all of which I rejected. An inquiry from the Munich *Abendzeitung* seemed to be of somewhat higher caliber: I was asked my opinion on Wagner's work and influence, and I thought I could answer that with a clear conscience. But yet again it was only the gossip about who would succeed my father as head of the festival that was printed.

The bookshop windows were crammed with Wagner literature, but the only significant title was Hartmut Zelinsky's *Richard Wagner: Ein Deutsches Thema.* On the other hand, I found the commentaries superficial in the ten-volume Wagner edition by Dieter Borchmeyer, who tried to gain status in Bayreuth with his remarks about *The Jews in Music.* Yet again there was a Wagner boom in the book market, but I wanted nothing to do with it.

Meanwhile, I had advanced in the bank to potential management material, and pressure to perform increased. In February I was allowed to speak in the Bayerischer Hof Hotel in Munich before Dr. Siegfried Gropper, known as "God the Father," director of the Deutsche Bank in Munich, and his humble retinue from affiliated Bavarian branches. My topic was strike insurance, from a liberal-left viewpoint. A few days before I had assisted Peter Glotz of the Bavarian SPD as electoral assistant in Munich's working-class district of Haselberg. Contrary to expectations, my talk was calmly received. Afterwards there was a dinner to which the trainees had been invited. Many of them wanted to seize the opportunity to play up to the big boss—all jolly and deferential. It brought to mind Heinrich Mann's novel *Man of Straw*. I was under no pressure to gain status and so conversed in a relaxed way with Gropper, even daring to contradict him when he entered the—for him—uncertain territory of art and music and started giving me some private coaching on Wagner. My friends among the trainees enjoyed the spectacle, while the others just stood agog at such lack of respect.

The meeting had one distinct advantage: I could present myself as a specialist on Italy, although I didn't even hint at the true reason for my interest. Lo and behold, after I had finished my basic training in the Munich credit department, my request for transfer was granted. The Munich bankers were glad to see me go and found me a new job at the Deutsche Bank in Milan. I could now plan my move to Cerro Maggiore.

16

My Italian Wedding

ost of my friends from Germany had already arrived for the *Polterabend*, the prewedding party, on 2 July 1983, the evening before my marriage. My new family wasn't familiar with this tradition. In Antonio Lazzati's little summerhouse with its huge garden, we celebrated in glorious weather until far into the wedding day. In the morning, before the church ceremony, it was mainly the Italian friends and relations who came into Mamma Antonietta's home. I was only allowed to talk to Teresina through a locked door, as the groom wasn't permitted to see the bride again until she reached the altar. However strange such rituals seemed at the time, I kept to them, and throughout the day Uncle Luigi discreetly whispered instructions.

The wedding guests gathered on the piazza in front of the Borretta church. My extended Italian family created a merry atmosphere that kept me from feeling any regret that my father had declined his invitation. My mother, however, did come, and she accompanied me to the altar, with Teresina following shortly after with her father's eldest brother. She and Mamma Antonietta were visibly upset that Papa Antonio could not be there, but as she came toward me to the wedding march from *Lohengrin*, which the Cerro Maggiore choir had learned for us in Italian, the church resplendent with roses, the months since July 1981 flashed again through my mind. To my right in front of the altar, curious and happy, sat my witnesses, Eva and my friend Louis Landuyt, a singer and music teacher from Luxembourg. The choice of my sister as witness represented my hope that we could start our relationship afresh. Behind us, in the nave, sat my mother and my cousin Christa as the representative of my mother's family, and behind them Bettina Fehr and the friends who had helped me in the difficult transition period from theater to bank: Eckard and Rosi Grebner, Dietrich Hahn, Ulf, Dodo, Walter and Maureen Siegel, Florian Lavermann, and their partners. On the left side sat my brother-in-law Enzo and my sister-in-law Francesca, and behind them, more of Teresina's family, including Mamma Antoniette, her brother Luigi, and Ernesto, Papa Antonio's third brother, all of whom are still particularly close to me. They knew from the beginning that it would be difficult for me, as a foreigner, to be fully integrated into Italian society.

The marriage ceremony was performed in German and Italian by our friend Father Giuliano. Teresina and I had chosen the text from I Corinthians 13 on the love that overcomes all obstacles. I was caught totally unprepared by the request to read out a text from the Bible for our German guests. The words were printed so small that I could barely decipher them. Added to this was my profound emotion, and so I improvised—much to the amusement of guests better acquainted with the Bible. When Francesca, quite unexpectedly, sang the Bach-Gounod "Ave Maria" with wonderful tenderness and pure intonation, accompanied on the organ by Franco Pasquali, the leader of the Ars Nova choir, there were few in the church who were not touched.

In those moments, full of hope, a new chapter began in my life. Behind me lay crises. I had even toyed with the idea of taking on Teresina's family name in order to make a visible break with my Bayreuth past, but she convinced me that this would be a pointless denial of my identity and that I should soon continue my path in my actual professional milieu. When I came out of the church with my new wife to Mendelssohn's wedding march, which I had selected in preference to my great-grandfather's wedding music, I felt a completely different Wagner.

The exalted mood was abruptly broken by loud cries from the Italian wedding guests and curious onlookers—"Evviva gli sposi!" [Here's to the newlyweds)—and a relentless hail of rice showered down on us, and all of a sudden wild merriment erupted. Before driving off to the wedding feast, we laid roses from the church decorations on Papa Antonio's grave and on the graves of other deceased relations—such a contrast to my family's indifference toward the dead, who were only remembered on official occasions, with an eye to the media.

Our honeymoon took us to a magical place in Crete, the cradle of European and Mediterranean culture. Surrounded by sweet-smelling, lush, flowering woodland and the chirping of crickets, in the following days we forgot the rest of the world and our worries.

In August 1983, however, we went to Bayreuth, together with Mamma Antonietta and Italian friends. As Father did not want to receive us in his house, Aunt Friedelind invited us to dinner in the chic Schloss Tiergarten Hotel. On hearing that we had no tickets for a festival performance, she called Father and demanded three tickets for *Tristan und Isolde*.

I took Teresina and Mamma Antonietta on a guided tour of Bayreuth, through Wahnfried Park, Villa Wahnfried, and the Festspielpark, where there was whispering behind my back. The festival court employees, once they were sure no one was watching them, greeted us with insincere friendliness.

In the Festspielhaus we encountered my father's army of yes men. When I asked to see him, to introduce Teresina and Mamma Antonietta, I was told that he could see only Teresina and me, briefly. In outrage I threw the *Tristan* tickets on the desk and left the room, shouting: "Either my father receives my wife, my mother-in-law, and me or I leave the Festspielhügel immediately! Who does he think he is? My mother-in-law is not going to be discriminated against here!" The guests waiting in the corridors pointedly turned their backs on us. When I indignantly asked Mamma Antonietta to leave the Festspielhaus with us immediately, she pulled me back with a strong grip and said: "Calm down! You're going with Teresina to your father. She certainly won't have another opportunity to meet her father-in-law. Don't think of me now." Gunda, my loving foster aunt, who thank God was on duty that afternoon, pulled Mamma Antonietta down beside her next to her desk in the telephone exchange and pushed Teresina and me onto the stairs leading to the first floor, in the direction of my father's office.

When Teresina and I arrived there, Gudrun greeted us with a gracious smile and offered me her hand to kiss. I shook it. Shortly after, we met Father. Without looking at us, he shook our hands. Then he started talking without pause and in a strong Upper Franconian accent, which Teresina could not understand, tactlessly comparing his second marriage with mine. I replied calmly but firmly: "Everyone has to make his own decisions." He didn't go into this. I remained silent for Teresina's sake, but tried to persuade Father by meaningful looks to change the subject. Instead he continued praising the second marriage as a source of renewal for a man. This torrent of words was only interrupted by one of his secretaries, who flung open the door to indicate to us that we should now go. Turning to my father, she said in a thick local accent: "Herr Wagner, you're wanted on the stage!" Father bowed deeply and hastily on saying goodbye, so that he didn't have to look us in the eye, and tore out of the room. As we left the room I recognized the secretary: she was the daughter of one of my nannies. We had met many times previously, but she didn't seem to know me now.

Teresina and I collected Mamma Antonietta from Gunda's office, and, as the performance was soon to begin, we hurried to our seats. Briefly I explained to Mamma Antonietta the story of the first act of *Tristan und Isolde* while we were heading for the stuffy family box, where Gudrun had rather tactfully seated me next to the lawyer who had drawn up the inheritance settlement.

During the intermissions we went to the festival restaurant, where most of those present pointedly ignored us, apart from Philip Wults, who was writing a history of the Wagner family and appreciated with great sensitivity what was happening. I waited impatiently for the end of the performance; the brief visit to my father and his lackeys had put me in a bad mood. I wanted to prevent

Mamma Antonietta and Teresina from taking home an even worse impression of Bayreuth.

Mamma Antonietta was pleased with the music and Ponnelle's production. However, when I asked her later how she found her stay in Bayreuth, she answered, concerned: "The opera performance was beautiful. But I don't think you could be happy in Bayreuth." On what she had had to put up with in Bayreuth as my mother-in-law she remained silent. This first trip was her last.

At the end of August 1983 I organized my transfer to Italy, paid for by the Deutsche Bank. The bank also enabled me to enroll at the expensive Bocconi School of Economics in Milan; but more important, they had given me an advantageous contract for a position in the credit department of the Deutsche Bank. Four weeks later I began my new life with Teresina.

I started work immediately and attended the Bocconi School every evening, pursuing both activities purely to earn money. The most valuable possession for anyone involved in the theater scene at that time was a membership card in Bettino Craxi's Socialist Party. I didn't have one. This type of corruption disgusted me. Besides, being a banker precluded me joining the operatic and academic circles, and my attempts to deny the image failed.

My superiors in the credit department made a varied impression on me right from the start. With one, Eleonore Finsterbusch-Horn, I was to develop a warm friendship over the course of time. The other superior, a man we only called "Semmel" [Bread Roll], made an awkward and stiff impression, and I soon suspected we would not see eye to eye. In fact it was through Semmel that I experienced firsthand what it means to be a subordinate in a bank hierarchy in which deviations from the prescribed norms are not tolerated. This system, which was only for the profit of the bank, stifled any individuality below the top-level positions. There were two options: submit or get out.

As I fully intended handing in my notice once my course at the Bocconi School had finished, I could afford to stand up to Semmel. After I had caught him repeatedly talking disparagingly about "the Italians," I requested he stop such discrimination: my family was

Italian, and I too felt insulted. That was the prelude to a series of spiteful gestures, for which I was fortunately well prepared. News of our feud spread like wildfire. Eleonore took my part, and our Italian colleagues started trusting us. Pleased to be able to offer them help, I advised them to join a union, but most were frightened of losing their jobs and scarcely dared demand changes. Semmel took the coward's way out and complained to the director, a former Luftwaffe officer, who now tried to intimidate me. But I soon brought my efforts to a halt by casually mentioning that as a side-line I worked as a journalist. Semmel and he then started preparing a report on me for the Frankfurt headquarters. Shortly afterwards, I noticed that Semmel no longer greeted me and seemed relieved if I closed my door, which was directly opposite his. Any contact was via the internal mailing system, and minutes of meetings filled whole files. I collected these documents, and in spring 1985, when I had enough valid material in my possession, I asked for a meeting at the headquarters in Frankfurt am Main. The ever-kindly Adolf Sievers saw only one way out in the short term: my transfer to Berlin. I asked for time to think it over.

17

Back to the Culture Jungle

*A*midst in-fighting and tension at the bank, Götz Friedrich, now the intendant of both the Deutsche Opera in Berlin and the Theater des Westens, made me an enticing offer. I was to write a program article for the Theater des Westens production of the opera *Aufstieg und Fall der Stadt Mahagonny* by Weill and Brecht in April 1985. I accepted the offer gratefully. I had unlimited resources to draw on: in fact, I had only to think of my experiences in the Deutsche Bank and in Bayreuth. I called the article "I Remember: The TV Memoirs Of Leokadja von Begbick." My story of Mahagonny, with its strong autobiographical allusions, was based on the idea that there is scarcely any difference in procedure between the banking and the opera world, where ultimately everybody is trying to outdo everyone else. I played off the decadent, bourgeois world of Wagner against the progressive forces in the opera scene of the Weimar Republic, hinting too that there was not much difference between the past and our own times.

Friedrich understood my allusions immediately, and he commissioned another article, this time for the program for his new production of *Götterdämmerung* in autumn 1985.

Re-entering the cultural scene at this time, I brought newly gained and valuable experience. My work in the bank had taught me more about economic and political forces, including those in opera.

Shortly after the publication of the article, my sister sent me an interview that my cousin Wummi had given to Karsten Peters, editor of the German edition of *Harper's Bazaar*. I had heard nothing from Wummi since my move to Italy. Entitled "I Always Have the Feeling Everything's Going to Happen Today," the interview contained statements I couldn't possibly endorse. Unfortunately, Wummi didn't just restrict himself to his own life and work; and his comments on my situation and attitude, although he didn't know my opinion on many things, made me angry. It proved once again that even Wummi and I had not learned to talk, really talk, to one another—a consequence of the distrustful and hate-filled atmosphere in which we had grown up. The interview certainly portrayed a reaction to long-endured humiliation.

I did, however, endorse his criticism of my father's work as festival director. When Peters asked him about the line of succession in Bayreuth, Wummi answered: "Wolfgang Wagner wants to be the longest and last festival head in our family. And actually I don't find that a very responsible attitude." So far, so good.

Not so good, however, was his response to the question of whether he wanted to be my father's successor:

"Yes, I would really like that. That's not just wishful thinking on my part, but a definite ambition."
PETERS: "Who other than Wolfgang Wagner could hinder you there?"
WUMMI: "Oh, Wolfgang can't hinder me there either, I think. It's just a matter of under what circumstances it happens."
PETERS: "Is there a practical possibility, then, of taking over the festival before your uncle's death?"
WUMMI: "He ought to bring me on board now, instead of waiting for the moment when catastrophe strikes or something else unexpected happens."
PETERS: "And he expressly rejects that?"
WUMMI: "He rejects it."
PETERS: "And does he give any reasons for that?"
WUMMI: "Yes, he says I should have worked my way up from the

bottom after my father's death. But he forgets that he made that impossible for me. I also find that it is more beneficial to make one's way outside a firm one belongs to, than inside."

PETERS: "Among the other 'Young Bayreuthers,' who aren't actually that young anymore, are there no other candidates?"

WUMMI: "Oh, yes, there's my cousin Eva, who is already heavily involved in arts administration, and there is my cousin Gottfried, who is not concentrating on administration anymore for the moment, though."

PETERS: "How is your relationship with them?"

WUMMI: "I have—amazingly for our family—very good contact and we get on very well. And there's no reason at all why two or three people couldn't take it on together."

PETERS: "Wagner directs Wagner—one generation after the other. Isn't that a sort of artistic incest?"

WUMMI: "Of course it's incest. But I'm of the opinion that amazing things can come out of incest as well. And in my case that is so: I get most of my ideas while listening to this music."

The following passages of the interview made me particularly thoughtful:

PETERS: "What characteristics would particularly apply to you?"

WUMMI: "Fury and vindictiveness."

PETERS: "And whom do you hate at the moment?"

WUMMI: "Myself most of all."

And then Peters came back to his favorite subject: "Do you want to be the heir of Bayreuth here and now, today?"

WUMMI: "Yes—rather the day before yesterday than yesterday. Wolfgang Wagner should stop dismissing the rest of the family as incapable. And if he were to look back on what he has done in the past, then I would say my qualifications are certainly worth more than his were then."

PETERS: "What makes your uncle act like that?"

WUMMI: "He must still be reacting to a distorted relationship, which—and I can only guess at this—goes back to that battle he had to fight as younger brother. I can't understand that, especially as my father has been dead a long time now. Wolfgang established himself a long time ago, and he's recognized. He doesn't have to fight for his reputation forever."

PETERS: "Was the enmity between big brother Wieland and little brother Wolfgang so great?"

WUMMI: "Yes, they were at daggers drawn."

PETERS: "Isn't it a bit the envy of the less gifted too?"

WUMMI: "It must be, I suppose, otherwise he wouldn't react the way he does."

PETERS: "What's his relationship with his own children, Eva and Gottfried?"

WUMMI: "That's the real tragedy of the whole story: he regards his own children exactly as he does his brother's children—they mean nothing to him. That is pretty alarming."[25]

The historical basis for doubts over my generation's claim to succession are for me further illustrated by an event that took place during the festival in summer of 1984. Friends told me of the exhibition "Wagner and the Jews" in Villa Wahnfried, and I received details a year later by way of an exhibition catalogue. For the following reasons I still consider the exhibition and its catalogue a falsification of history:

First, the inflammatory anti-Semitic essay *The Jews in Music* by Richard Wagner is presented totally without comment and without a critical comparison of the three versions.

Second, this essay is only the beginning of Wagner's anti-Semitic writings up to 1881.

Third, the historical development of anti-Semitism from Richard Wagner to Cosima Wagner, and then on via Houston Stewart Chamberlain to Hitler, Winifred, Wieland, and Wolfgang Wagner, was only partially demonstrated in text and pictures.

Fourth, the biographies of the so-called Jewish friends of Richard Wagner—Herman Levi, Samuel Lehr, Carl Tausig, Hein-

rich Porge, Angelo Neumann, Joseph Rubinstein, and Joseph
Joachim—and Wagner's Jewish artistic paragons, Felix Mendelssohn
and Giacomo Meyerbeer, were presented falsely.

These four points constitute an attempt to relativize Wagner's
anti-Semitism and to falsify it to the point of philo-Semitism.

Fifth, an indispensable element of the exhibition should have
been the inclusion of specialists on the historical connection between Wagner's anti-Semitism and the Holocaust.

Sixth, in the exhibition nothing is said about the connection between Wagner's anti-Semitic writings and the anti-Semitic content
of his stage works.

In its presentation of Wagner's anti-Semitism I found the exhibition's contempt for critical Wagner scholars such as Hartmut Zelinsky particularly unpleasant. Bayreuth was going in a direction that
I now combated. In a subsequent telephone call to Father I asked
him whether he was behind this shoddy attempt. "It's high time to
draw a line under this," he said, and hung up.

But before I could continue my attacks against the Festspielhügel, I still had my inner struggle to overcome, in which Teresina
selflessly stood by me. After serving notice at the Deutsche Bank
and receiving a surprisingly positive reference, I tried to keep my
head above water financially in whatever way I could. For a time I
worked as an insurance agent in Milan. After that I sold shoes with
some success at the Milan Shoe Fair for a friend in Cerro Maggiore,
who was a designer shoemaker. That gave me a bit of leeway for
work on Liszt and Wagner. All attempts at finding a job in the cultural scene via August Everding came to nothing, which didn't surprise me. I heard nothing from him except for a few pious phrases
with a lot of compliments. His interest was solely in Bayreuth family gossip, and I soon tired of asking him for favors. The only person in the opera scene who didn't abandon me was Götz Friedrich.

Because of the official historiography in Bayreuth and my desire
to continue my German-Jewish studies, I concentrated intensively
on the nineteenth and twentieth centuries. I also continued exam-
ining Liszt, fascinated by his contradictory personality: he was

Mephisto and saint, social lion and Christian socialist. He considered himself cosmopolitan, and had occasionally shown courage when he had to publicly stand by his convictions, but he was incapable of building up lasting family and intimate relations.

As I studied, a new, exciting world opened up to me, a cultural concept that I felt more and more to be a counterposition to Wagner. The contrasts thrown up by Liszt's confrontation with the outside world seemed extreme. He experienced reality as a contradiction to his artistic idea of the world. In vain, Liszt sought a solution to the conflict by retreating into artistic isolation. Through his work as avant-garde composer, pianist, music theoretician, opera director, conductor, teacher, and coordinator of all the essential musical trends of the nineteenth century, his effect on the music of his and our century is enormous.

I found myself confronting yet another giant out of my own family—but this one is far more likable than the one whose name I shall always bear like a millstone. I also realized while working on Liszt that I still had to find my own identity. It is not enough to read literature and music scores.

In the course of my research I drove to Eisenstadt in Austria, to the European Liszt Centre, which turned out to be an insignifcant little archive. In nearby Raiding, the composer's birthplace, I discovered that Bayreuth had already stretched out its hand in that direction and had reached the Liszt museum there. To me, though, it was important not to leave Liszt to sanctimonious Lisztians and all-powerful Wagnerians, but to interpret his work independently.

After the disappointing trip to Austria I contacted my Parisian cousin Blandine Jeanson. Her mother, Daniela Jeanson, had looked after the artist's legacy, and now Blandine was trying to continue that work. When I informed her of my Liszt studies, she gave me advice and told me of the coming international Liszt Congress at the Sorbonne in the autumn of 1986.

This was to be Teresina's first trip to Paris, and I anticipated showing her the great museums, especially the Jeu de Paune and the Louvre. I particularly looked forward to meeting with Blandine, whom I had not seen for years. Her sympathy and concern for my professional career and our conversations about our families' destinies helped me to find a non-Wagnerian family role.

In addition to my studies on Liszt's ethics as an antidote to Wagner, I was working on an article for Götz Friedrich on the final bars of *Götterdämmerung*. At that time I still didn't recognize the anti-Semitic overtones, especially in Wagner's drama outline *Jesus of Nazareth* of 1849, which had preceded *The Ring*. But I felt the end of *Götterdämmerung*, compared with the rest of the *Ring des Nibelungen*, to be a sort of artificially imposed music-theater epilogue, with an operatic happy ending.

I then received an offer from the head of the Richard Strauss Institute, Stephan Kohler, whom I had met in 1978 during rehearsals of *Ariadne auf Naxos* in Salzburg. Kohler is an open European with wide-ranging knowledge, not just on Strauss, and is personally courageous when it comes to awkward subjects. He wanted me to give a lecture on Strauss and Liszt. As I had just been working on Wagner's vague final message of love as the redemptive salvation of mankind in *The Ring*, I was interested in the ideas of transcendence and immanence in the symphonic poem *Ce qu'on entend sur la montagne* of the unorthodox Christian Liszt and in the *Alpine Symphony* of the bourgeois and onetime Nietzschean Richard Strauss. The point of departure of my theme, "Christ–Antichrist, or the Artist Between Transcendence and Immanence," was Kant's definition in his *Critique of Pure Reason* of 1781: "We want to name the principles, the application of which is held completely within the limits of possible—not merely actual—experience, immanent, but those which should go beyond these limits, transcendent principles."[26]

In preparing for the lecture I read the correspondence between Liszt and Nietzsche of January and February 1872. Nietzsche, who at the time was still strongly influenced by Wagner, misinterpreted Liszt as a Dionysian: that is, as a man who follows his own demon and gives his passions full rein because he is strong enough to master them. Liszt's answer was full of respect, but he wrote that he was a Christian. I then read in Nietzsche's essay *The Case of Wag-*

ner (1888) the way Nietzsche's judgment of Liszt developed. In the epilogue I found the following lines, which became important for my exposition of Liszt: "If Wagner was a Christian, then Liszt was perhaps a church father! The need for redemption, the quintessence of all Christian needs, has nothing to do with such buffoons: it is the most honest expression of decadence, it is the most convinced, most painful affirmation of decadence in the form of sublime symbols and practices. The Christian wants to be rid of himself. *Le moi est toujours haïssable* [The ego is always hateful]."[27]

I started to better understand a few things in Liszt's thinking when I read that at age sixteen the wunderkind had had a nervous breakdown and wanted to be a priest. His desire to escape from the world reemerged two years later, after his first love affair ended tragically. The composer's subsequent relationships ended tragically too, and Liszt was disastrous as a father, which accounts for the character of his daughter Cosima.

Liszt fought against the rigid musical forms of his time, but, like Wagner, he allowed discussion about music to peter out in vague interpretations. At that time I saw Liszt as the complete opposite to Wagner, which was very important for my further understanding. In October 1985, in a lecture to the choir of Cerro Maggiore, I declared myself totally in agreement with Liszt's ideas, against a dogmatic, intolerant exercise of religion and music. My audience was not enthusiastic. In fact, my new views were the start of my growing distance from the intellectual life of Cerro Maggiore.

In mid-December the conservative cultured classes of Munich heard my thoughts on Strauss and Liszt, in the presence of the Strauss sons, who were devoted to Bayreuth. Not only had I carried out my assignment, but I also had some money in my chronically low bank account.

It was only in the following year that I really discovered Liszt, though. In lectures and radio broadcasts in Switzerland, Italy, Belgium, France, and the United States, I was to be offered many opportunities to exchange views, and I gradually came to understand Liszt's attitude toward the Jews. His book *The Gypsies and Their*

Music in Hungary of 1859 with the crucial chapter "the Israelites" had certainly been prompted by Wagner's inflammatory and racist *The Jews in Music* of 1850. Liszt ends his book not like Wagner, with the "decline" and "suicide" of the Jews, whom he understood as a nation, but with the advice to them to reconquer Palestine through their "own efforts."

At the end of October 1986, after attending the not very satisfying Liszt Congress in Paris, Teresina and I went on to Luxembourg, where Louis Landuyt and his wife, Catherine, had invited us to a Liszt evening. With the assistance of the Luxembourg Ministry of culture, the German embassy, and—of all things—the Deutsche Bank, Louis had put together a well-balanced program of piano pieces, played by Catherine, and songs, which Louis performed, accompanied by his wife, in the Théâtre des Capucins.

I gave a lecture at the start of the evening, reading out mainly provocative quotations from Liszt's writings on all essential aspects in the life and creativity of the artist. An aggressive silence spread through the audience, which was composed primarily of bankers, when I read out the following passages from Liszt's article "Chopin's Virtuosity" of 1852, in which the composer berated bankers as the basis of a materialist society that demeaned artists and poets:

> Among the kings and princes of the financial world, on the other hand, everything is paid for in cash, even the visit of a potentate like Charles V, to whom, should he condescend to be accommodated by his banker, is offered his own bill to light his fire. Hence poets and artists need not wait in vain for a fee, which protects their old age from care. . . . The enriched bourgeoisie lets artists and poets founder in the voracity of materialism. Here women and men know of nothing better to do than to fatten them up, as a King Charles spaniel on the boudoir sofa is fattened, until, at the sight of their Japanese porcelain dish, they die of obesity. . . . The parvenus, who do not hesitate to pay for their gratified vanity, as they only feel great through the sums of money they have

lavished, may hear and see with wide-open ears and eyes, but they understand nothing of true poetry and art.[28]

Then, when I read out in Catholic Luxembourg Liszt's opinion of the Roman Church and his letter to the excommunicated social revolutionary the Abbé de Lamennais, a slight coughing became audible in the hall. But the audience remained polite and refrained from the heckling that I had been hoping for. In the interval afterwards I stood alone as a punishment. Louis and Catherine were amused by the audience's embarrassed silence. But then like a deus ex machina a representative of the Hungarian Ministry of Culture came up to me to inform me that on the basis of my work on Liszt I was to be distinguished with the Liszt Medal for 1986, the only German to receive it. Louis announced this news before the second half of the evening, the concert. Suddenly I was "in" and Teresina and I were paid court after the successful concert. People were amused by Liszt's "jokes" in precisely the way Liszt had intended, "with wide-open ears and eyes." A director of the Deutsche Bank said: "Those are just the opinions of an artist who understands little of the banking world. For you, as for your great-grandfather, our world would certainly be quite alien." I answered: "The banking world is alien to me, it's true, but I know it—I worked for three years in the Deutsche Bank." There was general amusement. No one quite believed me.

In 1987, I got a contract from the opera house in Bonn to act as dramaturg for a production of *Die Meistersinger von Nürnberg* in the 1987–88 season. The project required me to be in Germany, initially to do research in the Richard Wagner Museum in Bayreuth, but it was some time before I was permitted to visit there: the archive administration knew its master's voice and looked on my work with suspicion. A few violent scenes preceded my being able to read my own family's letters without submitting detailed reasons every time. My resentment of bureaucratic obstacles led me to look around a little more thoroughly in the archive, and I started again probing into areas taboo in Bayreuth: anti-Semitism, Gobineau,

Cosima Wagner, Houston Stewart Chamberlain, Winifred Wagner, Hitler.

That was also useful for my introductory lecture at a Toscanini symposium at the beginning of November 1987 in Parma. Harvey Sachs, the internationally acclaimed Toscanini biographer, let me choose my own subject, and I decided to talk on Toscanini's Bayreuth conducting style. Going through the *Bayreuther Blätter* and the festival programs from 1878 to 1943, I felt so nauseated by this pre-Nazi and Nazi reading matter I had to break off several times and go for a walk in Wahnfried Park. So that was the cultural soil of my own family! I had all the material I needed copied, knowing that there were (and still are) a lot of sources in Bayreuth that are supposed to be withheld from public view or which my father and his associates would like to keep under lock and key forever.

Every visit to the Richard Wagner Museum and Bayreuth was like a nightmare: the repression, the concealment, and the distortions of German cultural history had reached a stage that ensured evil spirits of the past remained long in the archive cupboards. Even my route from the archive in the Chamberlain House toward the city center took me along the Richard Wagner Strasse. And I was reminded yet again.

Before I left Germany I met Father in the Festspielhaus. I wanted to offer him an article on the centenary of Nietzsche's *The Case of Wagner* the following year. He answered shortly: "Send in your concept. Dr. Bauer will look through it." I was surprised that Oswald Georg Bauer, in spite of his new job as general secretary of the Bavarian Academy of Fine Arts (of which my father had been a strong supporter) still had influence on Father. His answer was equivalent to a rejection. Remembering how much Father despised Nietzsche, I asked: "Is Dr. Bauer the specialist on Nietzsche too now? When he was still working in the Festspielhaus, he already had his problems with Wagner." Father walked off angrily.

I knew that Bauer would be looking forward to rejecting my proposal, but I wanted his opinion and Father's in writing. I got them in April 1987: Father's comment was that the subject was still too charged with emotion and he consequently did not consider such

topics desirable in the Bayreuth program at the moment, especially
from a descendant of Wagner.

In Munich in August 1987, through my mother, I got to know the
Jewish Wagnerian Alfred Frankenstein from Tel Aviv. Mother had
been in contact with him for years and had often mentioned him.
His love of Wagner's music blinded him to my criticism of Wagner's
anti-Semitic writings and the role of the Bayreuth Festival in German culture and politics. He did not want to acknowledge that
Wagner, with his racist writings and his Bayreuth Festival, had
contributed his ideological part to the Holocaust. Unfortunately, he
didn't realize how shamelessly the festival was exploiting him in
marketing the new philo-Semitic Bayreuth. As part of this calcu-
lated attention, he was overwhelmed with festival tickets.

Like many of my Jewish friends who adored Wagner, Frankenstein could never completely understand why I did not identify
with my great-grandfather. Like many other Jewish Wagnerians,
he wanted to repress all this; I didn't. But in spite of all the contradictions, we liked each other—a feeling that he expressed when he
found out that I was investigating German-Jewish history. We
spoke abut Kurt Weill, and then the question came up about whether
I would give some lectures in Israel. Alluding to Uri Toeplitz, however, he pointed out that this idea would be difficult to put into
practice. Toeplitz had written in a concert program in Israel in
1966:

We speak of music to emphasize that we can only accept Wagner
as a composer, not the ideologist of the "total work of art," even
less so the theoretician, the writer of inflammatory works on cultural or political subjects, the unprincipled, egoistic, ambiguous
revolutionary, friend and exploiter of kings, friend of Jews and
arch Jew-hater—in short, the man who acted out of all the contradictions of his complex personality. We do not want people to
forget what the Nazis made of him, namely one of their spiritual
ancestors, but we should also bear in mind that we can never
know what Wagner himself would have said about it, because he
had been long dead when National Socialism emerged.[29]

That attitude was typical of the majority of liberal German Jews in Israel, though it was opposed at the time by the general population's radical rejection of Wagner, whom they equated with Hitler. None of this discouraged me, as I had gone my own way where my family and their past were concerned; and I owe Frankenstein and his wife, Esther, my first contact with Israel.

In July 1987 I sat in on some dress rehearsals in the Festspielhaus, among them my father's production of *Tannhäuser*. I had tried beforehand to correspond with him on it, but he hadn't even answered my letters. I realized yet again during the rehearsal that we were worlds apart, illustrated by our ideas of the Venusberg.

My interest now turned to an offer from France, from Orange. In conjunction with a *Ring* production at the open-air Roman theater there the following summer, I was to help, as dramaturg, to produce a video, organize an exhibition, and put together the program book. After an initial meeting with the festival's director, Raymond Duffaut, I noticed that there were scarcely any differences between the marketing methods in Bayreuth and in Orange, where the administration wanted above all to exploit my name. As I was not exactly inundated with offers at that time, and the idea of the video attracted me, I thought of the fee and said yes.

Back in Cerro Maggiore, meanwhile, I was told on the telephone that I had become one of the short-listed candidates for directorship of the opera house in the northern Swedish town of Umea. Lennart Rabes, the pianist and well-known interpreter of Liszt, who was working in Umea as repetiteur, had proposed me as candidate, and with no great hopes I had sent my details to Umea. I flew to Stockholm for the first time at the end of August and found it enchanting with its lakes and its architecture, untouched for centuries. I was received very warmly by Bertil Hagman, then dramaturg of the Royal Opera, the liberal politician Jan Eric Wikström, and Marietta Kardos, a prominent physician. Marietta and I soon developed a warm friendship—I later learned that as a child she had survived a concentration camp with her mother.

My new friends instructed me on what would be expected of me, and, once prepared, I flew on to Umea. I was impressed by the sight of the wild landscape of lakes and forests, and scarcely had I landed when I was met by the whole of the opera personnel. I was completely frank and emphasized that it was a privilege to work in the culture and opera scene, and that any form of cultural work was based on individual initiatives and responsibility. The cadre of Party Socialists in the opera house didn't approve of my views: they thought art should be fully organized from the cradle to the grave. Despite my opposition to such political nannying I was elected by an overwhelming majority as the new opera director. There was great disappointment when I decided, after discussions with Teresina, that I would prefer to continue my life in Italy rather than to do battle with party functionaries in beautiful Umea. Many of my friends and acquaintances were horrified that I had not seized such a unique opportunity in the opera world. But there was no question of my pursuing an uncertain future in a field that had become strange to me, at the expense of my private life. As a friend in Bayreuth told me, the Festspielhügel sighed with relief.

I now started preparing some radio broadcasts on Goethe's *Faust* in musical versions by Liszt, Berlioz, and Wagner, and also on Liszt's youthful opera *Don Sanche*. I also soon had a lecture to prepare on "The Cases of Nietzsche and Wagner" for the Bayreuth young people's festival meeting.

18

Bonn and Orange

reparations for the *Meistersinger* in Bonn and the *Ring* in Orange seemed good opportunities to establish new contacts in the opera business after an absence of six years. This new beginning did have its dark side, though: the then general intendant in Bonn, Jean-Claude Riber, had brought me in solely because of my name, and in the course of our preliminary discussions on *Die Meistersinger*, I noticed that we had nothing in common on the intellectual front. He reveled in the absurdly large budget of his federal-capital opera house, staked everything on the star circus, and anyone who didn't go along with it was frozen out. During one such discussion I saw the set model by Günther Schneider-Siemssen, whom André Heller had rightly called "Karajan's *Basteltante* [handicraft auntie]." The design was appalling: it reminded me of Bayreuth's *Meistersinger* productions of the thirties and forties. Schneider-Siemssen sensed my disapproval and retaliated by criticizing Wieland's *Meistersinger* of 1956. As this was one of my favorite productions, I could hold back no longer and said: "Where content and aesthetics are concerned we don't seem to have anything in common. Wieland's *Meistersinger* of 1956 will make theater history. This *Meistersinger* won't." With that, all further contact with the set designer came to an end. I realized that next year in Bonn I would have to concentrate on finishing the program.

Before that was the Toscanini congress in Parma and my lecture "Toscanini's Bayreuth Conducting Style." The great Italian conductor's tenure on the Festspielhügel was during the run-up to National Socialism, and I was interested in the political environment, in particular the role of my grandmother, who from 1923 had made Hitler presentable to the German bourgeoisie. In preparation, I reread Aunt Friedelind's autobiography of 1948, *The Royal Family of Bayreuth*, in which she describes the unbridgeable gulf that lay between her and my father.

Shortly before my departure for Bonn at the beginning of March 1988, I met the poet Karl Lubomirski and his Italian wife, the painter Enrica Lubomirski, at a reception given by the Austrian consul, Rudolf Novak, in Milan. What a humane contrast they made to the seedy opera world awaiting me in Bonn and Orange! From the outset our talk ranged over many levels, including an interest in the fate of others. I soon became familiar with Karl's colorful narrative style with all its nuances of subtly caustic humor and deep melancholy alternating with explosive joie de vivre. I knew after our first hours together that our paths would often cross. I read for him a poem from *La Zolla Di Luce* [The Clod of Light], a volume of his poetry that Enrica had translated with great sensitivity into Italian. Poems such as "The Tree," with the line "The tree of my life bears doubts," won me over immediately to his work. He too had been induced by the *italianità* of his wife to leave the narrow confines of his native Austria.

Although Karl had left Innsbruck irrevocably behind him, as I had left Bayreuth, we remained—whether we liked it or not, and Karl as a poet even more than I—marked by and dependent on German culture and language. Between us a quiet solidarity arose in opposition to the friendly but ultimately impersonal attitude of Italian Catholicism. Although it is clearly better for us to live in Italy than anywhere else in Europe, nevertheless we feel like cosmopolitan outsiders and nomads. How close we are in decisive questions became clear to me too when I read Karl's poem of 1990 "Auschwitz," in which he manages to say the unsayable as follows:

Here fell a great leaf
from the tree of death
greater still than Babylon
Jerusalem and elsewhere too
a leaf
that follows no winds
that lies and lies and lies
and when history itself is blown away
then only will perish
with its place.[30]

For me there is no doubt of his importance as a poet. He also became a trusty fellow fighter for German-Jewish dialogue in the controversy over the Wagner cult in Bayreuth after my trip to Israel in 1990. What will always bind me to Karl is his incorruptibility in humanitarian questions. He was discriminated against by self-styled popes in a pseudo-left-wing international cultural lobbying scene—something else we have in common.

The beginning of our friendship in March 1988 already had a good effect: I went to Bonn without fear of Riber and company. At first I stayed with my "second mother," Bettina Fehr, and as always we talked at length about Father, Mother, and Bayreuth. Bettina always tried to work toward mediation and conciliation, but over time she had realized that there was little I could do about what seemed an impasse.

Inspired by our conversations, on 14 March Bettina sent me to bed with Ralph Giordano's *Die zweite Schuld, oder Von der Last, Deutscher zu Sein* [The Second Guilt, or On the Burden of Being German] to read. She said, knowing me all too well: "This book will have a big effect on you!" She was right. I didn't read the 363 pages, I devoured them, for what I read in Giordano's book touched my very soul. The clarity of the content, its linguistic beauty, his nuanced historical, political, and cultural analyses, and his humanity overwhelmed me. Here, finally, was a German-speaking author who had something to say to me. His life of suffering had made him unusually sympathetic as a human being, one who stands up with the courage of his convictions against the German society of repression. He seemed to put into words everything that was important to me.

On 15 March I got up at seven, wide awake despite having had hardly any sleep at all. I couldn't resist waking up Bettina, who is not an early riser, by making a lot of noise during my morning ablutions. Still somewhat sleepy, she made coffee for me in the kitchen while I told her enthusiastically about my reading experience, asking impatiently: "Can't you ring Ralph Giordano?" Bettina laughed and said: "Now, at half past seven in the morning? Let's wait till nine!"

At nine she rang him up and introduced me in her charming, irresistible way, not only as "the Weill Wagner," but as someone very much hoping for a discussion of German-Jewish history with him. Three days later, at Giordano's invitation, Bettina and I went to Cologne. Having rung the doorbell, we waited outside until the door opened, and inside we saw a beautifully laid coffee table, among several other pieces of tasteful period furniture. Instead of a greeting by the host came the Prelude to Act One of *Tristan und Isolde.* Then Ralph Giordano came toward us. Pensively he said to me: "This music is one of my favorite Wagner compositions." I answered: "It's impossible not to be fascinated by *Tristan und Isolde,* but unfortunately we have to live with the other Wagner as well." He agreed and shook my hand.

I had intended asking Giordano about his life and work, but I didn't get around to it during the next three hours. He had a lot of questions about my life. And as we sat on the sofa in a relaxed mood, I noticed how his fine and melancholy features began brightening up while I was answering him. I found it so easy to open up to him, and talked as though to an old friend. When I told him about Winnie and Wolf, he gripped my arm and interrupted my flow with a question that annoyed me: "Are you really Wolfgang Wagner's son?" I hardly reacted, as I thought I had misheard, and carried on telling him about the correspondence between Hitler and my grandmother. With friendly obstinacy he repeated the question: "Are you really Wolfgang Wagner's son?" He was evidently asking about my father, so I countered laughingly with the question: "Why do you want to know that?"

He answered seriously: "I once interviewed your father in Bayreuth. I'm sorry to have to tell you that I didn't believe a word he said. There's no humanity in that man."

I answered: "You don't have to apologize—you're only saying what I've known and felt since my childhood."

Giordano reached for a copy of his novel *The Bertinis* and wrote in it: "For Gottfried Wagner—who I liked on sight." And then he said emphatically: "Whether you want to or not, you must write the story of your life. You owe that to your own generation and those to follow."

I didn't like this idea at all and said: "At the age of forty-one to write a sort of autobiography against the degenerate conditions in Bayreuth? Why? Who would be interested? To make myself even more isolated than I am now?"

Giordano replied: "You have nothing to do with the false Bayreuth of the Wagners, but you are a Wagner aware of his human and historical responsibility. Write your life story. Going over it will help you personally and one day may help you be reintegrated in Germany. I'll support you."

I was moved when Bettina and I left Ralph Giordano. I knew the meeting would have consequences for my life.

The day-to-day life in the opera house caught up with me again. My initial fears that Jean-Claude Riber might misuse *Die Meistersinger* in Bonn to promote himself proved to be founded. In mid-March I sat in on one of the rehearsals taking place on the small main stage. The set, which was partly assembled, was even more tasteless than the model. According to the idea that anything expensive must be good, Riber had hired stars from the international Wagner market, including René Kollo as Walther and Bernd Weikl as Sachs. They stood around bored in the rehearsals and feigned interest in Riber's arrangements, which they then supplemented with ideas and experiences from other productions. At first Riber made video recordings of these embarrassing scenes, to preserve it all for posterity. When I tried to bring to his attention mistakes in the way he was directing movement, he was insulted, as he was accustomed to everyone lauding his artistry.

My work on the large *Meistersinger* program book was going well; so as to remove any critical eye from his rehearsals, Riber agreed to all my suggestions for the program. He regarded me as a rival and did whatever he could to thwart me. Everything I did was overseen by his assistants. The dramaturge, Monika Rottmaier, who like me didn't take these repressive measures lying down, was eventually given notice. Riber and his associates hurt a respected opera repertory house through this soulless, interchangeable star system. Singers who ridiculed Riber in the cafeteria feigned admiration for his direction during rehearsals. Beneath all this hypocrisy, however, was the box office. I hoped that this system which was inimical to art, and which was prevalent not just in Bonn, would soon end, but this would not be the case.

I had only one opportunity in Bonn to protest against this state of affairs, and that was through the content and shape of my program book. I quoted from Wagner's writings and the *Meistersinger* libretto and wrote articles that opposed what was happening on the stage. I unmasked Riber and his associates through the revolutionary Richard Wagner and his avant-garde ideas on music theater, while Riber, in the federal capital, tried to present the composer as little more than a petit-bourgeois garden gnome. I felt not even Wagner and his ambiguous works deserved an accusation such as that. I quoted Wagner's letter of 14 October 1868 to Ludwig II, in which he complained about the production of his *Meistersinger*: "The utter wretchedness and deep decline into which the German theater has sunk is something I shall discover to an even fuller extent by what happens to this very work of mine."[31] This was precisely how I felt about the Bonn production.

The tension between me and Riber became more intense after an interview I gave the music critic Hans G. Schürmann of the Bonn *General-Anzeiger* appeared on the weekend of the premiere, under the title "The Other Wagner: Against the Flow Towards His Own Goal." In it, I criticized the opera "jungle" and advocated "achieving opera as a constructive group experience on the basis of indi-

vidual responsibility, motivation, initiative, and permanent evolu-
tion of professional competence and creativity." Instead of prompting
open discussion, my comments were followed by effusive compliments, which by being generally noncommittal reminded me where
I was: in Germany, the paradise of repression, where silence, especially in the case of Wagner and his *Meistersinger,* has well-known,
well-founded reasons. The *Meistersinger* premiere, on 17 April
1988, was just as one would have expected from the rehearsals.
The media and the public were taken in by the glamour of the famous names. In a last attempt to hurt me, Riber had tried to delete
my name from my program booklet. He also asserted that I made
no contribution to his "brilliant" *Meistersinger,* although the public and the media reacted positively to my booklet. Later, Riber had
to retract his calumnies in court.

In the short run, though, Riber was successful in hurting me.
The festival director in Orange, Duffaut, suddenly wanted me off
the production of *The Ring,* which Riber had been engaged to direct,
and offered to settle with me for half my fee. It ended in a quarrel.
I demanded to be allowed to fulfill my contract as dramaturg, and
Duffaut realized that legally, he'd have to let me. I delivered the
large manuscript for the program book, reasserted that any alteration must be discussed with me beforehand, and then left.

My next task was preparing my video *The Ring of the Nibelung,*
for which I collected a great deal of material. Inspired by events in
Bonn, I chose the subtitle *The Consequences of the Misuse of Power*
for the project. In my *Ring* story, Wotan and Alberich appear as two
crooks in a struggle for world domination. My method of narration
was to consciously address a public that understands opera and
Wagner as it is presented: as a stage for the self-presentation of alleged high society. I owed considerable visual inspiration to the pictures of the famous photographer August Sander. In a crazy
mixture of pictures from Botticelli through Roy Lichtenstein to
Coca-Cola ads I showed the decline of an apocalyptic society from
Red Square to Wall Street, ending up with the launch of an atom
bomb. Thierry Bénizeau saw to the technical assembly of my
meticulously wrought material.

Duffaut and Riber eventually altered the program book without asking me, contravening the contract. At the end of July 1988, my lawyer advised me to leave Orange and informed the media of this decision, which caused quite a stir. A few days earlier my *Ring* video had won first prize at the video festival in Biarritz. The subsequent legal action against the administration in Orange dragged on for four years and ended in a settlement, as I could not afford to continue the proceedings.

I now began to prepare a multimedia lecture for Bayreuth. In it I wanted to continue what I had begun in Bonn and Orange: an open attack on the Wagner moneymaking machine.

At that time I was living in Bad Kissingen and was in poor health. I was being treated by my friend the distinguished cardiologist Peter Deeg, whom I had know since 1960—the year my father had directed his first *Ring* on the Festspielhügel. He, like myself, had a strong father to contend with, one who had written a book during the Nazi period on the "court Jews" and had made a second brilliant career as a lawyer in Germany's economic miracle.

Throughout the first years of our friendship, as a point of principle, Peter and I avoided talking about the Nazi past of our fathers. Peter had been brought up by his father to be a conservative, but I knew that behind this apparently impenetrable conservative façade there were other qualities. They emerged when he married Jadwiga Angielski from Gdansk. Jadwiga, with her openness and radiant joie de vivre, altered Peter so much that, to my amusement, the effect of his years-long bachelorhood was completely undone. Their four lively children grew up in a stimulating German-Polish cultural environment. Jadwiga's cosmopolitan father, Stefan Angielski, had gone through Poland's Nazi occupation and been detained in a Stalinist labor camp in Siberia.

It was also about this time, in July 1988, that I got into conversation with Peter's father. Initially he had helped my father to draw up the Foundation charter of the Bayreuth Festival, until he discovered that they did not lead to a settlement of the succession within the family. That went against the grain with him as a strongly family-oriented man, as did the shoddy treatment of my mother in the divorce: he and his wife continued to help her from 1976 on. I was surprised when, during our conversation, he also began to talk about National Socialism and the Jews. With some emotion he fully acknowledged the horrors of the Holocaust as a terrible crime in German history. I had never heard this kind of admission from my father. His admission also had an effect on my friendship with Peter. Gradually, we began to talk about our fathers' past and openly discussed anti-Semitism in the Third Reich and our responsibility for coming generations.

In the middle of August 1988, within the framework of the Internationales Jugendfestspieltreffen (International Young People's Festival meeting) in Bayreuth, I gave my talk "The Cases of Nietzsche and Wagner." My politico-cultural collection of quotations from Nietzsche's *The Case of Wagner* and *Nietzsche Contra Wagner* created an icy atmosphere that I found difficult to cope with. Nietzsche's marvelous analysis of Wagnerians was received with silent fury. I described the reasons for the breakup of the friendship between Wagner and Nietzsche in 1878: Nietzsche could no longer stand Wagner's woolly, late-Romantic conception of life with all its ideological dynamite. I then turned to Nietzsche's description of the "Wagner neurosis," with its anti-Semitism, which he recognized early on as a danger. In summing up Nietzsche's convincing criticism of Wagner, his passionate attack on the opera public of his time and of the future, plus his gloomy diagnosis of "Bayreuth cretinism," which was already showing totalitarian aspects, I was clearly understood in the auditorium: namely, that I was getting even with the festival public of the dishonest New Bayreuth era. I garnished all this with provocative collages of Wagner's music and caricatures by Marc Sautet and Patrick Boussignac.

As I brought the lecture to a close, the atmosphere in the auditorium was as I had expected: edgy and aggressive. Bayreuth is a place full of resentment against anyone who does not share Wagner's ideas, and I had hoped to expose what a ridiculous prejudice that was by lecturing on Nietzsche, who rejected Wagner's cultural ideology in his years of philosophical maturity. Unfortunately I was unable to engage members of the audience in serious discussion. It was impossible to discuss Wagner, Nietzsche, and the Jews openly in Bayreuth. Members of the Friends of Bayreuth did not even attend the lecture, and many others I had invited did not come because they did not want to lose favor with my father.

After the lecture, Teresina and I stood with a few friends and acquaintances in the near-empty auditorium. As we left, a man came up to me with a friendly smile and said: "My name is Janos Solyom. Don't let yourself get discouraged by the reaction of this audience. I'm right behind your talk, which has to be unpopular here: you are not only questioning everything, but you are not allowing any repression of the past. Any form of truth hurts. You are unwelcome here, where nothing has changed." He shook my hand warmly, and we arranged to meet during one of the intermissions of *Die Meistersinger*, which was about to begin.

Janos was Hungarian by birth but became a Swedish citizen after escaping Hitler. When we met, he told us of his international career as a pianist and of his wife Camilla Lundberg's work as a journalist. The friendship among the four of us developed in defensive reaction to the dishonesty of the Bayreuth environment. We talked about Liszt and the misuse of his life and works by Bayreuth, and together made plans for the future. One of our joint projects was a much-admired Theresienstadt evening in Stockholm in 1994, in which Janos played piano works by Pavel Haas, Gideon Klein, and Viktor Ullmann in a uniquely intense way. His artistic and cultural richness and his tolerance made the hours with him irreplaceable. It was only in Stockholm that I learned that Janos is related to Kurt Weill and that the Nazis had murdered his father in Russia.

One day after meeting Janos, my *Ring* video was being played as another event in the Bayreuth Young People's Festival Meeting. The negative mood following my lectures had not abated, but because I was the son of the festival boss, it didn't come to a head. As I played my video several times over, a large section of the audience indignantly left the hall. Such conservatism among these young people did not surprise me. It was a reflection of the zeitgeist, in which there was no vision, no protest, simply career plans. Discussions with younger participants of the Young People's Festival revolved mainly around aesthetic details instead of the politico-cultural phenomenon of Wagner in Bayreuth. Older members of the audience were just as shocked by the video but, as one audience member told me, to my amusement, hoped that because of it I had disqualified myself as my father's successor.

The only positive outcome of my two events in Bayreuth was an offer from the *Neue Zürcher Zeitung* to publish my thoughts on Nietzsche. To my surprise, Josef Lienhart, president of the West German Richard Wagner Societies, invited me to show the *Ring* video to his Freiburg Society in the autumn of 1988. Shortly before my arrival in Freiburg, both my video equipment and the only copy of the video were stolen from the luggage locker at Hamburg railway station. So I had to talk about the *Ring* video without showing it. Before and after the talk, Lienhart enthused about the Wieland era in Bayreuth. That surprised me, as my father and his followers had done everything to banish his great shadow. Lienhart also seemed to appreciate my critical examination of the Nazi past and, in particular, my intention to accept the invitation to Israel, and promised to do what he could after the trip to promote discussion about Wagner's anti-Semitism in the Wagner Societies.

But I soon discerned that despite all my criticism of the Bayreuth Festival, he believed I would go to Israel as a pro-Wagner propagandist. I made it clear that that was not my intention, and on my return from Israel I heard nothing more from Lienhart.

19

On the Road with Nietzsche, Wagner, and Liszt

At the end of October 1988, after thorough preparation, I set off on a lecture tour that was to take me first to North America and then to Japan. My first stop was Washington, where I was to speak at George Washington University. Before that, the historian Stephen Gallup gave an impromptu party attended by stimulating academics from all over the world. From the first moment I felt at east in this environment, with its great expertise and kindly tolerance. During the party, passionate discussions had already broken out for and against Wagner, always conducted with a respect for the opinion of others. What a contrast to the German academic circles!

Just as stimulating were the hours I spent as a guest in the home of the Guenthers. Roy was the head of the music department at George Washington University and an excellent trombonist, and his wife, Eileen, a music teacher and distinguished organist. Roy is a happy mixture of scientific passion, which he easily conveys to his students, and pragmatism, having the capacity to carry through projects efficiently—a mixture I had seldom, if ever, encountered in Europe, but one that I consider important for effective teaching. Roy helped me with the preparation of my talk "The Cases of Nietzsche and Wagner" and with the discussion afterwards.

My next appearance took me to Chicago, where I was a guest of the Goethe Institute and the Chicago Lyric Opera. The conservative opera public reacted quite negatively to the recovered *Ring* video and Nietzsche's criticism of Wagner. Their number included a powerful German contingent, which had expected a eulogy to Wagner, and the Wagnerians in particular were disappointed. The discussion with some liberal intellectuals, who were particularly interested in the subject of Wagner and the Jews, was more constructive.

My last stop in the United States was of particular interest: in mid-November I landed in Los Angeles and was the guest of Michael and Miriam Meyer in their beautiful home in Pacific Palisades, overlooking Santa Monica. Michael, who is a history professor at California State University in Northridge, specializing in the Third Reich and Richard Wagner, was particularly interested in my theories on Nietzsche and Wagner. His Jewish mother had survived the Nazi period in Germany.

Cornelius Schnauber, head of the Max Kade Institute and the person who had suggested I visit Los Angeles, had organized a series of events on the subject of Nietzsche and Wagner in various cultural institutions in Los Angeles. As there were a large Jewish community and a Wagner Society in Los Angeles, the hall in the Goethe Institute proved too small, and half those who came had to be turned away. During my talk the faces of the Wagnerians close to Bayreuth became stony, although the subsequent discussion was begun by a young man who apparently mistook me for a relative of Adolf Hitler and became quite abusive. After I corrected him, there followed an objective discussion on Wagner's and Nietzsche's conflicts with Judaism between various groups in the audience, of whom many were German or Austrian emigrants. This subject made the Wagnerians uncomfortable, and at first they kept quiet, many of them having only come to stare at me as a museum piece. Not very diplomatically, I cut short the pro-Wagner eulogizing à la Bayreuth, which the Wagnerians in the audience misinterpeted as a typically powerful Wagnerian character trait. What would now await me in Japan?

I finally set off for Tokyo at the end of November 1988. I was pleased to be met at the airport by two representatives of the Japanese Wagner Society: the Germanist Tomoyoshi Takatsuji and Mrs. Yasuko Miyake. Yasuko's husband, a musicologist, had provided an analysis of the form of *Tristan und Isolde* for the Bayreuth Festival.

I had scarcely put down my bags in the guest room of the Goethe Institute when the first reception of the Wagner Society took place in my honor. There I finally met Tatsuji Ivanbuchi, a professor of German at Gakushuin University, with whom I had already corresponded and who had translated my book on Weill and Brecht, on whom he is an internationally recognized authority. Now he came up to me in person: a frail gentleman in an elegant three-piece suit. With a faint smile, he warmly shook my hand. He immediately offered me the "du" form of address, which, being quite uncommon in Japan, pleased me. "Buchi," as I was to call him from now on, is a cosmopolitan nomad in everything he does, thinks, and feels. Come what may, his presence served as a shield in a country that, despite all the familiar Western traces, I found rather disconcerting.

My first, well-attended talk, sponsored by the Wagner Society at the Tokyo Goethe Institute, on Liszt and Wagner, went smoothly, possibly because I refrained from too-critical discussion points.

An excursion with the enchanting Yasuko, which began at five in the morning in Tokyo, was unforgettable. In splendid weather we sped to Kyoto by Shinkansen, the famous Japanese high-speed train, to see the imperial residence. The beauty of the palace, its gardens, the temple, and the shrines fascinated me. Small, irresistibly smiling schoolgirls in black-and-white uniforms asked if I would have my photograph taken with them, and when Yasuko told them something about me, they hummed "The Ride of the Valkyries," beaming. It was not the time to tell them my opinion on the necrophilia of the opera scene, and for Yasuko's sake I said "cheese" like a good European tourist.

At Gakushuin University on 29 November, in a marathon event, I presented both my talk on Nietzsche and Wagner and my *Ring* video to a Japanese-European academic audience. When I subsequently showed the video at Keio University, the reaction of the women students surprised me: they giggled behind their hands at the erotic scenes. This then turned into general amusement. The end, however, where the dropping of the atomic bomb on Hiroshima symbolized the end of *Götterdämmerung*, visibly moved all the students.

20

Hitler and Wagner?

arly in 1989 preparations began for the centenary of Hitler's birth. Leo Haffner, one of the leading producers of cultural programs for the Austrian radio channel ORF Vorarlberg, had prerecorded a discussion with Karl Lubomirski and me back in autumn 1988 on the subject of German culture, tradition, and politics, which could not avoid mention of Hitler and Bayreuth. Haffner, an Austrian Jew, was interested in the consequences of anti-Semitism beyond Germany, and he proposed that I give a talk at the beginning of April in the ORF studio on Hitler and Wagner.

While I was preparing the talk, I became more and more aware of what consequences this subject had for me personally. It is the most painful chapter of my family history, which I then tried to face publicly for the first time. I didn't want to take refuge in the world of art, like Father and Uncle Wieland, and separate Wagner the theatrical genius from Wagner the ideologist. Enough Wagners before me had been similarly led to such a fateful repression and ultimately to the denial of individual responsibility, so I now asked myself why I hadn't been able to speak more openly to my grandmother and my father on the subject of Hitler and Wagner. After all, if my grandmother had accepted Hitler's proposal of marriage, I could have been called Gottfried Wagner-Hitler! (Historian

Robert Wistrich records the proposal in his *Who's Who in Nazi Germany*, 1982.)

Hitler and Wagner are therefore part of my life, a connection that created in me a strong identity crisis. With doubts at that time about myself as a Wagner, a German, and a post-Holocaust Christian—and through a degree of uncertainty about the theme—I settled on a lecture title in the form of a question: "Adolf Hitler and Richard Wagner?"

The lecture was my first, unsuccessful attempt to dissociate Wagner's work—in particular *Parsifal*, which was open to several interpretations—from his anti-Semitic writings. I quoted a line from Wagner's regenerative article "Heroism and Christianity," in which he wrote about his *Parsifal:* "The blood of the Saviour, the issue from his head, his wounds upon the cross—who impiously would ask its race, if white or other?"[32]

Despite the historical connection between quotations from my great-uncle Chamberlain, Grandmother Winifred, and Hitler from November 1923 up to his official statement from the "Wolf's lair" in January 1942, I still had not understood or—from a modern viewpoint—wanted to understand the full consequences of the terrible total vision: namely, that Richard Wagner himself had already contributed his part to the inextinguishable link between Bayreuth, Theresienstadt, and Auschwitz. At that time I didn't want to regard Richard Wagner as co-responsible for being connected with Hitler.

Today I must acknowledge that I cannot uphold the final sentence of my talk of April 1989 in the Vorarlberg studio of ORF: "Wagner and Hitler? I hope the 'and' strikes you as odd. . . . Wagner belongs to art, Hitler to the criminal records file."

That month I embarked on my first lecture tour of Norway, Iceland, Denmark, and Sweden. The animosity toward the subjects of Wagner and Nietzsche and the *Ring* cycle, the discussion of which I opened with my video, was noticeable everywhere, for Richard Wagner was still connected with the memory of the Nazi invasion and German occupation in the 1940s. But once people understood that I was neither a member of the master race nor intended to harp on about Wagner's unique greatness, the ice began to melt.

Having made it clear that I rejected not only the Wagner cult in Bayreuth from 1872 to 1945 but also the repression of the Nazi period of the New Bayreuth era, I was then mostly received with great openness, warmth, and interest.

In Iceland in particular I realized that Wagner's use of Nordic mythology only very superficially corresponded to Scandinavian culture. I also learned that Nordic mythology has nothing to do with Hitler's delusion of the Nordic race.

The less conventional the audience, the more open the discussion on the politico-cultural phenomenon of Wagner and the Nazi period. Media interest was high. Only in Arhus and Stockholm did I meet Wagnerians who, in their woolly worldview and through their pilgrimages to Bayreuth, did not want to talk critically about their "Master."

On my return flight from Stockholm to Milan I realized how much the Wagner affair is obscured in Scandinavia by the fact that they have not yet come to terms with the Nazi past.

In July 1989, while I was preparing for my trip to Israel, I went with Teresina to the premiere of my father's new *Parsifal* in Bayreuth. This time we were the guests of the then managing director of the Upper Franconian Chamber of Industry and Commerce, Helmuth Jungbauer, and his wife, Helga, who remained unperturbed by the intrigues against me. Jungbauer supported the opposition theater group Studiobühne Bayreuth, which had made a name for itself through its refreshingly disrespectful treatment of the Bayreuth Wagner tradition.

On the Festspielhügel word had got round about my invitation to Israel to give talks on Wagner, and the usually cool tolerance of our presence now turned icy. With great sensitivity the Jungbauers sensed the atmosphere, and their friendly attitude toward us now became warm and open on public occasions as well as in private. When we were escorted by them, we benefited from Helmuth's reputation as a powerful yet warm man who is not impressed by my father or his sponsors. Even my father's yes men had to accept our presence at official receptions in the opening week of the festival. Whereas in previous years Teresina and I had been used to being invited only to the "state reception," we found ourselves at the table of the guests of honor after the *Parsifal* premiere, which all the other invited guests had to pass, including my father and his wife—although they managed not to see us.

People at our table asked me for my opinion of the *Parsifal* and, aware that the tabloid press was within earshot, I answered with careful objectivity. I referred to the end of the opera when Parsifal sings "redemption for the redeemer," and in which, according to Wagner's instructions, Parsifal, as the new, Aryan Christ, celebrates the Last Supper as a sign of salvation. Contrary to Wagner's conception, Father had allowed Kundry, the main female character, to survive in the male Christian temple of the knights of the Grail. Parsifal had disappeared among the crowd of knights. In other words, my father was re-directing Wagner to make his grandfather seem less anti-Semitic and mysogynistic. Such misinterpreted democratization, which my father created to avoid negative criticism of his festival meant that in the Grail there was no individual, but only the knights' collective responsibility—a thought that appalled me in light of the evil done by thousands of individual Germans in their quest for redemption. Clearly my audience understood my point, for they kept silent and then changed the subject.

In 1994 Peter Deeg informed me that Father had changed the end yet again: Kundry, as female Messiah, now offered the goblet to the knights of the Grail as redemption. This was New Bayreuth repression at its most extreme.

After that, we saw *The Ring* directed by Harry Kupfer and conducted by Daniel Barenboim. Watching the absurd opening scene in which the chorus was a stampeding horde in a thick mist under a figure that insiders later informed me was supposed to be Wotan (without the Rheingold music), I realized that the festival could no longer have any meaning for me. The whole *Ring* concept was portrayed as an eco-swindle story of Messrs. Wotan and Alberich between two fictional atomic world wars. Not surprisingly the end of this most absurd interpretation was in keeping with the rest of the production: to the "redemption-through-love" motif, drunks and drug addicts burped in a sort of East German railway restaurant.

I bumped into Barenboim, after the *Götterdämmerung*, in the Bürgerreuth Restaurant. He had expected a compliment for his brilliant production, but I had to tell him I had never seen such nonsense. He feigned interest in my opinion and promised a meeting in the following days. Unfortunately, he did not keep his word.

y first meeting with Professor Herzl Shmueli, on 3 August 1989 in Zurich, was a complete contrast to that last visit to the Festspielhügel. We had first started corresponding in May 1988. This musicologist had dared hold seminars in Tel Aviv on Wagner as far back as the 1970s, arousing great public interest. The early Romantic period was one of his main areas of study, so he could not avoid the "Wagner case."

Shmueli had grown up in Istanbul, in a traditional Jewish family, and had attended the German school there. At the beginning of the 1930s he emigrated to Israel. He studied mathematics and then, from 1950 to 1952, musicology in Zurich. Why Zurich? "Despite all my love for German culture, instilled in me by my education in Istanbul, it was impossible for me to study in Germany after Hitler," he explained.

At our first meeting in August he asked me about my life: "Doctoral thesis on Kurt Weill in Vienna. That doesn't seem to me to be a typical choice for a Wagner after Hitler." With that our intimate critical dialogue began, culminating in my being invited to give four lectures in Israel in January 1990.

At the beginning of September 1989, I accepted an invitation from the International Music Festival of Montreal to a multimedia talk on "Faust, Goethe, Wagner, Liszt: Poetry and Music." I informed my cousin Winifred Arminjon-Lafferentz of my arrival.

Winifred, named after my grandmother, was the second daughter of my father's younger sister, Verena Lafferentz.

We had only met each other briefly as children, after which my family had made any further contact impossible; my father spoke of Aunt Verena's family in Nussdorf on Lake Constance as negatively as he did of Aunt Friedelind's. He had told me on one of our walks in Arosa at the beginning of the sixties that Aunt Verena had been "a favorite of the Führer" and that her husband, Bodo Lafferentz, had organized the wartime festivals as assistant of the Labor Front chief Robert Ley. I never quite believed this version of the story.

And so we met again, weighed down by the family burden and encumbered by untruths from our time as children and teenagers, just before my trip to Israel. After discussing my talk on *Faust*, we finally came around to the subject of our family's past. I could speak openly with Winnie. The humiliations she and her family had had to suffer on visits to Bayreuth made me feel ashamed. We both knew that Festspielhügel politics had made personal discussion, even within our own generation, impossible ever since the Wagner Foundation had been set up and the public war of succession ensued. The willfully contrived "discussion" on succession was one subject we avoided.

Like me, Winnie suffers from the Nazi past. As a painter, she deliberately goes her own professional direction. We both view a critical handling of family tradition, and a search for one's own identity through one's own work, as a constructive alternative as well as a chance for dialogue between us in the future. Deeply sensitive to the shadow of our family's Nazi connection, Winnie herself has studied Jewish history as a result.

After returning from Montreal I continued working on my Wagner lectures. I had applied to the Ministry for Foreign Affairs and the Goethe Institute for financial support for the project but still had not received an answer. Eventually it became evident that neither organization would sponsor my work toward reconciliation in Israel.

At the beginning of October 1989 I presented to Herzl Shmueli my proposed topics for the University of Tel Aviv lectures: my video *The Ring of the Nibelung, or The Consequences of the Misuse of Power*, "The Fall of the Gods, or *Épatez le Bourgeois:* The Anti-Wagnerian Musical Contemporary Theater of Weill and Brecht," "The Cases of Nietzsche and Wagner," and, finally, "The Wagner I'm talking About: An Approach to Wagner's Personality and Work." Explaining this choice, I wrote among other things: "My intention remains, calmly and patiently, to make my contribution to a continuing dialogue in small steps on the subject 'Wagner and German culture.' I am fully aware of my responsibility and cannot understand why the West German institutions in Israel (Goethe Institute and West German Embassy) do not support my conciliatory work, in which I have been engaged now for two decades."

Fortunately I received committed help from Herzl's successor as the head of the music department of the University of Tel Aviv, Shai Burstyn, whom I fully informed of the contents of the lectures, as I didn't want to give offense to my host country. I also asked him a question which, for me, was critical: "Would it be very tactless to present a few—small—musical examples from Wagner's music at the university?" He agreed to it, although he anticipated protests.

Finally everything was ready, and on 2 January 1990 Teresina and I flew to Tel Aviv. In the crowded plane there was a confusion of tongues in which modern Hebrew predominated. We listened fascinated, unable to understand, but secure in the knowledge that we could always make ourselves understood in English or some other language. Traveling at the invitation of the university, I did not feel like a tourist, but rather privileged. Reading through the Israeli landing card for German visitors as the plane approached Tel Aviv, I came upon the following question: "Were you a member of a party in the period from 1933 to 1945?" Which I interpreted as: "If German, were you a Nazi or not?" A perfectly justified question, I felt, as guilt and shame flashed through my head. When the pilot announced that we would soon be landing at Ben Gurion Airport, I became uneasy. Despite all the trust so prevalent in my correspondence with Shai and Herzl, I was still a descendant of the anti-Semitic Wagner family from Bayreuth. What people would I meet?

How would they react to my grandmother's, my father's, and my uncle's Nazism? Would they regard me too as a Nazi Wagner?

Herzl and Shai greeted us with a friendly "Shalom" and from the outset, showed us nothing but solidarity and readiness for dialogue, which took away a lot of my fear of behaving wrongly. They talked about the itinerary—"our coming Wagner events"—which Shai and his colleagues had planned down to the smallest detail for every day of our stay.

We agreed that in my talks I would not touch immediately on critical subjects such as Wagner's anti-Semitism, Hitler, Bayreuth, and the Holocaust, since Herzl and Shai knew the audience would address these topics without our help. I was to understand my talks more as a starting point for subsequent discussion. Added to this was the fact that my appearance in Tel Aviv and Jerusalem was taking place only two months after the fall of the Berlin Wall.

In a good-natured rush Shai and Herzl took us to the Grand Beach Hotel in Tel Aviv, where immediately after my arrival I gave an interview to Hanoch Ron from the main evening newspaper, *Yediot Acharonot*. Ron was well prepared for the discussion. He set the tone and the content, which were then, with variations, followed by other interviews and audience discussions until I flew back on 14 January. For him, his colleagues, and the audiences, my opinions on *The Jews in Music*, on Hitler and my family, on my upbringing in Bayreuth as a Wagner after the Holocaust, and on whether Wagner should or should not be performed in Israel were important. While I was answering Ron I became aware of the responsibility that, from now on, I had publicly to bear in this country. I was no longer prepared to show any consideration for the opinions of my father, who had viewed my trip to Israel with grave misgivings: I had told him about my intended lectures, suspecting that they would have repercussions both for our relationship and for me personally.

The interview with Hanoch Ron opened the floodgates. The journalists were mostly understanding, sympathetic even, about my desire for dialogue, which helped me answer difficult questions in a more relaxed and balanced way.

But I still found it difficult to answer the question of whether Wagner's works should be performed in Israel: I had no right to interfere in Israeli domestic policy, but people were not convinced by this, so I suggested that there should be a democratic vote on it in the music institutions. I also expressed an understanding of the victims of the Nazi terror who no longer wanted to hear Wagner, Hitler's favorite composer and I criticized the undemocratic action of the conductor Zubin Mehta, who in 1981 had attempted to perform Wagner as an encore after a concert, against the wishes of the majority of the audience. The public stopped his performance with shouts and booing after only a few bars of music.

During all the discussions in Israel my exhaustive work on Weill was viewed sympathetically, as it had been in New York. The significance of such an explosive mixture—Weill and Wagner—was grasped; it even amused people. Weill's dismantling of the Bayreuth Wagner cult had much in common with my attempts to knock my great-grandfather off his pedestal.

The fact that I grew less afraid to face the Israeli media was due most of all to Teresina, who supported me with devotion and believed fully in the purpose behind my trip to Israel. Her solidarity seemed to carry over to the other members of the audience and even to the interviewers. People often addressed Teresina in Hebrew because it was assumed that she was Jewish. She then said, smiling: "I am only an Italian from a Catholic family." When I told this to Herzl later, he said: "Your story is so extreme, people assume you could only be married to a Jewess." Just as important as Teresina's help was that of the few friends and acquaintances who gave me their open support both during and after this decisive time.

The intensity of my discussions in the first afternoon and evening increased over the following days; my actual series of lectures didn't begin until 7 January. The idea that we could quietly tour Israel beforehand proved wishful thinking: even during our two-day visit to a kibbutz, Caesarea, Masada, and Arab villages with Herzl and Shai, we talked constantly about my lecture subjects. As Herzl, an expert on this topic, convinced me, in Israel

Richard Wagner was inseparably linked to Hitler and Nazi Germany. But emotion would not prevent him implementing seminars and lectures at the University of Tel Aviv on this "aberration" in music history.

During these discussions I began to realize how much I had changed. In order to rescue that anti-Semite Richard Wagner, I had tried to ascribe the blame only to his children and grandchildren. Now I understood that this repression of reality would not hold water. Meanwhile, I have learned that I was in a similarly contradictory situation to my Jewish friends who are Wagnerians. But today I also know it is not possible to split Wagner into the genius composer on the one hand and the leading ideologist on the other, as his weltanschauung belongs inextricably to his work and his life.

A discussion of my experiences and responsibility developed imperceptibly: in Israel I realized I could no longer just articulate my political and moral position indirectly, by grappling with Jewish-German culture. My time in the ivory tower of liberal-left thought was over. I demanded greater personal credibility through deeds. In Israel there were limitless opportunities for undertaking this seriously, as time and again we came to talk about individual fates, about people who had been driven out of Germany by persecution and suffering to Israel and elsewhere.

While my hosts, their friends, and my lecture audiences described their life stories, I became more open to the truth of the Nazi atrocities than I had ever been before. Out of the dark, vague yet frightening, gigantic shadows of six million victims, individual stories emerged. The desire grew in me to take up a clearer position on our shared history and on our joint responsibility for the present and the future. I now started to see Israel as a central motif in the mosaic of my life. I remembered again my time in New York in the Kurt Weill Foundation; the connections between German history, the chronicle of my family, and my contrary lifestyle finally became clear to me. I wanted to translate the trust and understanding that so constructively had been offered to me by canvassing for German-Jewish dialogue among my own countrymen too. My fears, insecurity, and anxiety dissolved as my insight increased.

One of my first important public appearances took me to Jerusalem, where I had been asked by Israeli radio for an interview. The producer Danny Or'Stav gave me a warm welcome and told me he would first introduce me to the listeners in Hebrew. His introduction centered, as Shai told me later, on my life and the lectures. He commented with obvious sympathy on my book on Weill too and the time I had been working at the Kurt Weill Foundation in New York. But the only thing I understood of the introduction was the repetition of my grandfather's first name, Siegfried, which Danny had obviously confused with mine. When he asked me how I liked it in Israel, I answered: "I like it here very much, but my name is not Siegfried, it's Gottfried! I am the great-grandson, not the son, of Richard Wagner!" I did not want to be identified right at the outset either with my grandfather Siegfried or with the blond beast and mad heroic figure from *The Ring.* My reaction caused general amusement and was possibly the reason my first radio interview in Israel went so well.

I was very pleased to hear later that only two months after this interview, Wagner's music was played again on Israeli radio. Though I oppose the performance of Wagner's anti-Semitic works, such as *The Ring, Die Meistersinger,* and *Parsifal,* I believe that playing some of his other works will encourage critical discussions about his music and its consequences. Unfortunately, the radio aired "The Ride of the Valkyries," which I rank among the most sinister and questionable of compositions. And yet our mission proved effective: Wagner was no longer just a taboo subject, laden with emotion. Now a differentiated politico-cultural discussion developed. This was probably the best thing that one could achieve for Wagner's music in Israel.

Four days later I was interviewed in Jerusalem by Ram Evron for Israeli television. Before the taping, he told me that he was in favor of Wagner's works being performed in Israel. I disagreed, which amused him and prompted him during the interview to ask more about my rebellion against my family. Via Weill and Grandmother Winifred we came finally to the question of how to deal with Wagner's essay *The Jews in Music*. I categorically condemned the work and advocated a more discriminating historical approach.

The effect of the television interview was almost immediately noticeable: the next day in Tel Aviv, total strangers came up and spoke to me. When I reacted to this with surprise in an optician's shop, the optician said in perfect German: "Herr Wagner, don't you know how small our country is? We show our guests Israel in the morning, and in the afternoon we wonder what on earth we can do with them. So don't be surprised that we saw you on television yesterday. Your coming here is important not just for the 'Jeckes,' the German Jews. Keep up the good work!"

My first lecture also took an unusual course. My introduction to my video on *The Ring* had been planned to take place at noon at the university. However, a university employee informed me discreetly that there had been protest telephone calls from fanatics opposed to my visit, so they were considering giving me a bulletproof jacket or protecting me behind bulletproof glass. I refused. Teresina asked me to do something for my safety. "I am not Eichmann. I have confidence in my hosts," I reasoned. It didn't make Teresina any calmer, but she accepted my decision.

Instead of an audience of eighty, as planned, four hundred turned up, and we had to move to a larger hall. Furthermore, security measures were increased: the audience was searched, and two young Israeli soldiers were posted with guns in the larger but still crowded hall. Despite the demand, though, the first row remained unoccupied: fear of contact with a Wagner descendant. I remembered a book with the title *Who's Afraid of Richard Wagner?* that I had been given shortly before the talk began. Without really thinking about it, I said: "There are still some empty seats down here. Who's afraid of Gottfried Wagner?" Liberating laughter broke out, in which I joined. Laughter continued during the video, even at those parts that at previous talks across four continents, I alone had found amusing. Shai's introduction in Hebrew had seen to that. He presented my interpretation of Wagner's tetralogy faithfully: as a story of the criminals Wotan and Alberich in a struggle for power.

My lecture on Weill and Brecht the following day went quite differently. The fact that someone with my family background had the chutzpah to talk at the biggest university in Israel on Weill's contemporary musical theater as a countermodel to Wagner's *Gesamtkunstwerk* filled the hall. The well-known Israeli singer Adi Etzion, accompanied by her husband, Jonathan, at the piano, sang Weill songs at the end of the evening—very reminiscent of Berlin in the 1920s.

An elderly lady from Berlin, who introduced herself only by her first name, Isolde, asked me: "Herr Wagner, why don't you give your talks in our beautiful German language?" Rather confused, I answered: "Because the majority here in Israel speak English." Isolde soon came up to me again and said: "You can imagine why I'm called Isolde. Yes, my family loved Wagner's music, and I love Wagner too. I still remember the wonderful productions in the Kroll Opera under Otto Klemperer, and Bruno Walter's *Walküre*." Isolde turned out to be an accomplished Wagnerian, such as I have only seldom encountered. She beamed at me like a kindly grandmother and said finally: "You can't imagine what your visit means to us Berlin Jews." We hugged one another in silence and unsuccessfully fought back tears.

A crucial test for me was the last lecture, with the subjective title "The Wagner I'm Talking About." Following Herzl's advice, I tried to explain Wagner's significance in European music theater and music history. I preceded this with an attempt to come to terms with my own past in Bayreuth. I had started to understand the course my life had taken, but still separated Wagner's ideology and life from his stage works. I am still surprised today by the generosity and goodwill of my audiences. Anyone casting a critical eye over what I said at that time, reading nervously from my notes, could quite rightly have accused me of not having considered Wagner's anti-Semitism carefully enough. In particular, my statements on "the purely human, the myth" and "redemption and pity" I regard today as the result of my own repression, as an unsuccessful attempt to relativize Wagner's anti-Semitism in order to make my own family's past more bearable for myself. What I said at that time on Wagner no longer has anything to do with my present state of mind. It was probably also my last, unsuccessful attempt at self-repudiation, in an attempt to comprehend my father's position.

At the end of my lecture I quoted from Richard Wagner's floridly dishonest letter in diary form of 1 October 1858 to his friend Mathilde Wesendonck. In the letter, based on an imperfect understanding of Arthur Schopenhauer's philosophy, he presents himself as the saint of universal pity, writing, among other things:

> After all, we know what exists around us only inasmuch as we picture it in our imagination, and as I imagine it, so it is for me. If I ennoble it, it is because I myself am noble, if I feel the other man's suffering to be deep, it is because I myself feel deeply when I imagine his suffering, and whoever, by contrast, imagines it to be insignificant reveals in doing so that he is himself insignificant. Thus my fellow-suffering makes the other person's suffering a reality, and the more insignificant the being with which I can suffer, the wider and more embracing is the circle which suggests itself to my feelings.
>
> But here lies an aspect of my nature which others may see as a weakness. I admit that unilateral actions are much impeded by it; but I am certain that when I do act, I act in accordance with my essential nature, and certainly never cause pain to anyone intentionally. This consideration alone can influence me in all my actions: to cause others as little suffering as possible. On this point I am totally at one with myself, for only in this way can I hope to give others joy, as well: for the only true, genuine joy, is to be found in the conformity of fellow-suffering.[33]

Wagner has here repressed his own, pitiless anti-Semitism, which was later to culminate in the demand for a Jew-free Germany.

I declared then:

> Here [i.e., in Wagner's egocentric definition of pity] lies too the key to the final artistic message, which we find in the clos-

ing bars of *Parsifal*. This statement represents for me the distinct possibility to interpret Wagner's work responsibly, which of necessity contradicts his existence as an artist in a "human, all too human" theater world. Mixing up biography and work means, in Wagner's case, to manipulate the interpretation of his stage works, as well as falsifying his personality. This happened in the past when his work was abused for ideological-political reasons and Wagner's artistic aims were disregarded. I regard it as my duty, as a music journalist, opera director, and also as Wagner's great-grandson, to refute this. By upholding this point of view, I shall always fall between two stools in Bayreuth. So let us always approach Wagner as the man he was: as a genius of opera in the nineteenth century, without whom the cultural history of Europe is unthinkable.

On reading my text of January 1990 today, I can only shake my head at such repression and inability to judge the Wagnerian legacy as a whole. I was still rooted in the family tradition. I had to liberate myself from it, that much I already knew, and it became clearer to me in Israel during discussions. At the time it was more a matter of demonstrating through my talks that I was interested in an ongoing dialogue: that I wanted to escape my isolation and learn. Most of the audiences understood this hidden message and accepted me without mistrust, in spite of the lack of clarity in my remarks. With the trip to Israel, I began once again to try to come to terms with Wagner's anti-Semitism. I had to gauge his effect on the Bayreuth Festival as well, and acknowledge that I could no longer uphold my position.

During this painful reexamination of my own knowledge and conscience I distanced myself from essential landmarks in my youth and my student years. I felt removed from the interpretations of Ernst Bloch, Hans Mayer, and Claude Lévi-Strauss—in other words, those prominent Jewish authors who had been misused in the New Bayreuth, in order to repress and distort the past and responsibility.

But back to Israel and January 1990. More important than the lectures were the countless discussions with members of the audience, which through lack of time I unfortunately could not tape. But important episodes remain in my memory, like the meeting with Alfred and Ester Frankenstein in their beautiful house in Ramat-Gan. I also owe to them the initial contact with Herzl Shmueli. Not even my pointing out my great-grandfather's anti-Semitism could reduce Frankenstein's passionate veneration for Wagner, which takes him back again and again to Bayreuth for the festival. And yet, surrounded by the classics of German literature, with coffee and cake and music and discussions on German culture, I felt so at home at the Frankensteins'. It was a shame that this discussion took place in Ramat-Gan and not in Berlin. Germany suffered a great loss when it drove out or murdered people like Alfred Frankenstein.

How differently the meetings went with the Wagnerian Harry Riss from the United States, who only told me years later that there had been Nazi victims in his family. He had immigrated to Israel in the mid-fifties as a Zionist. He believed he had discovered in me, as Wagner's great-grandson, several things that had nothing to do with me and little with the "genius Richard." Today Harry accepts my rebellion against the Wagnerian legacy in Bayreuth.

Far more discriminating and complex were my discussions with the musicologist Peter Gradenwitz. My mother had given me a copy of his book *Musical History of Israel*, written at a time when he shared my criticism of Wagner and was very interested in the tensions within my family—a subject I was willing to comment on only up to a certain point.

On our only free evening in Israel we were invited to a concert given by the famous Israel Philharmonic Orchestra, founded in 1936 by the violinist Bronislaw Huberman. The program included works by Grieg, Boccherini, Danzi, and Mozart; Mika Eichenholz conducted. But the evening was by no means relaxing: shortly before we went into the big concert hall, there was a bomb scare, and we all had to evacuate into a side street.

After the all clear, we went to the box office to pick up our tickets. We were warmly received there by the head of the PR department and taken to our places. The young lady then went onto the stage, where some of the musicians were already tuning up, spoke to the first cellist, and pointed at us. He stood up and beckoned to us. Rather shyly we went up to him. He gave us his hand from the stage and said in English: "I'm all in favor of performing Wagner in Israel. We are very glad you are here. Thank you." I answered. "But under the right conditions and with broad agreement." He agreed, smiling, and invited me to come backstage after the concert to meet Mika Eichenholz and cellist Lynn Harrell, the soloist that evening.

Even more touching was an invitation from the Tel Aviv Central Music Library, which also contains the Bronislaw Huberman archive. Nehama Lifschitz, director of the library at the time, and her colleagues showed me with justifiable pride the treasures of the book collection, among them a picture of Arturo Toscanini and Huberman on the beach at Haifa in 1938, only half a year before Kristallnacht. What was then called the Palestine Orchestra played Wagner's music until that night of pogroms, works such as the preludes to the first and third acts of *Lohengrin*. I spoke about Toscanini's collaboration with my grandfather Siegfried on the new production of *Tannhäuser* in Bayreuth in 1930, and about Toscanini's resignation: after the Nazis seized power in January 1933, he refused to perform in Germany anymore, although Hitler had personally asked him to conduct again in Bayreuth. With great cordiality Nehama gave me a copy of the book *An Orchestra Is Born*, a unique collection of documents on Jewish musical and cultural history in what was then Palestine and is now Israel. The book, with its friendly inscription, is one of the most beautiful mementos of my first, short trip to Israel.

In spite of the hectic rush of events, we did not want to miss out on a visit to the Diaspora Museum in Tel Aviv. Teresina and I had the privilege of being shown around by Judith Etzion and the composer and music journalist Benjamin Bar-Am. The clarity of the display of Jewish culture and history through texts, photos, and films impressed us, as also did Judith Etzion's explanations. The connection between Jewish and German history, and my own family's part in that history, was brought vividly to mind there. The Diaspora Museum has an extraordinarily detailed and extensive data bank available to any visitor to the museum. I typed in the keyword "Wagner" and received four printed sheets of interesting information. I learned, for example, that there were also Jewish families with the name Wagner, who were first recorded in the seventeenth century in Leipzig and Frankfurt am Main, among other places.

I also learned that there had been a Jewish community in Bayreuth since the beginning of the thirteenth century. In 1933, 261 Jews were resident there, which meant .7 percent of the population of Bayreuth. On 10 November 1938—Kristallnacht—the beautiful synagogue, built in 1760, was destroyed, and the homes and shops of Jewish citizens were plundered and devastated by the SA. The following day the population of Bayreuth attacked their Jewish compatriots and desecrated and destroyed the Jewish cemetery. On 27 November 1941 fifty Jews were deported to Riga, and on 12 January 1942 the last eleven Jewish citizens of Bayreuth were taken to Theresienstadt.

Angrily, I thought again of how I had been deceived as a child by my family and most teachers. Where were the good burghers of Bayreuth and my family on 10 and 11 November 1938? We left the Diaspora Museum in silence.

Our encounter with Holocaust survivor Moshe Hoch, the head of the Institute for the Preservation and Study of Jewish Museum of the Holocaust, in Yad Letslilei, was also distressing. His description of his persecution as a child by the Nazis rekindled images of the National Socialist past in all its cruelty. The old question nagged at me of how it was possible for such a highly developed nation to turn into criminals.

The attitude of the German media during and after my stay in Israel was peculiar. Most of them knew very little about Wagner's anti-Semitism, as was evident in their reporting. Their main concern was sensational headlines, presenting me as Siegfried in the fight against Fafner. This didn't help me in my efforts to achieve a more discriminating image of Wagner in Germany and Israel, or to come to terms with the family history. The German reports from Israel only served to increase my isolation.

As I look back, there is little left for me to report of the Germans I met in Israel. Hans-Heinrich von Stackelberg, the West German cultural attaché, was—not just in my opinion—the wrong man in the wrong place. Despite the success of my lectures he could not be persuaded to change his mind about me.

The Israeli media made much more effort to understand me and my concerns. The journalist Hanna Yaddor, for example, summed up my visit in the evening newspaper *Ma'ariv*, under the headline "Thank You for Your Courage," on 16 January 1990: "The talk of the music world in Israel in the last ten days has been the visit by Dr. Gottfried Wagner, the great-grandson of the German composer Richard Wagner. . . . He did not meet with any hostility, but with affection and friendship. . . . People recognized him from the media in the street and gave him gifts. In a letter someone wrote to him: 'Thank you for your courage.' . . . He hopes very much to come back to Israel for a longer period. Here he has already gone through his baptism of fire. Now all that remains for him perhaps is to counter a few hateful remarks from members of his family."

Hanna Yaddor's prediction was to prove correct.

22

Father's Last Letter

After my return from Israel in mid-January 1990 I found it difficult to concentrate. I kept thinking of the possible consequences of my trip and knew that Bayreuth would react after the first wave of reports in the German and international newspapers.

At the end of January the president of the Richard Wagner Society, Josef Lienhart, called me up from Freiburg wanting to know more about my trip. I described the positive results and experiences, the great interest of the Israeli media and audiences. Finally, I declared confidently, a new stage had begun in the discussion about Wagner in Israel. I noted down the themes of our conversation and sent a summary by fax to my father:

Dear Papa,

This evening Herr Lienhart rang me and informed me of the following, to his regret and stressing his appreciation of my work and his kind regard for me: that you had, on the basis of a one-sided selection from various West German newspaper articles on my Israel trip and on the basis of your right as head of the festival, demanded that either all existing invitations from Richard Wagner Societies to me are withdrawn and ruled out for the future, or you would publicly distance yourself from those societies. He also says your boycott of the Richard

Wagner Societies, if they should choose not to observe your
demand, would take effect from the next plenary assembly of
the Richard Wagner Societies [on 30 January 1990].
Furthermore, you have been sending Herr Lienhart the said
articles highlighted in yellow and with your comments against
me since mid-January by express registered post. I cannot
believe that you would have given such instructions. I ask you,
as my father, to act in this instance, especially as your
instructions affect firm offers from Richard Wagner Societies
now and in the future. I request that you respond before the
end of the week by fax, in view of the very slow postal service.
Awaiting your reply, I remain with kind regards,

> *Your son*
> *Gottfried*

The official reply came two days later. Father wrote to the effect
that he had informed the Richard Wagner Society and its local sections that he would not take part in any of their events if it remained possible for me to give talks under the auspices of the
society, as his participation could be construed as sanctioning my
views on the development and the artistic standard of the Bayreuth
Festival, which he found unacceptable. He referred here to an article in *Die Welt* of 11 January 1990, in which I had stated that since
Wieland's death the Bayreuth Festival had become a cross between
a stock exchange and a scrap-metal market. Furthermore, I had
emphasized that politics and commerce predominated, to the detri-
ment of music, drama, and poetry. Of course, Father did not want
his threat to boycott Richard Wagner Society events to be understood as an "instruction," for which, in fact, he had no legitimate
right, but rather as an expression of his own personal "preference."
None of this, Father maintained, had anything at all to do with my
lecture tour in Israel.

What I had said on the possible consequences of the Foundation
charter on the further participation of the Wagner family in the
administration of the festival (quoted in the *Süddeutsche Zeitung*
on 17 January 1990) Father dismissed with the remark that I ob-

viously lacked thorough knowledge of the sense and content of this charter. He also said that if I really did have such critical thoughts about my grandmother, as I had asserted in various statements, I should have declined my share of her financial legacy as "dirty money" back in 1981.

At the end of his letter, referring to his overall responsibility for the Bayreuth Festival, he drew a hard and fast line of separation between father and son.

To avoid later accusations that I was simply trying to provoke my father out of petulance, I attempted to explain my position to him after receiving this letter, but to no avail. I sent copies to friends and others who I assumed were interested in resolving what was now a public conflict. Even looking at it today, the letter spells out to me that he was never interested in a genuine exposition of his own past and responsibility as father and as head of the festival. The newspaper quotations he mentioned, which by no means always corresponded to my statements, were taken out of context, incomplete, and based on an arbitrary selection of articles. An objective assessment of international press reports produces quite a different picture. But neither on the Festspielhügel nor among the majority of the German media is there any desire to acknowledge this.

One need only look at the press coverage of my trip to Israel—in Israel, the United States, and Germany—to see how positively it was generally viewed. The *Neue Zürcher Zeitung*, for example, featured an objective report of the trip on 8 February 1990, titled "Richard Wagner in Israel: Signs of a Rapprochement":

Potential access to Wagner and his work will certainly continue to improve for future generations, and consequently opportunities will increase for the performance of Wagner's works again in Israel. That real steps have already been taken in this direction is illustrated by the invitation at the beginning of this year to Richard Wagner's great-grandson Gottfried Wagner (son of the grandson Wolfgang) by the University of Tel Aviv. In four lectures, this Wagner descendant was able, as doctor of musicology and director, to talk about his personal approach to his ancestor's works and about his conflicts with those works. Gottfried Wagner was born in Bayreuth shortly after the war (1947). He was confronted early on with the problems surrounding the political and cultural position of his family. Of course, it was neither his nor his hosts' brief to resolve here and now questions about Wagner or the performance or nonperformance of his music in Israel. On the part of the university it was the musical interest, keeping discussion alive on this important composer, which was clearly in the foreground, and on Gottfried Wagner's part there was a serious attempt at rapprochement, as he expressed it in radio and television interviews. Without these premises the encounter could scarcely have taken place in such a generally positive atmosphere. It should be noted in particular that this encounter with Wagner's great-grandson took place in a much broader framework than the university milieu had originally planned; interviews on Israeli radio and television, reports by the national and international press, confirm the necessity and the significance of such steps. In Israel too in those days the word "glasnost" was used when referring to the reception given to Wagner.

At the same time I received an official statement from Shai Burstyn in his capacity as head of the music department of the University of Tel Aviv. He wrote: "I should like to thank you for your efforts in ensuring your visit to Tel Aviv University was so successful. The capacity crowds which your lectures drew, as well as the interest shown by the press, are clear indications that the topics of your lectures are of great interest to the Israeli academic public and, indeed, to a large part of the Israeli population. . . . [The lecture series] was a project well prepared and well delivered. I wish you success in the future development of the ideas you conveyed in your lectures here."

Comparing the international reactions and those of my father and his friends, I realized it was pointless to expect constructive discussion. I had to continue the course I had begun in Israel in spite of all resistance. Amid all the personal, cultural, political, and ethical differences, I still longed that he would be prepared one day to meet me just as a father.

But as he showed no inclination to listen to my opinion, and his instruction to the Wagner Societies led to the cancellation of previously agreed contracts, I felt I had no option but to respond. In mid-February 1990, with the aid of my lawyer and constant friend Inge Lehmbruck, I wrote:

> *Dear Papa*
> *. . . So I must acknowledge that, using the most severe pressure, namely the threat to boycott any events of the Richard Wagner Society, you have prevailed on the president, Herr Lienhart, to cancel any events in which I am involved— three lectures in Freiburg, Baden-Baden, and Karlsruhe. In other words, you have thought it right not to discuss with me personally what I have actually said and why, but instead to take a course of action via third parties which has had repercussions on my material existence. I must emphatically deny your remark that I accepted "dirty money" (not my expression) as inheritance from my grandmother. What I received from the inheritance at the beginning of the 1980s was approximately 85 percent (exactly DM 83,509.27 before tax) my grandfather Siegfried Wagner's legacy, and the remaining 15 percent (DM 12,500.00 before tax)—the figures can easily be verified by the executor, Thorwart—from Grandmother's legacy, which I have always regarded as merely a part of the Wagnerian property coming from Great-Grandfather Richard.*
> *Gottfried.*

As this registered letter was returned to me unopened, Inge Lehmbruck wrote to my father: "I have to draw your attention in due form to the fact that my client, who is economically largely dependent on his lecturing activities in order to earn a livelihood, would not hesitate to defend himself with all legal means, including court action, if attacks on your part on his professional career should be repeated."

My father's secretary acknowledged receipt of this letter without comment.

Breaking off his relationship with his own son did not stop my father from using his influence to make life in the music world difficult for me. Via his countless contacts and connections—always acting via third parties—he brought about precisely what Inge Lehmbruck had warned him of. In his 1994 autobiography, *Acts*, he offered a coherent formulation and justification of his position— and inadvertently helped my own position, as people became interested in my version of events. In the blurb of the German edition my father writes:

> In the vast amount of literature on every conceivable subject relating to Wagner and Bayreuth, there persist, in particular where the twentieth century is concerned, so many clichés, tenacious prejudices, half-truths, and quite infamous lies. There are as many blatantly uncritical voices in favor as there are unobjective voices against. Rage, violent emotions of love and hatred explode, all on a relentless scale, so that often enough an adequately sober view is obscured or at least clouded. It seems to me it is high time finally to bury the legends and end the empty talk. My autobiography is intended in the widest sense to offer testimony of greatness experienced and pain suffered, of course from my quite subjective viewpoint, but at the same time substantiated by documentary evidence and accurate records, which have until now largely remained unpublished. The unusual, outrageous, not to say sensational is no figment of my imagination, but lies in the established facts themselves.

I read this text several times, as I didn't understand it. Father emphasizes that he is writing from his "quite subjective viewpoint"—in other words, he is not aiming at an objective autobiography—its credibility reinforced by "documentary evidence." But the choice of documents and their sources, which are arbitrary and vague, remain open to criticism. His "subjective viewpoint" apparently includes a selection of "documentary evidence and accurate records . . . largely unpublished" until today. Ultimately, *Acts* does not succeed even as a subjective account. Rather it could be called an arbitrary interpretation of father's own life.

I grasped this on a first reading. On a second reading I placed the blurb like a pattern over the sections which for me were crucial, in the professional and personal areas, where our differences of opinion were concerned: his interpretations of the anti-Semitism of Richard Wagner and the Wagner family; his interpretation of Hitler and the Holocaust and the consequences of these on our relationship today. I wanted to know why he represses his own past and the past of his own family—as head of the Bayreuth Festival, as a Wagner, and as my father.

Acts demonstrated to me how he had succumbed to the contemporary mood in repressing his own past by dealing far too arbitrarily with his grandfather's romantic philosophizing. It became clear to me, too, how in judging Father's romantically written autobiography, I orientated myself toward rationalism and knowledge of the Enlightenment. I share the opinion of the philosopher Karl Popper, who in his 1967 essay "On the Subject of Freedom" writes in his understanding of rationalism and the Enlightenment against the philosophizing of the Romantics:

> As one of the last stragglers of rationalism and Enlightenment, I believe in the self-liberation of man by knowledge. . . . For in my backwardness I can see in the philosophy of the Romantics and in particular in the philosophy of the three great leaders of German idealism, Fichte, Schelling, and Hegel, nothing but an intellectual and moral catastrophe—the greatest intellectual and moral catastrophe that has ever befallen the German and European intelligentsia. This catastrophe, this intellectual and moral chain reaction, had, I believe, a disastrous and stultifying effect, which like an atomic cloud is still expanding. It provoked what Konrad Heiden in his book

on Hitler years ago called "the age of intellectual and moral dishonesty." . . . What I mean when I talk about reason or rationalism is nothing more than the conviction that we can learn by criticism of our faults and mistakes and in particular by the criticism of others and ultimately by self-criticism.[35]

Father doesn't acknowledge the idea that only critical discussion allows us to see our own ideas from different angles and judge them objectively. He will not recognize that, as Popper describes it, "the sensible, the critical approach can only be the result of the criticism of others and one can only achieve self-criticism through the criticism of others." Instead, Father wants to impress, forgetting that in art Richard Wagner is not the only "guiding light of mankind."

His language is vague and complicated. In his attempt to legitimize his own power he inadvertently refers to the third, secret instructor, to the Mephisto of the Nazi opera world, Heinz Tietjen. In the Führer's Bayreuth and Berlin he learned as Tietjen's assistant to recognize every means for holding on to power—a skill that was then, in reconstructing the economic miracle that is New Bayreuth, to smooth his path to becoming intendant of the festival for life. For the great organizer there was no zero hour.

There is a pattern of repression of his past throughout his book. He trampled on the dignity of those who could not protect themselves and who refused to be wholly subjected to his will. One need only read the pages on which he passes judgment on his brother, Wieland; my mother (who, when all is said and done, was a supportive wife for thirty-three years); his sister Friedelind; his sister-in-law, Gertrud; and the "unqualified" fourth generation. Here he applies the phrase "Do unto others as you would have them do unto you" only to himself, when he talks of "pain suffered" and presents himself as a victim. One moment he dons the martyr's mask, another the victor's. Like a conjuror, he makes the mass murderer Hitler vanish into the mythological fog. Thus "Uncle Wolf" remains the "kindly human being" that Winifred believed him to be—Winifred, with whom Father steamrollered the Foundation charter.

He says nothing about the historical connection between his

grandfather's anti-Semitism and Hitler, despite the copious material explicitly documenting the private relationship between the Wagner family and the Führer. So where is this important segment of the "accurate records"? Nor has my father included in his book correspondence with Wieland. That would have been important for an understanding of what the New Bayreuth was.

Central scenes are missing in *Acts*, although all those concerned know about them. In this way my father has thrown away a great and unique opportunity of being credible to himself and to the world. Does he care nothing for the solidarity of the honest, valuing instead the applause of those who simply follow fashion?

I stick to Democritus' aphorism: "I prefer an austere life in a democracy to wealth under a tyrant." This knowledge also gives me the freedom to leave a door open to him. Why should we not be able to "learn by criticism of our faults and mistakes and in particular by the criticism of others and ultimately by self-criticism"? In this way my father could discover himself.

23

The Ban from Bayreuth

My father's personal and professional attacks on me had negative and positive consequences. One positive result has been my focusing no longer just on Wagner and Jews but on the history of Christianity and Judaism. The cultural and spiritual enrichment this has entailed has had a significant effect on my personal and professional development.

On the negative side, opportunities for me in Germany dwindled. Word of our rift spread quickly—and precisely in those places where I had previously had prospects. Everyone in the music world who wanted to offer me work now knew that doing so would attract my father's enmity. Why spoil things with the Festspielhügel? Still, in many circles, my father's attitude toward me was considered excessive and indefensible.

Set against the peculiar relationship Germans have with Richard Wagner, however, my position turned out to be complicated. Wagner is for them pregnant with meaning, his works heavyweight and earnest. Irony and self-irony have never been a forte of the Germans. For them Wagner is either a sacred national relic or a Nazi monster. He is always taken seriously, and he arouses more emotion than any other composer on earth. The reason for this lies in those conflicts contained within the works, life and jumbled weltanschauung of Wagner himself, who misused music as a vehicle of propaganda; he plays with the German soul, which is continually taken in by idealistic concepts of world improvement. As long as fundamental discussion on Wagner's attitude to the Jews is avoided in Germany, every aspect of the zeitgeist can be accommodated in him. But anyone who, as a post-Holocaust German, finds this wild mixture of theatrical "redemption," racism, antifeminism and Teutomania in Germany not only outdated as a cultural model, but also dangerous, will meet with violent resistance—not only among the Bayreuth Wagner cult community.

Where arguments about Wagner are concerned, Germans very quickly lose their sense of humor. With Wagner the German soul becomes exalted. Woe betide anyone who questions Wagner—especially if he comes from Wagner's family and thus commits the most infamous form of fouling one's nest.

My father and Josef Lienhart succeeded in curtailing any discussion of my trip to Israel at the Federal Congress of the Richard Wagner Society in Mannheim at the end of May 1990, although some local sections wanted to talk about it. But the majority of those present followed Father's and Lienhart's line and, in fear of losing their ticket quota for the festival, moved quickly on to the next item on the agenda.

Typical of this attitude was a letter from the chairwoman of the Saarbrücken Wagner Society, Otti Maurer, once a close friend of my grandmother's. On 6 June 1991 Frau Maurer informed me, presumably with approval from Bayreuth, that on the basis of the—for her—shocking newspaper reports over the last year, she had proposed to the working session of the Richard Wagner Society in Hanover that the main assembly discuss whether it was still appropriate, after my "derogatory remarks" on the Bayreuth Festival, my father, and my grandmother (whom she had loved very much) to invite me to speak before the Richard Wagner Society. One must ask oneself, she wrote, whether it was worth jeopardizing the friendship of the head of the festival and of his sister Frau Verena Lafferentz for the sake of one young man, even if he was a member of the Wagner family. Frau Maurer did not participate in the session, however. Her final sentence echoes Father's "dirty money" accusation, reproaching me (in the form of a question) for having profited from the inheritance that Winifred Wagner had held together.

In all fairness, the attitudes of most chairpersons of the German Richard Wagner Societies were mixed. They regarded my critique of Richard Wagner in Israel and its consequences with some understanding. But if it was a matter of the opinions expressed to me in private being voiced in their own local society or even to President Lienhart, they lacked the courage of their convictions.

A commendable exception and example of steadfastness came from the Munich Wagner Society. Its then president, Jürgen Dreher, wrote to me that the very announcement in the annual program had led to renewed threats from Gudrun and Wolfgang Wagner, which would certainly have thrown the federal chairman and the local chairwoman in Hanover into a state of some panic. In spite of this, they were looking forward to my "rapprochement with Richard Wagner" and were not going to let themselves be pressured by the head of the festival, and had resolved to stand up to him.

In spite of the topic of my discussions, the name Wagner caused people to be hostile toward me. After that lecture in Munich in January 1991 a man was waiting for me outside in the street dressed in leather trousers, green loden coat, and Bavarian hat, with an enormous Alsatian dog—a man who had put in an appearance once many years ago. When I got into my car he shouted at me, pointing to his dog: "My Wolfi will get you yet, you Wagner swine!"

One of the audience members in Munich later wrote me a letter revealing to me the dilemma in which one group of Wagnerians found themselves. The Jewish Wagnerian Heinrich Frank advised me, with reference to the fourth commandment, to stop criticizing members of my family, especially Winifred Wagner and Chamberlain. People knew of my views on the matter, and no one would assume that I had moved away from my criticism of the woman who had run the festival from 1933 to 1944, were I to avoid the subject in future. My answer to Frank included the following:

My statements, always based on public documents and facts, correspond to my understanding of tradition . . . and my con-

science and knowledge as a Wagner after Auschwitz, who will
never be prepared to remain silent for reasons of professional
expediency out of blind obedience to a questionable family
tradition. . . . I have known since my childhood that in so
doing I find myself outside the norms of the "morals and tolerance" of a "certain German establishment," which represses
its own past in self-alienation. . . .

You speak of the fourth commandment in connection with
my grandmother. . . . Anyone who claims to have been hon-
ored as father and mother must have acted convincingly
through a correspondingly responsible former life and firm
actions as a private and public person in the interests of the
future of the children. . . . Why do you think I get no answer
from Bayreuth to my letters and have been declared persona
non grata there? . . . The reconciliation with a certain establishment cannot and may not rest on repression, as occurred
in the case of the exhibition "Wagner and the Jews" in 1984 in
Villa Wahnfried. . . . You could play a part in mediating my
mission to a different, open German establishment, which,
thank God, exists.

Unfortunately, my position and Heinrich Frank's remained ir-
reconcilable. As a German Jew, he wanted to suppress discussion
about Wagner's anti-Semitism because it would involve for him a
large degree of self-criticism and discussion about how Jews could
admire the music of a man who hated them. When Frank implored
me to stop criticizing my family, he was, I believe, really trying to
prevent a more profound discussion about being a Jewish Wagnerian. I do not believe, however, that it is morally responsible to make
a distinction between Wagner "the great artist" and Wagner "the
anti-Semite." For that reason, it is impossible for me to remain
silent on the deeds of my grandmother and Chamberlain.

One thing I did learn from my correspondence with Frank was to
use the word "mission" less in connection with my activities. Even
then I did not understand my work as a mission, simply as a contribution to finding out the truth about Richard Wagner.

Another interesting episode took place in mid-August of 1991, at a conference in Weimar on the subject "The Case of Richard Wagner in Israel and Germany." Herzl Shmueli also took part, and before the start of the discussion in the Autonomous Cultural Center the chairman of the Richard Wagner Society in Weimar, Eberhard Lüdde, asked me: "What line should we take? All the Wagner Societies at home and abroad have been instructed not to invite you to functions." I answered: "Thank you for the hint. Whether you or other Wagner Societies want to invite me or not must surely depend on you yourselves."

Other representatives from Wagner Societies turned up at my *Lohengrin* premiere in Dessau in May 1995. Here again, the picture was not uniform. The Berlin society obviously toed the Bayreuth line. The *Neue Zürcher Zeitung*, which applauded my concept of a critical reading of the text, then poked fun at the organized booing against me. Two soloists fell in with the anti-Gottfried mood, after months of pretending during rehearsals that they agreed with my concept. Subsequently they were reluctant to be named in the documentary film *Herr Hitler's Religion*, televised from September 1995 in various countries, which shows scenes from my *Lohengrin* in which Wagner's "New Christianity in the direction of *Parsifal*" is clarified, to the horror of the Bayreuth faithful. The administration and the majority of the ensemble of the Dessau theater shared my opinion.

I had a particularly difficult time in Bayreuth, not least regarding my correspondence with the mayor, Dieter Mronz. In December 1989 I had sent him, for his information, the introductory texts to my lectures on Wagner at Tel Aviv University. On 26 March 1990, having heard nothing from him for three months, I wrote again:

Dear Dr. Mronz,
    In our talks during the opening week of the Bayreuth Festival at the end of July 1989 you expressed definite interest in my desire for reconciliation in Israel (cf. also the interview of 18.8.89 in the Nordbayerischer Kurier*) and promised to send me your views on the "case of the Chamberlain-Furtwängler*

Strasse." For that reason in my letter of 21.12.89 I referred,
among other things, yet again, to my forthcoming trip to Israel
and enclosed the summaries of my three lectures and of my
Ring *video presentation with the intention of evoking some*
reaction from you. . . . Your continuing silence on the
matter . . . which surely also concerns the citizens of Bayreuth,
gives me cause for concern.
   With kind regards,
   Your Gottfried H. Wagner

One month later I received a four-page letter from Mayor Mronz,
in which he congratulated me on the success of my journey to Israel. His remarks on the Chamberlain affair, however, are indica-
tive of the intellectual climate in Bayreuth. With reference to the
municipal councilman Werner Kolb, a member of the Greens, who
in 1989 had courageously pleaded for a renaming of Chamberlain
Strasse, Mronz arrived at a position toward the Bayreuth municipal
council: on the basis of the fact that the present generation must
also be suffering under the heavy burden of the Nazi dictatorship,
he pointed out that in Bayreuth a new, more profound sensitivity
toward this problem had developed. That in turn led, among other
things, to confidently freeing themselves from such burdens as the
disputed street name, instead of encumbering themselves with new
guilt complexes and burdens on top of the old.
   On July 5 I replied to Mronz:

   I find it not only regrettable, but in every respect scandalous,
   that it has taken twenty-three years to change the name of the
   Chamberlain Strasse. The example of the Chamberlain Strasse
   shows that we are not capable of "confidently freeing ourselves
   of such burdens as this street name."
   The words "confidently freeing" in this connection make me
   feel uneasy. Whoever "stubbornly clings" to names like
   Chamberlain in Bayreuth and elsewhere shows what sort of
   person he is. "New guilt complexes and burdens" will certainly
   continue to exist if these antidemocratic powers are not

publicly opposed with personal courage and pluralistic-democratic means and people are still not prepared, especially in the period of German reunification, for a thorough acceptance of the past and genuine mourning through firm action—without remembrance ceremonies, which often function as rather dubious alibis. The city of Bayreuth could, for example, find a twin city in Israel. After discussions with people there you would certainly, as I did, alter your opinion and attitude to this fundamental subject of German history. I regret that on the basis of my knowledge and conscience, I am forced to acknowledge that in this sense neither the commemorative text on the Reichskristallnacht [in Bayreuth] nor the volume Wagner and the Jews *corresponds to my ideas.*

With thoughtful regards and constant readiness for dialogue I remain,

Yours,

Gottfried Wagner

P.S. On the basis of my objective critical statements at the University of Tel Aviv, among other things on the style of leadership of my grandmother as head of the festival in the Nazi period, I have been declared persona non grata by circles close to the festival (letter of 2.2.90), including the federal president Lienhart, blacklisted in Germany, and my work has been slandered as a "settling of private scores."

The international professional world and the press, particularly in Israel, has still to deal with this. This will certainly not be awkward for me, as among other things the manipulated selection of press quotations against me will probably have to be aired. As persona non grata I no longer have access to the Festspielhügel, it is true; but surely I do still to the archives of the city of Bayreuth? Can I, if I am hindered in my researches, apply to you? Also on this subject, "can we confidently free ourselves from such burdens?" On the basis of my experiences, I fear not.

Mronz never answered this letter. I was not surprised that I was unwelcome at that time in the Richard Wagner Archive and that my work was not encouraged.

Just as revealing is another episode, this one concerning Bayreuth University, which I naïvely believed was independent of Festspielhügel politics. Professor Walter Gebhard of the German department wrote to me in June 1993 in connection with a "possible lecture" that he considered the time (before the granting of an honorary doctorate by the university to my father) inappropriate, not least because the reaction of the festival administration to a critical lecture was difficult to predict. I did well to cancel the lecture. The university's attitude was clear, not only from the fact that it had granted the doctorate to my father, but also from the content of the ceremonial speech that well-known figure on the left Walter Jens had given in January 1994 on the occasion of the eight hundredth anniversary of Bayreuth. Jens rejected the findings of independent research into Wagner's anti-Semitism and told the representatives of the city of Bayreuth and of the Festspielhügel at some length what they wanted to hear. He performed what the Wagner scholar Hartmut Zelinsky aptly termed a "flight into vagueness."

Yet another icon of the German cultural scene joined the Bayreuth game: August Everding, Germany's most powerful intendant. In April 1990 I had written to him in the hope he would support my discussion of Wagner in Germany after my trip to Israel. Everding, ever the cultural politician, responded noncommittally. But things did not stop there. He managed, in opposition to the head of the Richard Strauss Institute in Munich, Stephan Kohler, and the chairmen of the patrons circle of the Richard Strauss Festival in Garmisch Partenkirchen, Dr. Manfred Frei and Christian Lange, to see to it that my invitation to the symposium "Richard Strauss: An (Un)heroic Life" in July 1991 was cancelled. Word was spread around that I was "difficult, verbose, and dangerous."

A planned lecture on "The Case of Wagner in Israel and Germany" at the Bavarian Academy of Fine Arts in Munich in 1991, which the composer Günter Bialas had championed, also came to nothing. I had written to Bialas in May, enclosing numerous documents on my trip to Israel. He had been very interested in the subject, but at the end of June 1991 he wrote to say that he found himself unable to invite me to give a lecture without the consent of my father, who was a member of the academy's music department. According to Oswald Georg Bauer, secretary of the academy, the tensions between me and my father were (still) too great to invite me.

My experiences with the media were not much better, whatever the individual reasons. In autumn 1991 Tilman Jens, Walter Jens's son, rang me and asked for an interview in my home in Cerro Maggiore on the subject of my journey to Israel in 1990 and Wagner's anti-Semitism. The interview was then televised under the sensationalist title "The Inheritance War: Trouble in the House of Wagner—Wolfgang Wagner Is Angry" in November, on the cultural program *titel, thesen, temperamente* [title, topic, temperament]. My cousin Nike deputized as spokesperson for the fourth Wagner generation, although Nike's opinions and mine diverged where Bayreuth was concerned.

Shortly after the broadcast I wrote Nike a letter, to initiate dialogue again after a silence of several years. Unfortunately she did not reply. For years she has reinforced her claim to the succession by criticizing the festival as run by my father. In an interview in the summer of 1995 she stated: "As in every institution a period of government should not go on too long. There is an urgent need for new ideas, a new artistic will, a new vision. The future of Wagner is at stake. That is what I stand for, and I am ready to take it on." But she did not present a program for dealing with Wagner's ideology and the anti-Semitism in his work and theories.

Until then Nike had avoided being involved in the Bayreuth politicking against me, and in that respect she differed agreeably from the other two women in the family who have ambitions of inheritance: Eva and Gudrun. Both worked closely with Father and were tarred by the brush of his power politics. Two principles of my father's rule his pupils almost as much as their master: one can be described as "control from the rear"; the other is that in dealing with the public, you should leave your sentiments ambiguous. Neither Eva nor Gudrun has the will or the ability to come to terms with Bayreuth's Nazi past—something Eva has already proved by allegedly losing the copies of the films from the motorcycle sidecar that I had entrusted to her.

Tilman Jens should have reported this during his program. Of course, he also gave my father the chance to make a statement: "I can't turn the Bayreuth Festival into a playground for Richard Wagner's great-grandchildren. I can only appoint someone here who in my view has something to offer Bayreuth. We are not a training center for the Wagner great-grandchildren."

JENS: "Does that mean that you are sort of the last representative of the great Wagner family?"
FATHER: "No."
JENS: "You are the last Wagner?"
FATHER: "No, I have never maintained that. And I can't understand why I am blamed because my nieces and nephews can't read and understand that."
JENS: "Okay, but if you say that at the moment nothing will come after . . ."
FATHER: "I'm sorry, what I was trying to say was that, there is no one from within the family who, based on achievement so far, is any better placed than an outsider . . . with respect to what they could contribute to Wagner's work."
JENS: "Do you see something like a generational conflict in the great Wagner family?"
FATHER: "I can only say the following: from the outset my brother maintained that older and younger generations don't work well together."

Talking about me, and the fact that I no longer receive festival tickets, he said: "In many of the public talks he has given on tour, my son has made very negative comments about the present structure of the festival. Among other things he has claimed that my colleagues are just alibi Jews and that I have been indulging in negative nationalist tendencies. That is an arrogant and terribly false accusation, and furthermore a degradation of this circle of colleagues. That is totally unacceptable."

JENS: "So he doesn't get tickets anymore?"

FATHER: "As I have said, I can't receive him here because of my colleagues. If he says such things, attacks everyone, including myself, and acts so negatively, he should not be allowed in the house."

JENS: "How do you feel, playing the role of wicked father, or wicked uncle?"

FATHER: "Excuse me, I am not wicked! It is only one of a very small group. . . ."

JENS: "Your family . . ."

FATHER: "What do you mean, my family? Excuse me. Family is a haphazardly compiled community . . . which happens to have originated from the same root. At some stage one's own personality emerges, one develops, and then one makes up one's own mind about things."

JENS: "Herr Wagner, you are now seventy-two. People usually retire at sixty-five. Why haven't you retired yet? Do you have any idea when you intend to do so?"

FATHER: "Adenauer started to rule Germany at seventy-five and voluntarily retired fourteen years later."

JENS: "Is that some indication of your plans?"

FATHER: "You will see. You are young. One day you will read it in the newspapers, and I presume television will report on it too."

In conclusion, Jens remarked: "The patriarch will decide on his successor jointly with a commission. One may assume that none from the circle of his children, nephews, and nieces will feature among the candidates. So, a family tradition is coming to an end. Wouldn't that be a very typical Wagner story! Fifteen years ago Wolfgang Wagner married for the second time. Now there is Frau Gudrun and Katherina, their daughter. In a few years she will have reached her majority—and she would not be the first female chief in Bayreuth. Nothing changes. Rejoice! Wagner without end!"[36]

Judging from interviews in January and August 1990, I had the impression that a critical discussion of Richard Wagner's anti-Semitism might be possible on Bavarian Radio. But a statement I had made during the August interview—"Post-Wieland Bayreuth has nothing to do with [Richard Wagner's] idea of the festival"—was then used as grounds to cancel all collaboration on the planned project. The harmony—in other words, the long-term business association—between the local radio station and the Bayreuth Festival was not to be jeopardized.

In February 1996, the Vienna-based journalist Hellfried Brandl managed to arrange a broadcast with me—not knowing who at WDR radio were close to Bayreuth—on the subject of Wagner, Bayreuth, and anti-Semitism as part of the Bavarian Radio family program.

An interview with Wolfgang Seifert, a former employee of West German Radio and Free Berlin Radio, went less favorably. I knew of Seifert through his exculpatory article "Zero Hour for New Bayreuth" for the West German Radio, which was printed after it was broadcast in February 1970. Research documentation for this had been provided by Father's former assistant director and house dramaturg, Dietrich Mack. At the end of October 1993 a program was broadcast on four decades of the Bayreuth Workshop. In it my statements were distorted and taken out of context. Seifert also dismissed my comments on the "multicultural future of Bayreuth" simply by using my father's words: "That is not suitable for Bayreuth."[37] And, with servility, he drew attention to Father's influence in the Foundation Council of the Bayreuth Festival.

My experiences with a number of leading German newspapers were similarly negative. The London correspondent of the *Frankfurter Allgemeine Zeitung*, Gina Thomas, in April 1995 reacted defensively in print to remarks I had made on the program *Wagner Versus Wagner*, televised at the beginning of the month by the UK's Channel Four. She did this without any knowledge either of my work or of modern research into Wagner's anti-Semitic writings, which I quoted. As opposed to objective discussion, she gave free rein to her resentment and kept deliberately silent about the fact that other critical experts, such as Barry Millington, the editor of the *Wagner Compendium*, Paul Lawrence Rose, and Dan Bar-On, had also been interviewed in this program. But it was the following remarks in particular that caused greatest astonishment:

> The *Times* devoted half a page to Gottfried Wagner's childish objections and left his assertions uncontradicted. Other newspapers gave him, someone who likes to present himself as the victim of persecution, a lot of space. . . . Not even the faintest doubt is expressed on his exaggerated assertions. His English interviewers blindly believe him. Full of sympathy, the opera critic of the *Times* describes how far Bayreuth's influence extends: Gottfried Wagner, whom the keepers of the Grail wrongly described as a nest-fouler, is even largely denied access to the German media. . . . Abroad the ignorance of those giving him commissions works in his favor, and they are only too happy to have their own clichéd ideas confirmed.[38]

The German reviews, influenced by Bayreuth, of my *Lohengrin* production in May 1995 were of a similar tone. Since May 1977—in other words, since the reviews of my first production, *Fidelio*—nothing had changed. Most of the reviewers aligned themselves with Bayreuth and wrote in a style devoid of all objectivity: unfortunately, often of any competence in the field either. I will always listen to valid, quality criticism, and I shall come to examples of those in time.

Something far more ominous now came to my attention. The American conductor John Edward Niles, with whom I had been in contact since 1990 regarding various projects on Jewish composers murdered during the Nazi period, informed me at the beginning of October 1992 that his brother Thomas, a high-ranking official in the American diplomatic service, had received hints that my Italian family and I were on some sort of international Nazi organization blacklist: "I am very concerned [for] your personal safety. My brother and some of his colleagues were informed that there are people who want to bump you and your family off. I'm not someone who easily gets alarmist, but I must beg you to be very careful." He said we would be in danger if I continued my critical lectures on Wagner's anti-Semitism, particularly in Germany. This information scarcely surprised me: since my trip to Israel I had been constantly pestered by phone calls at night and death threats.

At that time I was preparing a lecture which the German Council of Industry of Commerce had invited me to deliver in Bonn, introduced, at my request, by Ralph Giordano. Concerned about my family, especially as the activities of neo-Nazis in Germany at this time had greatly increased, I asked John Edward Niles to get detailed information for me on the various neo-Nazi groups. I also asked Minister of State Helmut Schäfer from the German Ministry of Foreign Affairs for help. The list of reasons I supplied, at the beginning of December 1992, included the following: "Since my lecture tour to Israel on Wagner in January 1990 I have regularly received anonymous telephone calls from Germany, in which, among other things, I am abused as 'Jew-lover.'" After the publication of a magazine article on my trip to Israel I was viciously attacked by the *Nationalzeitung*. In March 1992 I received death threats in the United States from skinheads, so that I had to give one lecture under police protection. Niles told me of a discussion he had had in the States with an extreme right-wing German lawyer who apparently lives in Switzerland. He learned from this dubious gentleman that people in Germany were very angry with me for getting involved in matters concerning the Holocaust and Wagner. Minister Schäfer ensured my safety. But it left a bitter aftertaste when, in December 1992, we were driven around Bonn and Cologne in an armored limousine with guards.

24

Anti-Semitism and Opera Business

ince January 1990 Wagner's anti-Semitism had been the focus of my investigative research and the main subject of my lectures. Although demand for my talks in Germany was rather meager, there was lively interest abroad, especially in Jewish communities, and so I increasingly distanced myself, even intellectually, from Germany.

Abroad, where repressive mechanisms are not all-powerful, one could discuss Wagner more freely. And discussion was most objective where hosts and audience had nothing to do with Bayreuth. If they did, there was renewed confrontation, but that seldom happened. Yet I must describe a few exceptions, which illustrate how deeply anti-Semitism has penetrated elsewhere.

For example, an American Nazi called Max Orlando wrote to me a few days after my Israel journey: "'The era of the American Weimar Republic' is coming to an end. . . . Who needs Washington DC and Moscow? US, Biopolitics USA—our triumvirate E[ustace] Mullins, R[obert E.] Kuttner and myself—welcome in the twenty-first century. Wagner music is of no consequence. . . . Wagner's anti-Jewish position was instinctive, as the host to the parasite, i.e., *The Biological Jew* [written by] E. Mullins, published in 1968." Orlando enclosed with his letter the "research results" of his study of biological racism at the McArdle Laboratory for Cancer Research at the University of Wisconsin. I had strong doubts about the authenticity of these documents.

Other fanatics tried to bring me back to the "right path" of Wagnerian hatred of Jews, or simply threatened me. Being called a "dirty traitor and friend of the Jews" in nighttime phone calls has become part of life for me ever since.

In March 1992 in Dallas I gave my talk "The Case of Wagner in Israel and Germany." My hosts were Southern Methodist University, the Goethe Center, and the local Richard Wagner Society. Two ladies on the committee of the society, both keen Bayreuth visitors, were eager to tell me, in private, what I should and shouldn't say: no politics, not a word on Wolf and Winnie, and lots of enthusiasm for the neo-Christian case of the redeemer Richard Wagner. I thanked them and delivered my lecture against Wagner's anti-Semitism with even more passion. One of the two ladies exploded and ran shrieking from the hall. Before slamming the door behind her she shouted: "Scandal! Scandal!" But the majority of the audience were on my side, and one member of the Wagner Society apologized for the incident. At the end of the lecture, my hosts immediately invited me to give another talk.

Two separate experiences, involving James Levine and Daniel Barenboim, made clear to me exactly how far Bayreuth's connections reached. After delivering my lecture on Wagner in Israel and Germany at the City University of New York at the end of February 1992, the music historian George Jellinek, who also worked for *The New York Times* radio station, WQXR, invited me for an interview. He asked me in particular about *Parsifal*, as the interview was to be aired during the intermission of the Metropolitan Opera's live radio broadcast of that opera conducted by James Levine on 28 March 1992. The interview went smoothly, and Jellinek said he was "very happy." I subsequently alerted friends to the interview—among them Pierre Béique, founder of the Montreal Symphony Orchestra, and Larry Mass, doctor and contributor to the magazine *Opera Monthly* in New York. The North American media reported on the upcoming broadcast and my part in it.

On 28 March, however, Pierre informed me that the interview with me had not been broadcast that afternoon, because I had apparently been "ill." Larry looked further into the matter and wrote in *Opera Monthly* in October 1992, under the title "Met Cancels Gottfried Wagner":

> *Opera Monthly* has learned that Richard Mohr, producer of the Texaco-Metropolitan Opera Radio Station, cancelled an interview with Gottfried Wagner, the great-grandson of the composer and outspoken critic of Bayreuth. The interview was scheduled to have run during the 28 March 1992 broadcast of *Parsifal.* George Jellinek, who had interviewed Dr. Wagner for his WQXR radio program and who had additionally conducted the prerecorded interview for the broadcast, confirmed that the decision to cancel was made because Dr. Wagner was judged to be "too controversial." While Jellinek did not want to be quoted as opposing the cancellation, he referred *Opera Monthly* to Mohr, who gave the following explanation: "It was a defective tape. You can interpret that as you wish."[39]

Jellinek had informed me in May that the decision to cancel had apparently had something to do with the Met-Bayreuth connection. However, he enclosed a list of radio stations that had broadcast the interview—thirty-three stations in the United States and a few in Canada—which confirmed yet again how strong North American democracy is. It is not impressed by connections.

Following well-meant advice, I desisted from writing a letter of protest to Mohr. But I couldn't accept this kind of attitude. When I received a check by way of compensation for a sum six times higher than the agreed fee, I wrote to Jellinek: "I shall send the check from Texaco-Metropolitan Opera International Radio Network to Unicef and try in that way to turn something bad into something good. I hope you can understand my reaction."

Despite my "too controversial" contribution, only three days after recording the radio interview I gave a long talk on *Parsifal* in the renowned music conservatory of the University of Cincinnati. My arguments were no different from those in the interview with Jellinek, but not one member of the audience felt provoked—nor could anyone have had a reason to. Afterwards, I received a friendly thank-you letter from the conservatory. A visit by Henry Meyer, the eminent violinist and former member of the La Salle String Quartet, was very welcome, too. On this occasion he presented me with a copy of his autobiographical sketches with his best regards. Henry, a Jewish survivor of the Holocaust, had been a teacher of James Levine in Cincinnati, Levine's hometown.

My outspokenness has also made an impression on Daniel Barenboim, the one-time wunderkind pianist and protégé of Otto Klemperer. (There have been several critical studies of his brilliant career, such as Norman Lebrecht's *The Maestro Myth*, Klaus Umbach's *Geldscheinsonate*, and Stephen J. Petit's *History of the London Philharmonic Orchestra*.) In an interview with the Israeli newspaper *Yediot Acharonot* published in summer 1992, Barenboim took issue with my exposition of Wagner, the Bayreuth Festival, and Judaism. In June 1993, he told the Spanish newspaper *El Pais*, regarding the neo-Nazi and xenophobic violence in Germany, that "if the Nazi phenomenon becomes widespread," he did not want to "stay a day longer" in Germany. I would have had some sympathy for this statement were it not for the fact that one year earlier, German neo-Nazis had been very prominent during the festival in Bayreuth. Until today I have not heard of any statement by Barenboim on this, or on the historically distorted 1984 exhibition, "Wagner and the Jews," in the Villa Wahnfried. And would he really leave Germany, where in Bayreuth and Berlin they lie at his feet?

At a time when the local and international media were criticizing Germany for its rise in neo-Nazi activities, Barenboim remained complacent. In an interview with the newspaper *La Repubblica* in November 1993, entitled "Daniel Barenboim Rejoices and Is King of Berlin," he said: "But I, as a Jew, defend Germany." To compound this, in an interview with *Opera Monthly* (May/June 1993) he made every effort, in quite the Bayreuth style, to understate Richard Wagner's anti-Semitism: "We must remember that Wagner's anti-Semitism was intellectually fashionable in the nineteenth century and he cannot be held responsible for the actual atrocities committed half a century later by those who misused his ideas."[40]

Leonard Bernstein, with whom I had met in April 1990, just a few months before his death, would never have said such a thing. On the contrary, he openly stressed his deep aversion to conducting at the Bayreuth Festival under my father's administration and never compromised on Wagner's anti-Semitism or accepted the New Bayreuth's policy of repression; and he enthusiastically supported my trip to Israel.

But Barenboim had said these things, and I decided to defend myself against his attacks. In a letter to the editor published in the July/August 1993 issue of *Opera Monthly*, I proved once again Wagner's anti-Semitic attitude, in which he was not simply following the beliefs of the time. I described the ultimately catastrophic effects of this fanaticism in Germany, criticized the Bayreuth Festival, and even talked about the neo-Nazi gatherings in Bayreuth in 1991. I declared that Richard Wagner, through his inflammatory anti-Semitic writings, was co-responsible for the transition from Bayreuth to Auschwitz. Moreover, I supported Elie Wiesel, who in *The New York Times* of 12 January 1992 had criticized the way Barenboim excused Richard Wagner from guilt.

In the end Franklin Littell, president of the Holocaust, Genocide and Human Rights Institute in Philadelphia and co-founder of the universally recognized organization The Holocaust and the Churches, joined the argument. In an article that was printed in various American newspapers, he wrote:

> But what happened at Bayreuth, that major fortress of cultural revisionism? Gottfried Wagner, the great-grandson of the famous composer, has a letter in the July/August issue of *Opera Monthly* that probes some of the deeper issues of this center of revisionism. He is responding to an article in an earlier issue of *Opera Monthly*, in which the vaguely Jewish Daniel Barenboim has attempted to lift the burden of willful and wicked anti-Semitism from Richard Wagner's record. . . .

Gottfried Wagner will have none of it. He knows the bitter anti-Semitism of his great-grandfather as a personal burden. He knows the correspondence of Winifred Wagner and Hitler (from 1923 to 1944). He knows the bitterly anti-Semitic passages in his great-grandfather's letters and in Cosima Wagner's diaries. He asks why, if his anti-Semitism was so harmless, the skinheads chose Bayreuth for their major rally in August of 1991. . . . We know about Bayreuth's past, and we can be thankful that Gottfried Wagner and his allies won't let that record be hidden for commercial and political purposes. There is a great deal going on in and around "Bayreuth" today.[41]

Among the reactions were articles in *The New York Times* in mid-August 1993 and the English magazine *Opera Now* in January 1994. In a long letter to James R. Oestreich, the music editor of *The New York Times*, I criticized what was a very inaccurately researched article by John Rockwell on the festival and the family, published on 15 August 1993 with the title "The Gods Sit There and Wait for Another Ugly Twilight." Rockwell had asserted:

Relations seem to be most bitter between Wolfgang and his son. Gottfried has taken to denouncing his family's history of anti-Semitism, most prominently on a visit to Israel, the first by a family member—this despite the fact that the two most prominent conductors at Bayreuth today are James Levine and Daniel Barenboim. Wolfgang, calling it shameful to stigmatize the conductors as "alibi Jews," banned Gottfried from Bayreuth in 1990. "Henceforth, both in Bayreuth and elsewhere," he wrote by fax, "an absolute distance between you and me must be maintained." Now, Gottfried says, his letters to his father are returned unopened.

Part of my letter to Oestreich read:

Mr. Rockwell does not appear to have seen my recent letter published in the July/August edition of Opera Monthly. *In this*

*letter I express my opinion of the roles of Daniel Barenboim
and James Levine and the hypocrisy of their involvement. Your
report only quotes my father's statement, i.e., that my criti-
cisms constitute a shameful stigmatization of Barenboim and
Levine as "alibi Jews," but fails to let me respond. The Wagners have profited twice, in my grandmother's and now in my
father's time, by denying any personal responsibility in the
Nazi era as well as after the Holocaust. The former victimizers have become the new falsely pro-Semitic heralds of today,
thanks to people like Barenboim and Levine, the children of
the victims, and to the common big-business enterprise—
the "Redemption" Bayreuth Festival. The article also fails
to mention my twenty-year struggle to help create better
German-Jewish relations, as well as my co-founding of the
Post-Holocaust Dialogue Group. I have dedicated my life to
fighting the evil of the Wagner legacy, attempting to give the
public a better understanding and reconciling the important
issues that still pull us toward my great-grandfather's art. . . .
None of these events, nor my father's intrigues over the "royal"
succession to the Bayreuth Festival can hide one brutal truth:
a reunified Germany has a responsibility not to falsify its past,
to face up to the Wagner family's important cultural role in
the Nazi tyranny and to fight discrimination against those
who, like me, are not willing to engage in a profitable music
enterprise.*

This letter was not published.

The *Opera Now* article was false and slanderous. Robert Hartford wrote in connection with my father's seventy-fifth birthday
and as promotion for the latter's book *Acts*, under the heading
"House of Cards": "it is Bayreuth's heir apparent, Gottfried, who is
making the most mischief. Gottfried has adopted a fashionable
theme: his family's attitude towards Jews and, on the profitable
principle of telling people what they want to hear, he has been lecturing his way around America—and Israel too, the first Wagner to

set foot there—denouncing Bayreuth as still in the thrall of Nazi ideals and anti-Semitism. He has made especially vicious attacks on conductors Levine and Barenboim, both Jews, alleging 'Uncle Tom' compliance in working at Bayreuth."

At the end of January 1994 I sent my reaction to *Opera Now*, in which I restated many of the points from my unpublished *New York Times* letter and reasserted my criticism of Barenboim and Levine.

Mr. Hartford's comments on me and my work are mostly wrong, slanderous and reflect his lack of knowledge of the subjects involved. Here are a few examples of false statements made about me: 1. The issue of Judaism and Wagner has been troubling me for more than twenty years and I am, among others, a co-founder of the "Post-Holocaust Dialogue Group": as such this issue neither constitutes "a fashionable theme" nor a "profitable principle." 2. The author is not informed about the places where I have spoken or will speak on these topics, for example, this year at the United States Holocaust Memorial Museum and Ben-Gurion University. Are the distinguished institutions which invite me not able to select their speakers, or are they just inviting me to tell them "what they want to hear?" 3. I have never said that Bayreuth is "still in the thrall of Nazi ideals and anti-Semitism." My critique is on quite another level. 4. With regard to Messrs Levine and Barenboim, the author is apparently ignorant of my comments, e.g., in my letter to the editor of *Opera Monthly* (July 1993) or in my August 1993 interview with *Musica* Nr 4 (Kassel). I do not stand alone in my criticism of either Barenboim or Levine: see, for example, Elie Wiesel's criticism of Barenboim in *The New York Times* (Jan. 12, 1992). Finally, I will repeat, patiently, again and again, to journalists who are either unwilling or unable to understand me: I do not claim any aspirations to be my father's heir at the Bayreuth Festival.

My letter was printed in full in the March 1994 issue of *Opera Now*.

25

Eugenio, My Son

I t was while I was preparing for my trip to Israel at the end of December 1989 that, Teresina, Mamma Antonietta, and I saw television coverage of the arrest and execution of the Romanian dictator Nicolae Ceauşescu and his wife, Elena. The feature was followed by the first reports on the ill treatment of children in Romanian orphanages. We could scarcely believe that, post-Hitler and post-Stalin, a European state could have committed such crimes for two decades, with the knowledge of Western and Eastern politicians and humanitarian organizations, without provoking a storm of indignation.

Not until 1991, in a book by the child psychotherapist Alice Miller, *Breaking Down the Wall of Silence*, did I find an explanation of the reasons behind such a barbaric development. Miller writes: "Ceauşescu's deeds and his political career right from the outset, were ruled by the idea of redemption through destruction. Without having had similar motivation in childhood, one will not become a dictator. Just like Hitler, Stalin and others before him, Ceauşescu must constantly have heard that it was for his own good that he was being beaten, tortured, and spied on and his soul destroyed. As a child he could never have been able to see through the lie. These unexposed lies later become the fundamental principles of the tyrant." Miller writes further how the child who believes these lies to survive and who does not repudiate them in adulthood becomes himself a tyrant, assuming the belief forms they learned from their dictatorial parents. What the Ceaușescus did as "loving parents" to their people, who were living in indescribable hardship, is well known today. But during his lifetime, Ceaușescu expected grateful homage. In childhood his parents had disappointed his need for love and attention; he represented the pain of their neglect and abuse. As an adult he was unable to relieve that repression in a normal adult way. Instead, he abused his nation of children in the "guise of national salvation."[42]

And so I found myself thinking of the children of Romania and wishing I could save at least one of them from his abusive home.

All the important events in my life of recent years have somehow had to do with my journey to Israel—even the way I found my son.

In early January 1990, we read in the *Jerusalem Post* that since the execution of the Ceaușescus, it was possible to adopt children in Romania. After much discussion, Teresina and I decided to apply to adopt a child from Romania as soon as we got home in mid-January. After months of bureaucratic procedures, we flew to Bucharest at the beginning of June with the necessary documents. It was just a few days before the miners' revolt.

The squalor of the city took our breath away. The depression of the period following the "revolution"—which was unfortunately nothing but a putsch by onetime Ceaușescu vassal Iliescu and his thugs—also had its effect on us. Damp, stinking soot even penetrated the shops, where we couldn't even find mineral water or milk to buy. Hordes of neglected children ran after us begging, as they had seen by our clothes that we came from the West.

We spent the first night in the Intercontinental Hotel, right on University Square, where the students were camping out in protest against Iliescu. As we didn't speak the local language, we were constantly being swindled, and when the hotel tried to charge us higher prices than those quoted by the official travel agency, we decided to move to a simpler, cheaper hotel on the street leading to the university. The first floor was given over to child prostitution, and from our room we witnessed a group of militant Iliescu thugs beating former members of the secret service, Securitate. The police arrived too late to prevent a murder.

Finally the moment came. On 6 June we drove with the wily Romanian lawyer George Alexandru, who had been procured for us by the Italian embassy, to Orphanage Four in the workers' district of Bucharest. The Ceauşescu regime had left total desolation there too. The orphanage was a prison, surrounded by high fences and barricades. In the filthy, dark interior of the concrete building there was a stench of urine and ammonia. There was not a single picture hanging on the walls. No toy to be seen. No children's voices to be heard.

Equally cheerless was the office of the director, who, in her contempt for "her" orphans, was typical of the still omnipresent spirit of Ceauşescu. She made it clear to us that if we didn't want any problems in getting a child, there would be "little extras," cash and presents, to hurry her signature.

The door opened, and three children were introduced to us, one after the other: Elena, then Christoph, and finally Eugenio. Eugenio was in a pitiful condition. He was emaciated and his belly was very distended. His skin was pallid, raw, and dirty. His pale blond hair was thin in patches, and his teeth were covered with a black coating. His muscles were so underdeveloped that he had to keep sitting down out of exhaustion: he reminded me of Jackie Coogan in Chaplin's film *The Kid*. His clothes were a pair of underpants several sizes too large and a shirt of synthetic material which was full of holes. His shoes were enormous—so big, in fact, he could not walk properly. But Eugenio gave me a faint smile which lit up our first moments as future father and son.

The reality of the orphanage was brought back to us by the harsh voice of the director, who said: "As you are already forty-three, you could have Eugenio—he's one of our oldest children."

What had five-year-old Eugenio had to endure! His mother had given him up immediately after birth. The Ceauşescu state classified him as a delicate child, of the "second" category. The more robust children in the "first" category were destined to enter the service of the Securitate, while the delicate children, who did not

appear up to this "heroic" task, were shunted off to squalid orphanages. We yielded to the director's blackmailing in order to liberate Eugenio from his hell.

At that moment Eugenio noticed Teresina, who was sitting on a
chair in the cramped room. They looked curiously at one another.
Teresina gave him some chocolate. With difficulty, he climbed onto
Teresina's lap and, smiling, tucked into what were probably the
first sweets of his life.

After an odyssey through a Bucharest court, where we had to sign
further adoption documents, we finally visited Eugenio two days
later as his new parents. He had suspected something was happening and called both Teresina and me "Mama": having been brought
up only by women, he didn't know what a father was. We gave him
a little plastic truck, which he hugged, beaming, although at the
same time scared that someone could take the toy away from him.

Then we went for a little excursion outside the orphanage. He had
clearly never been out of his prison: everything was new for him. He
reacted with a mixture of joy and fear to a rooster, a bus, a crane,
and the crowds who scurried silently past us with impassive faces.

The first time I tried to pick Eugenio up, he trembled with fear.
I put him down again carefully, and later he told me that he had
only ever been picked up by the nurses when he was being taken to
a dark room after having been beaten.

We had to take him back to the orphanage that June, because the
documentation was not yet complete; and naturally we were afraid
we would never see him again. Iliescu's mob of miners were beginning to "cleanse" the streets of students, and foreigners were unpopular, despite their coveted dollar bills. At one point, we were
afraid we wouldn't make it to the airport and had to bribe a taxi
driver to take us there.

It wasn't until 30 August 1990 that Eugenio officially became
our son, by decree of a Bucharest court. It was also my father's
birthday. So Eugenio became a Wagner on his grandfather's birthday. He was baptized in December of the same year.

I sent Father a photo of Eugenio, which was sent back without
comment.

Even before our second trip to Romania, in September, I interpreted the strange coincidence of significant dates in the lives of grandfather and grandchild as a point of departure for a new chapter in my life. On the basis of my own childhood, I knew that I should never allow the shadow of Ceauşescu to become all-powerful for Eugenio, as the shadow of Hitler had been for me.

The day we collected Eugenio from the orphanage will remain unforgettable. He clutched our hands tightly and left without a word to anyone, without looking back once. Thanks to the wife of the Italian ambassador, Giovanna Amaduzzi, and their excellent colleagues, we were able to fly back to Rome immediately.

A new period began in our lives, to which we began gradually to accustom ourselves. During the first year of our life together, whenever Eugenio spoke of his past he always started his story with the words: "And then I flew home with Papa and Mama." It was difficult for him to find his own identity. In everything he did he lacked the life experience of a child who had grown up under humane conditions. For the first five and a half years of his life, he had had no family and had never experienced any kind of love.

Child therapists such as Jean Piaget, Alice Miller, Hans Aebli, Ashley Montagu, Alfred Adler, David Kirk, and many others, whose works I had read before Eugenio's arrival, did describe fascinating theories and models, it is true. But day-to-day life proved just how difficult it is to realize good intentions. I had a lot to learn as a father, and it was not just to come from wise books.

Eugenio had not learned any language, and in fighting to survive in the orphanage he had assumed several antisocial behavioral habits. He had to learn how to live in a family. Here his new cousin Alberto, who was the same age, helped him; in fact, they grew up like brothers. We tried to teach Eugenio what good and evil, right and wrong were, which also meant that we had to test our own standard of values.

It was particularly difficult to get Eugenio out of the habit of cringing, proto-military obedience, which he had been broken into and which was now increased by his fear of being sent back to the orphanage. His servile eagerness to obey was replaced by the need to learn how to cope with freedom. And for me this whole period felt like a daily tightrope walk between liberating knowledge and bitter experiences from my own childhood.

Following my own experiences, I also wanted to avoid any repressive teaching methods. The risks of misunderstanding and of overreaction were always present for me: I had to remember constantly that Eugenio was experiencing out of phase everything that had been missing from his early life. This also affected the way he played, the way he learned, and his need for love. In this way, we were able to experience things we would not have had with another child.

I also tried to satisfy his very personal needs with bedtime stories. But Eugenio was not interested in Grimm's fairy tales. Instead he wanted me to tell him his own life story again and again, but only from the moment he had called us Papa and Mama, and each time he heard this wonderful "fairy tale," he wanted lots of fresh details. He was probably satisfying his backlog need for warmth—although he got plenty of this in our Italian household. Eugenio's integration into the family took place with the high drama and alternating hot and cold emotions that are possible only in Italy. I envy him that: I would like to have grown up in a *famiglia italiana* too.

In raising my son, a new process of integration began for me also. My thinking, feeling, and acting all changed greatly. Eugenio confronted me with the real responsibilities of planning a common present and future. A lot that once seemed important to me, including the Bayreuth past, was put into context or simply lost all significance. Above all, I had to learn to be patient.

Outside the family, the process of integration didn't always go smoothly. A positive start in the family and at kindergarten were followed, once he started primary school, with phases of isolation, caused by his former enforced passivity and lack of motivation. In everything he did, Eugenio had to activate all his energies in order not only to absorb what was new in any school day, but also to fill the gaps and the deficit in experience from his past. As his teachers did not know how to help Eugenio by motivating him as an individual, his five years at primary school often proved an endurance test.

Neither the teachers, the nuns, nor the parents of the other children showed us much solidarity: any deviation from the prescribed syllabus or discussion on more liberal educational methods was rejected, and hidden resentments came out into the open. For example, it was maintained that I, as a "foreigner and intellectual" with my family background, could not understand the people of Cerro Maggiore. Fortunately, my Italian family didn't let this upset them.

Eugenio immediately understood my criticism of what was happening in the school and would ask: "And what is your opinion of the story I heard today in school?" He also understood the somewhat alienated position we found ourselves in, and whenever I had differences of opinion with the teachers, before I went into the consultation room he would plead with me, "Please, Papa, *piano, piano!*—he was obviously worried I would tell the teachers too plainly what I thought of them. He had every reason to fear this: I got very annoyed when they kept trying to tell me my son was at the bottom of the class. "We'll see how Eugenio will turn out!" I told them. "My teachers too always wanted me to believe I was untalented. Eugenio's horizons are already opening up today beyond the signpost marking the end of Cerro Maggiore."

Teresina and I were not prepared to take such nonsense from teachers we believed to be inadequate, and a close friend of ours, the pediatric neuropsychotherapist Anna Maria Carugo, arranged for us to visit one of the leading pediatric clinics in Milan. She led Eugenio through some ordinary developmental tests, and the results were very reassuring and gave every cause for optimism.

The more Eugenio was integrated into our family, the more clearly he articulated his interest in his own past and in my family. We had certainly expected the questions he asked us, but were still moved when they came. He gradually understood that before the time with us he had not had any family life. We could only soften the pain of the loss of an essential part of his childhood by pointing out that he was after all now living in our family. Although he showed amazing understanding, his reaction made it clear just how much he needs me and how much I still have to learn to be a steady and balanced father.

One day, as we were visiting Papa Antonio's grave, he suddenly asked where his other grandfather was buried.

I answered: "Your grandfather Wolfgang isn't dead. He's living in Germany."

He wanted to know why this grandfather didn't come and visit us.

I became nervous: I didn't want to paint a gloomy picture of my father in this, the first discussion. So I said: "Grandfather sees lots of things differently from us. His theater, his friends, and his new family keep him very busy, so he hasn't any time left for us."

Eugenio didn't say any more and when we got home he disappeared up to his room for some time. When he came down he declared hotly: "If Grandfather Wolfgang doesn't have any time for us, then I don't want to see him, his theater, or his new family either!"

His reaction moved me very much. I picked Eugenio up and said to him: "Who knows, maybe Grandfather will talk to us one day."

He didn't believe me.

On that October evening my work on this book faltered. I felt like giving up, and wrote to Ralph Giordano that evening:

I ask myself more and more often for whom am I actually writing my obituary—this book—in my isolation in Italy, which prevents me from living. In one thing you have perhaps deluded yourself: that I could write my book as well as do other things. I find working on it such a strain that I scarcely have any energy left for anything else. I have severely overestimated my inner strength for this constant overcoming and breaking through of inner walls. . . . I stare into the past of a family that was never mine, and to my horror this too often isolates [me] from the present in my own family who love me, and I see no opportunity of building up a future for myself that corresponds to my needs. . . . It all seems more and more uncertain to me, and my isolation is increasing. For a long time, my concern has been not for myself, but for the future of my Eugenio, for whom I would like at least to ensure an education. For his sake I shall continue to hold on. On him I project my hopes for a better tomorrow, and he will always be confident of my love.

Ralph Giordano answered me at once by fax:

I have been aware of your growing despair. . . . You are indeed right to "take stock." You are running up against brick walls and only injuring yourself by doing so. That is one thing. The other is the social, financial situation, and that is depressing enough. The worst thing is that your gifts are lying fallow, as it were, not getting established—that there apparently exists here in Germany no demand for what you are, do, and want. You yourself have already distanced yourself very much from it, and I don't know whether you would be up to the constant fight, or rather guerrilla warfare, you would have to wage here. I've been born into it, so to speak, and so I'm used to these conflicts with the outrageous, albeit only up to a certain point. I too sometimes consider flight, to a different, less problematic place, to jobs that give pleasure too. At the same time I know that I am "nailed" to this country and will never get away from it. The same holds for you too, even if you are not living geographically in Germany, nevertheless the whole weight of it is squatting on top of you, as it were. And that is not going to alter either. . . .

I too was only able to "stop the wheel of fate" at forty-one, so I lived long enough "on the outskirts." Yet, without the period up to that point nothing would have turned out well afterwards. Life's just like that—it's the blows of fate that form us, and not the strokes of good luck. That doesn't mean of course you have to be stuck in difficulties all the time. But it does mean drawing useful lessons from it, in overcoming it. Don't see things as too black or too rosy—but think that your book could achieve something! Keep at it; there you can achieve something real, purposeful, a crucial stage in your life. I know how difficult it is when you're oppressed and ha-

rassed by so many other things. But I also know how a degree
of fatalism can save one. . . . once you've finished it, you will
no longer be the same person, the status quo ante will be bi-
ography, life story, and you will continue to hang on to the
threads of that, but in a new stage. . . . To try is the essence of
life—if you know why you tried. All these components apply to
you and what you are capable of. You can do it. Don't give up.
Fight. Use the time. For Eugenio's sake, yes. But also for your
own!

The final sentences in particular strengthened me in my conviction that we can learn from criticism of our faults and mistakes, in
particular through the criticism of others and ultimately too by
self-criticism, as Karl Popper says.

I thought of the grandfatherly letter Ralph Giordano had written
to Eugenio on his eighth birthday, on 30 April 1993. In it he wrote:

I wish you all the best for your birthday today—presents and
a lot of happiness, the greatest and most precious of which is,
as I know very well, the love of your mother and your fa-
ther. . . . Their greatest happiness is to know that you love
them back with your whole heart. . . . While I'm sitting here in
my home in Cologne and writing to you for your birthday, I
look over my shoulder and what do you think I see? You! On
lots of photos that all have a place of honor and that I look at
several times every day. I can see Eugenio laughing, I can see
Eugenio alone, but then together with his father and mother
too, and all three of you are a wonderful sight! And that is the
way it should continue to be.

The idyll of a "happy family" has to be constantly worked at, as
Eugenio and I both know: for us, as father and son, there is no
other way but that of dialogue.

26

On Tour with Richard Wagner's Anti-Semitism

The trip to Israel and its repercussions had a marked influence on my work, evident from simply looking through the lecture subjects and articles I have written since 1990. The essential themes were: "As a Wagner in Israel," "The Case of Wagner in Israel and Germany," "Richard Wagner's Anti-Semitism: Contradictions and Consequences for German Politics and Culture," and "Wagner and Antifeminism." All closely interconnected, they document a constant process of development, which is both complex and almost inexhaustible. The four basic themes formed the basis for lectures on the reception of Wagner in and around Bayreuth. Complementary to these were themes such as "Does Wagner's Gesamtkunstwerk Idea Still Have a Future?" "Lamas and Kundry's Images of Genius: Notes on Elisabeth Förster-Nietzsche's and Cosima Wagner's Falsifications and Their Consequences up to the Present Time," "Toscanini, Wagner, Hitler," "Redemption for the Redeemer: Thoughts on Wagner's *Parsifal*," and "Wagner's Bayreuth, Bayreuth's Liszt: Art as Ideology and Art as Liberation," as well as theoretical thoughts on Wagner's *Lohengrin* during my Dessau production of that opera.

In contrast, although still closely connected, are my other main subjects: Kurt Weill and Viktor Ullmann, who was murdered in Auschwitz in October 1944 and whose epoch-making compositions I have been intensively researching since 1990.

In my lecture at the 1995 Bruckner Festival in Linz, entitled "The Destruction of Creativity in the Arts: Conformist Music— Nazi Ideology and Music as Political Propaganda," I pointed out in particular the historical connection between Wagner's anti-Semitic writings and Hitler's racist lunacy and culture, right up to Joseph Goebbels's guidelines on music.

Purely "aesthetic" subjects with psychological aspects, such as a lecture on Mozart, or on Goethe's *Faust* in compositions by Liszt, Schumann, and Wagner, served to keep me financially above water and open doors for the subjects I was really interested in. The tension of Wagner, on the one hand, and Weill and Ullmann, on the other, was central to my interests. For me it meant ultimately the exposition of the two-thousand-year-old conflict between Judaism and Christianity and the Bayreuth temple cult as an expression of romantico-religious redemption mania, according to Richard Wagner, and with all its consequences, up to Auschwitz. I understood the whole development more and more as the consequence of a perverted Christian anti-Semitism, which had reached a climax with Wagner in Bayreuth.

The historian Friedrich Heer opened my eyes to this painful knowledge. Reading his words helped me come to terms with the anti-Semitic past of my family. In his book *God's First Love: Christians and Jews Over Two Thousands Years*, Heer, an Austrian Catholic, proves, fascinatingly, that "the concepts of Jew-hating and Jew-killing were based on Christian theology, taught by the most eminent fathers of the church."[43] Heer comes to the conclusion that "Auschwitz and Hiroshima are based on a thousand-year-old theological tradition."[44]

The more knowledge I gained through ever more enthusiastic historical study, and in discussions on human experiences, the more firmly I distanced myself from the bogus Christian traditions of my family in Bayreuth—traditions that had lost all credibility after the Holocaust.

The break also prompted in me a search for new ethical guidelines. Any form of religion claiming sole powers of redemption, any fundamentalist ideology became intolerable to me. My question, based on knowledge and experience, became: How can I achieve total understanding of other, different ways of thinking, feeling, and acting? I feel it is through knowledge, by which mankind liberates itself, as Popper has said. My view of the world broadened and I accepted that there are many paths to paradise on earth and in heaven. They should, however, be based on active sympathy with all those deprived of their rights, irrespective of sex, nation, color of skin, and belief. The word "race" disappeared forever from my thinking.

Heer says:

Christianity today is rather like a tree, or a forest if you will, on a mountaintop: uprooted by a storm. . . . The reason for this alarming fact is that Christianity is not rooted in the soil from which it stems—from Jewish piety, the Jewish fear of God, love of humanity, love of earthly pleasures, joy in the present and hope for the future. . . . A true revival, a rebirth of Jewish piety, could possibly depend on whether the synagogue would assume the role of mother in the Mother Church and elder sister of the younger daughter churches. The return of Jesus the Jew to the community of His brothers who have borne His cross as crusaders from the fourth century to the twentieth century—this could be an event of extraordinary and vital importance.[45]

I found new ethical impulses in Reform Judaism, which interestingly enough arose in Germany, in the wisdom of the Psalms, as it arose out of Jewish historical experience and deep piety. For example, Psalm 142 of the Jewish Bible, an instruction from David when he was in the cave:

I cried unto the Lord with my voice; with my voice unto the Lord did I make my supplication. I poured out my complaint before him; I shewed before him my trouble. When my spirit was overwhelmed within me, then thou knewest my path. In the way wherein I walked have they privily laid a snare for me. I looked on my right hand, and beheld, but there was no man that would know me; refuge failed me; no man cared for my soul. I cried unto thee, O Lord: I said, Thou art my refuge and my portion in the land of the living. Attend unto my cry; for I am brought very low; deliver me from my persecutors; for they are stronger than I. Bring my soul out of prison, that I may praise thy name: the righteous shall compass me about; for thou shalt deal bountifully with me.[46]

Belief in God contains disbelief. This is expressed, for example, in a passage from Psalm 139, in the Jewish version: "Surely the darkness shall cover me; even the night shall be light about me. Yea, the darkness hideth not from thee; but the night shineth as the day. . . . How precious also are thy thoughts unto me, O God! How great is the sum of them! If I should count them, they are more in number than the sand: when I awake, I am still with thee."[47]

The poem "Prayer" by Ilse Blumenthal-Weiss, which she wrote in 1945 after her time in the concentration camps of Westerbork and Theresienstadt, is inconceivable without Jewish piety. It summarizes my thinking:

> *I cannot hate.*
> *They strike me. They kick me with their feet.*
> *I cannot hate. I can but pray*
> *For you and me.*
> *I cannot hate.*
> *They throttle me. They pelt me with stones.*
> *I cannot hate. I can but weep.*
> *Bitterly.*[48]

Ilse Weiss's husband and son were murdered in Nazi concentration camps.

My quarrel with Christian anti-Semitism includes that of Richard Wagner and his descendants. What sparked further investigation into the subject was a letter from Marcel Silberstein of Basel, who wrote to my host Shai Burstyn at Tel Aviv University in mid-

January 1990, only a few days after my lecture tour in Israel: "Wagner's anti-Semitism can be segregated neither from his general personality nor from his music." He added this statement to Hartmut Zelinsky's article in *Musik-Konzepten* in 1978 with the title "Richard Wagner's 'Ordeal by Fire,' or 'The New Religion' of 'Redemption by Annihilation.'" Zelinsky's assertion that Wagner was partly responsible for the rise of Hitler and National Socialism in Germany I neither could nor would yet believe in 1990. My hesitation and the unease that Zelinsky provoked in me with his revolutionary thesis, first formulated in 1975, I can only interpret today after years of painstaking preoccupation with the subject. It was my fear of an irrevocable break with my own family—above all with my father—but fear too of the end of the repressed childhood dream, to go back to Bayreuth and take part in a critical appraisal of Wagner in Bayreuth. Fear of a loss of identity. And fear of the international opera business, with all the Bayreuth connections on which I would be dependent as opera director.

By 1992—after my own lengthy investigations into the connection between Bayreuth and Auschwitz—I became painfully aware that there was no way past Zelinsky's findings.

I do not share Zelinsky's philosophical understanding of the historical link with Hegel in the politico-cultural phenomenon of Richard Wagner: Wagner had no solid philosophical basis and thus remains a dangerous, self-appointed pseudo-philosopher. But otherwise Zelinsky's work represents a turning point in international Wagner scholarship. His pioneering work is the courageous act of an ostracized loner who has my sympathy and respect. As he writes: "Present-day Wagner admirers deceive themselves on Wagner's anti-Semitism—either they ignore it totally, in order not to sully their image of the genius . . . or they treat it as a sort of whim of genius, which is rather embarrassing and curious, but certainly not to be taken seriously."[49]

The self-deception of most Wagnerians was repeatedly confirmed on my travels in recent years. But since the publication of Zelinsky's article in 1978; Ulrich Drüner's doctoral thesis, *Richard Wagner's Artistic Creation Between Ideology and Myth*; the painstaking historical study *Race and Revolution* by Paul Lawrence Rose (1992); and above all the interdisciplinary standard work *Richard Wagner and the Anti-Semitic Imagination* by Marc Weiner (1995), a slow change has come about in a minority of Wagnerians and a majority of those critically interested in the man. The subject is being taken more and more seriously, as Weiner illustrates in detail the close connection between biography, theoretical writings, and the stage works through thorough analyses of the music scores. The anti-Semitic writings, as an essential part of the politico-cultural phenomenon of Wagner in their unique effect, cannot and should not be overlooked any longer after Auschwitz.

My personal summing up, from experience and knowledge of the causes of the conflict, comes to this: Wagner's idea of a festival and its realization in Bayreuth signify a loss of reality and humanity. In this sense I, as a great-grandson of Wagner, have become an anti-Wagnerian. I became aware of the difficulty of presenting my knowledge of Wagner objectively, as a descendant of Wagner. At the beginning of my lectures I described my special situation to my audiences. The following not very academic introduction to one of my lectures reflects this:

"Anyone addressing Richard Wagner's anti-Semitism finds himself confronted by complex problems. Wide-ranging, interdisciplinary knowledge and a passion for individual responsibility are required, that must be put to the test in the selection and presentation of documents. Equally important is looking to the personal motives in dealing with the subject, as here one is touching on deep layers of human experience and suffering."

About myself as a speaker: "I am aware that I am speaking to you as a great-grandson of Richard Wagner, who was Hitler's cultural model. So I am speaking here not only as a music historian. Richard Wagner's anti-Semitic writings cast their shadow over my life. The subject contains fundamental questions such as repression, 'not wanting to talk about it.' denial, and the falsification of real links between German culture and politics in which Richard Wagner plays a decisive and inglorious role. Whether I like it or not, the subject is part of my existence. It is linked to something I consider typical of the German mentality—namely, the separation of the private and the public sphere in the discussion and translation of fundamental ethical positions. I refuse to condone such separation and consider it dangerous on the basis of historical experience and knowledge, and as a Wagner after the Holocaust; we are dealing with humanitarian values and individual responsibility. Anyone demanding open, unbiased discussion on this theme and humane dealings with those of different opinion will not only run up against resistance and rejection; he will also find himself exposed to slander, existential problems, and threats, which are a mask for all kinds of intolerance."

Equally unacademic was my practice in the lectures of projecting texts, showing films, and weaving in musical examples. Often the lectures were followed by lively debate, but sometimes too by an icy silence.

Between 1990 and 1995 I toured as the anti-Wagnerian great-grandson of Wagner, giving lectures in Germany, Switzerland, Austria, England, Italy, the United States, and Canada. Critical thoughts that required critical comment from the listener on basic ethical questions in art and politics polarized audiences. Their reactions varied. They were polarized: either quietly, indirectly, or openly critical of Richard Wagner or, on the other hand, of my interpretation of his work and personality. Many were disturbed in particular by the fact that I, as a descendant of Wagner, was so critical of him.

The various nationalities, cultures, ages, religions, and historical, political, and personal backgrounds of my audiences influenced their reaction, as did whether or not they were experts or opera fans. From this wide variety, I learned to beware of crude generalizations, and I slowly began to adjust for each particular audience. But one thing never did alter: a Wagner descendant talking critically about Wagner can always expect surprises.

Sometimes the reaction was extremely emotional, which stemmed from the Nazi past: repression, denial, silence, falsification. The example of Wagner, his anti-Semitism, and the Nazi involvement of my family in Bayreuth clearly illustrate that each individual bears personal responsibility. Anyone talking about Wagner and the Germans of necessity questions the self-confidence of many Germans.

Frequently Wagnerians who endured my criticism only because I am a great-grandson retreated into personal anecdote and experiences of Wagner and the Festspielhügel. In this way they didn't have to question their image of the composer. Instead they tried like missionaries to bring me onto the "right" path for the "Bayreuth case." I always tried to stay polite and didn't see much point in discussion.

The minority of German anti-Wagnerians behaved quite differently toward me. Despite their ideological aversion they were interested in the composer, and seemed surprised to meet a Wagner such as myself, and consequently we had some very intense and stimulating discussions.

The invitation to give a lecture on "Wagner's Anti-Semitism: Contradictions and Consequences for German Politics and Culture" in mid-December 1992 at the German Congress of Industry and Commerce had a political motive: Germany's international reputation had dropped that year as a result of crimes committed by neo-Nazis (the arson attack in Solingen and other violent actions). Leaders in business, politics, and culture wanted to create a liberal image. A critical Wagner who spoke against his great-grandfather's racism, presented by Ralph Giordano, one of the most important German-Jewish voices, seemed to be perfect for this.

The audience was confronted before the lecture with pictures from my traveling exhibition "From Bayreuth to Theresienstadt-Terzin," to the sounds of the music of Viktor Ullmann, which was followed by a visual analysis of a color slide of Arno Breker's Bayreuth Wagner bust, to the sound of "The Ride of the Valkyries." Ralph Giordano then gave his opinion on Bayreuth and the connections of the Festspielhügel and their negative influence on my work before introducing me. My lecture concentrated mainly on Wagner's anti-Semitism.

The reaction was a mix of discomfort smattered with a few polite yet familiar objections. As usual, people congratulated me in private and promised to support me "indirectly," because, as I heard many times that evening, one must take into account the sponsors in Bayreuth, Father, Barenboim, and Levine. The press reacted kindly, though there was no clear statement on my criticism of the New Bayreuth.

I realized that discussion about Wagner would be at the expense of my professional future in Germany. When I mentioned this to Ralph Giordano, he said: "Criticism of German politics and culture can only be expressed in Germany, and in the case of Wagner, only by a Jew. As an oppositional Wagner, you have no chance here at the moment. But I hope that will change one day."

I answered: "Just as German anti-Semitic philo-Semitism à la Bayreuth connections?"

He nodded.

To my surprise, an ongoing interest in my work has developed in Austria since 1989. Since 1992 I have regularly given interviews on Austrian television. I have known Gaby Flossmann, who works for the cultural division of television station ORF 2, since 1968. Our firm friendship has had a common theme: German-speaking Jewry and coming to terms with the consequences of National Socialism in Germany and Austria. Wherever she could—and that is by no means always easy where my subjects are concerned—she has managed to report in detail on essential stages of my work round the world.

In Vienna I met the sociologist Michael Ley and his wife, the painter Charlotte Ley-Kohn, with whom I not only discussed the effects of the Holocaust on the next German, Austrian, and Jewish generations, but also carried out projects such as the filming of my Dessau *Lohengrin* production as part of the documentary film *Herrn Hitler's Religion*, directed by Petrus van der Let.

In marked contrast to my experiences in Germany, I am met with continuing interest in the themes of my work in Austria. In Vienna, and again at the time of my lecture "Nazi Ideology and Music as Political Propaganda: The Hitler-Wagner Case" at the Bruckner Festival in Linz in 1995, I didn't have to restrain myself in my comments on Hitler, Vienna, and the Austrian Nazis. Instead, I encountered the special way in which they were dealing with their own thousand-year-old history: behind the insults—the derisive use of double-edged flattery—a caustic black humor and self-mockery always shines through, something most Germans lack. This attitude is particularly prominent in Austrian Jewish culture. I know today why I wrote my doctoral thesis on Weill and Brecht specifically in Vienna and not in Berlin. The mordant humor of the two iconoclasts of the last days of the Weimar Republic before Hitler's master-race twilight—fully comparable with the lack of direction in the period after the fall of communism at the end of the 1980s—makes me prefer Vienna to Berlin even today.

The Swiss—the Zürichers in particular—and their Wagner, to whom in 1849 they so kindly granted nine years of asylum: what do they have to do with Wagner's anti-Semitism? One thinks of Mathilde Wesendonck and her immortalization in *Tristan und Isolde.* Swiss anti-Semitism? Yes, here too there have been painful historical events that people do not like to talk about in Switzerland. In particular in the Nazi period, when Switzerland turned away Jews fleeing from Germany, and money stolen from Jews disappeared into Swiss bank deposits, many Swiss were blameworthy. But one should guard against prejudice.

In Switzerland too, people are prepared to come to terms with the dark chapters of European history as well as their own pasts. Such willingness was demonstrated in October 1992 when I was invited by my patron and friend Albi Rosenthal, the legendary musical antiques collector and patron of the arts, and Walburga Sia Strecker, daughter of the founder of the Nietzsche Colloquium in Sils-Maria in Switzerland, to speak about Cosima Wagner's and Elisabeth Förster-Nietzsche's distortions of history. My target was not only Cosima's and Elisabeth's falsifications while they were still alive. I also spoke of Richard Wagner's autobiographical falsifications, and pointed out the continuity in dealing with German and individual history in my family right up to today. Whether Richard, Cosima, Winifred, Wieland, or Wolfgang—they all used and use history in the interests of their power-political and economic aims. Elisabeth Förster-Nietzsche behaved similarly with regard to the Weimar Archive.

After the lecture, several German academics in the audience remained awkwardly silent, but the Swiss philosopher André Bloch, organizer of the Nietzsche Colloquium, presented me with a key to the Nietzsche House in Sils-Maria as a token of his appreciation, with the words: "No one's forbidden to enter the house here. You are always heartily welcome."

My reception in Zurich was equally generous. At the Paulus Academy in November 1993 I spoke, as I had in Sils-Maria, to a group of Swiss with a sensitive awareness of history on the subject of Wagner and anti-Semitism. Right next to the lectern on a stage was a piece by the artist Thea Weltner, *Children's Shoes and Breadbins*, a reminder of the murdered children of Theresienstadt. The *Israelisches Wochenblatt* and the *Neue Zürcher Zeitung* reported the event objectively.

After the lecture, an Orthodox Jew invited me to his home, where we discussed my ideas on directing *Lohengrin*. He regarded *Lohengrin* as a Messianic figure and showed me a painting of a tree in the desert with a church tower driven into its trunk: Judeo-Christian cultural history with all its dark shadows. This picture and the mysterious discussion inspired me later on in the visual concept for my *Lohengrin* production in Dessau: two pillars of a cathedral are set on two tree trunks.

In Italy there is scarcely any discussion of Wagner and Judaism, and people in the country of the Vatican have shown only detached interest in my lectures, whether they touch directly or indirectly on the subject. Their confusion over Wagner has been fueled by the influence of Bayreuth and by inadequate translations, and not much is likely to change this. Media reports are restricted to the occasional account of bomb attacks and violence in Israel, which cannot promote discussion about anti-Semitism. It is no wonder that I have often had to pack my suitcases in order to exercise my task as "historian with the wrong subject" elsewhere in the world.

It is still a wonder how unconcerned people are in Italy about coming to terms with their own anti-Semitism: it wasn't until 1994 that the subject became the focus for a discussion within the framework of a traveling exhibition, "The Lie of Race." The Catholic

Church has been one of the most important bulwarks of European anti-Semitism since the fourth century, and its role during and after Mussolini was hardly commendable. It took the Vatican forty-three years to grant Israel diplomatic recognition in 1993! Unfortunately, I do not read anything of this in my son's history books.

On my many journeys in North America I encounter great interest in my subject. There the mix of many ethnic groups is based on the principle of diversity while recognizing equal rights for all. In spite of all the criticism leveled at it, I consider the American model capable of development and improvement. There is still something of the pioneering spirit in the United States—a curiosity, spontaneity, and unaffectedness that was also expressed at my lectures and in discussions afterwards.

The knowledge, quality, and quantity of research regarding the subjects I deal with are particularly impressive there: all the important work after Zelinsky and Drüner comes from the U.S.A. The works of Paul Lawrence Rose of Pennsylvania State University and Marc Weiner of Indiana University outshine anything that has been published on the subject in Europe. And in many colleges and universities the liberal spirit prevails in the sense of militant diversity.

Such diversity along with the integration of Jewish groups into the various institutions—or at least the recognition of German-Jewish history as a subject—are instrumental in the acceptance of problematic subjects. By generating invitations for me, North American German communities showed that they are still influential. Because of its Nazi period Germany itself has aroused interest. People like hearing the "rebel against his own clan," not least because it reminds them of TV series like *Dallas* and *Dynasty*. Precisely because of my family background, a lot was expected of me, and my performance was fundamental to the judgment cast on my lectures: a fair precondition. I look forward to every trip to North America, as I do to visiting Israel, my elective home, and to returning to Italy.

I also feel at home at George Washington University in Washington, D.C. The director of the musicology department, Professor Roy Guenther, embodies the "liberal American," and I esteem him as a colleague and a private individual. The fact that my lectures "Wagner—Nietzsche," "Weill," and "Wagner in Israel and Germany" took place in the capital of the United States had positive consequences which I shall come back to.

Furthermore, I was able to appear in numerous universities throughout the United States and Canada, and I still enjoy a lively exchange of opinions with many academics I have gotten to know on lecture tours.

In many cities, too, the local Goethe Institute and American branches of German firms have supported me. Two Jewish-American cultural institutions—the Hebrew Union College in Cincinnati and the United States Holocaust Memorial Museum in Washington, D.C.—played a major role in my trip to Israel and my dispute with Wagner's anti-Semitism. When I spoke in February 1992 in the Mayerson Hall of the Hebrew Union College, a world-renowned Jewish theological institute, on "The Case of Wagner in Israel," I knew that there had been resistance to my invitation. That this resistance was discreetly overcome was the work of Abraham Peck, lecturer in modern German history and Judaism, administration and programming director of the American Jewish Archive in Cincinnati, and author of numerous articles on German-Jewish history of the nineteenth and twentieth centuries. Cincinnati not only is the American twin city of Munich, with a large proportion of Americans of German origin, but also has a significant Jewish community. German and Austrian Holocaust survivors live there, who know the history of the Wagner family very well.

After the lecture these people, who were quite particularly affected by German race mania, came up to me with great openness, even warmth. The director of the Hebrew Union College, Alfred Gottschalk, was among them, and he, for one, now had no more objections to future collaboration and my point of view.

Afterward, the mother of James Levine was introduced to me as a member of this group. To my surprise she asked me if I thought it right that her son was conducting in Bayreuth. I answered: "Only your son can answer this question."

A further landmark was an invitation to speak at the United

States Holocaust Memorial Museum in March 1994. The museum's administration was already familiar with my work before making contact in autumn 1993, and in particular with a long article in *The Washington Post* from April 1993. This interview, by Judith Weinraub, who had researched her subject thoroughly from November 1992 to April 1993, is for me one of the fairest accounts of my story.

The lecture evening itself further demonstrated the spirit of mutual trust and interest. Despite a snowstorm, the hall was well filled, and the discussion was of a high caliber, not least due to the presence of Paul Lawrence Rose, investigator of Wagnerian anti-Semitism. Here, as in other Jewish institutions in North America, I found sympathy and a desire for ongoing dialogue, which actually gave me the energy to continue my work in Germany too and find it meaningful.

27

The Post-Holocaust Dialogue Group:

And in the Beginning was Auschwitz

ounding the Post-Holocaust Dialogue Group was also connected with my trip to Israel. Franklin Littell had heard of my lectures on Wagner in Tel Aviv through the media, and in the summer of 1990 he invited me to the twenty-first annual congress of his conference, The Holocaust and the Churches, at Stockton College in New Jersey, which was to take place in March 1991. He asked me to speak on my experiences in Israel, the story of the Wagner family, and German history in relation to Wagner as a politico-cultural phenomenon.

I was only vaguely aware of the sensitive nature of the organization and the other guest speakers, having gathered some knowledge of it since the end of the 1960s through descriptions of friends and acquaintances and having read a lot on the subject of the Holocaust. Until my trip to Israel, though, I had not met any experts on the subject.

I began to understand the intellectual ambience of the meeting from the opening session on 3 March 1991. The organizers' open-mindedness was evident in their choice of vice president: Hubert Locke, professor of political science and sociology, is an African-American Christian. But Locke by no means suppressed the problems of his own group. He is the author of numerous works such as *The Detroit Riot of 1967* (1969) and *The Care and Feeding of White Liberals* (1970). When I asked him why he, as a black, had become vice-president of the organization, he answered: "The Holocaust is the culmination of experience with totalitarian systems, which can always be repeated if we don't watch out. As such it is independent of categories such as skin color, nation, religion, and ideology."

At this first meeting in 1991 I took part in all the discussions I could, and my own lecture met with great interest. Right at the start I had an unforgettable encounter with the respected liberal senator Paul Simon of Illinois, who had been one of the Democratic Party's presidential candidates in 1988. We were introduced after his impressive opening speech on contemporary human rights. He shook my hand warmly and said: "Hey, Gottfried, I have a photo of you at home that I took in Wahnfried Park in 1951 when I was an officer in the U.S. Army. I lived in the Siegfried Wagner House for a few weeks as a kid and you were always hanging around. But how come you're talking here about your lecture tour on Wagner in Israel, with your family history?"

I answered: "I think it's high time we talked about the effects of the Nazi period in Bayreuth after 1945."

We subsequently continued our frank discussion by letter.

In those three days in March I met a lot of people with whom I either developed a warm friendship or have since occasionally exchanged opinions. I became friendly immediately with Franklin Littell and his wife, the historian Marcia Sachs-Littell, and with the host and the organizer of the event, G. Jan Colijn, director of general studies at Stockton College, and Henry Knight, professor of religion at Tulsa University. They introduced me into the various groups and to two participants who interested me in particular and gave me a warm welcome. One of these was Abraham Peck; the other, the Reform rabbi Steven Jacobs from Huntsville, Alabama, who has published a considerable number of works on Jewish faith and history. Both men are sons of Holocaust survivors.

My lecture on the evening of 4 March, to a full hall, was another baptism by fire after Israel. Afterwards, Abraham and Steven approached me, and we talked until early in the morning and decided to organize ourselves as children of Nazi victims and Nazi crimi-

nals. What unites us even now is summarized in the six points of
the program of our Post-Holocaust Dialogue Group. As our slogan
we took the words of the Jewish judge and Holocaust survivor
Samuel Gringauz in 1947: "Our tragedy must become the starting
point of a new humanity."

We presented our six-point program at the Twenty-third Scholars Conference on the Holocaust and the Churches in Tulsa, Oklahoma, in March 1993. It was prepared by another board member,
the composer Michael Shapiro, for future official registration as a
nonprofit organization. The text of the articles reads:

1. We, the children of the victims and the children of the victimizers, see the Shoah/Holocaust as a unique rift in Western
   and world civilization and the starting point of a new moral-
   ity in terms of thoughts, feelings and actions.
2. We stand opposed to the repressing and silencing of any and
   all discussion of the Shoah/Holocaust and the continuation of
   any and all prejudices and hatreds resulting from the activities of our parents and grandparents both now and in the future and directly attributable to the trauma of the Shoah/
   Holocaust.
3. We fully believe that the sharing of our own unique burden of
   this tragic past in a continuing present and future dialogue is
   of vital concern, independently of any religious, ideological,
   and/or political group. With our dialogue we give concrete
   evidence how our generation, and those after us, will confront
   the challenges presented by the Shoah/Holocaust and its ever
   present influences.
4. We begin our dialogue with tolerance, respect and self-critical
   awareness as the children of the victims and the children of
   the victimizers. Our mutual willingness to share our burden is
   coupled with our unhesitating commitment to overcome our
   present ignorance, prejudices, and misconceptions, and to
   present to those who are open and receptive a model for present and future trust and understanding.

5. We see ourselves as an international activist organization whose avowed purpose is not only to inform others of the Shoah/Holocaust through scholarly conferences and publications, but to fight both theoretically and practically against any kind of totalitarian dogmatism religiously, politically, and ideologically. We stand for the adoption of human rights for all human beings, fully believing that we are responsible for our own actions, ever mindful of the "different other."

6. We hope by our humanitarian actions and our scholarly work to influence governments and nation states, thus lessening fear of present or future repetitions of the Shoah/Holocaust, striving at all times to realize our goal of a world living together in peaceful tolerance and appreciative of all diverse humanity.

After establishing the group in Seattle in March 1992 there were not only annual meetings with the aid of Franklin Littell's organization, but conventions with other internationally recognized organizations: Remembering for the Future; Christianty and the Holocaust; the National Workshop on Christian-Jewish Relations; the Evangelical Academy near Frankfurt am Main; and the international Institut Au Coeur de la Communication (ACC). The international media—except in Germany—has also shown great interest in recent years. Unfortunately, the percentage of Germans of my generation in our group is still very small in comparison with that of members with a Jewish background, but overall our organization is growing, and membership spans three continents.

One of the reasons for its international appeal is the fact that we have developed a mutual appreciation of the different psychological, historical, and family backgrounds. Membership comprises women and men with very different professional, national, religious, and political backgrounds, and the choice of themes for our symposia reflects this. In choosing discussion topics we also examine the statutes of our organization in a spirit of self-criticism. So that we could talk about our identities as post-Holocaust Germans and Jews, we had to come to terms with our experiences in life and our family chronicles in their historical context.

Abraham and I were molded by the liberal political developments of the late 1960s. As former "sixty-eighters" we had common intellectual orientations, toward such intellectual Jews of the Frankfurt school as Max Horkheimer, Theodor Adorno, and Hannah Arendt. But in our coming to terms, we by no means nostalgically romanticized our own student years. Rather, we were self-critical and set new targets for responsible actions as the children of Nazi victims and Nazi victimizers. In spite of all the biographical differences, this joint learning process went surprisingly smoothly.

It also became clear to me at this time though that my idea of a reconciliation between Germans and Jews is not realistic: reconciliation is only possible between perpetrators and victims. No guilt can be bequeathed to us, the children of the victimizers, let alone a direction for reconciliation.

Even so, Abraham and I have been corresponding almost weekly since March 1991. Our exchanges on life and reading matter are very intense, and as far as we can, we involve other members or those interested in our organization. Dan Bar-On, for example, whom we met for the first time in March 1993 in Tulsa, has been important in this critical process of self-questioning. He presented us with six questions about the effect of the Holocaust on our lives: When and how were we confronted with the Holocaust? How did we cope with our lack of roots? How do we deal with social alienation and being different? Can we empathize with the role of victims and victimizers? Are we living our own lives without the shadow of the Holocaust? Have we found a middle path between the desire to live and the desire to die, through knowing about the Holocaust?

We needed time to answer such complex questions seriously and finally wrote down our thoughts some months later. While I approached each question individually, Abraham answered Dan Bar-On's questions in the form of an article.

It is also instructive how Dan Bar-On judges the dialogue

between Abraham and me. He describes it as "microcosm of the German-Jewish dialogue" and writes:

> Gottfried Wagner and Abraham Peck are brave people. Their parents would never have been able to talk with one another. Only fifty years have passed since the ancestors of one were deeply involved in the atrocious act of attempting to annihilate the ancestors of the other. The survivors gave a solemn commandment to their descendants, never to forget and never to forgive. Why does Abraham try to break this commandment? Why does Gottfried try to break through the silence which came over the German people after the crime became public knowledge: silence that is a mixture of shame and the desire to shrink from responsibility for the murder, to forget and to be forgiven? . . . For their own sakes, they are looking for a dialogue which, though breaking their fathers' commandments, will help them articulate their internal quest for hope.

He then analyzes what the Holocaust has brought about in our lives: being uprooted in our childhood from our environment, isolation and mistrust:

> Gottfried found . . . his intellectual harbor in the post-War Jewish and gentile writers who tried to grapple, genuinely, with questions similar to his own about "Who is Wagner?" However, he had to pay a high price for his courage and was ostracized from his family and his homeland. He has a new personal sanctuary [in Italy] which protects him from the storms awaiting him in the open sea. . . . After describing painful childhood memories which have shaped their life stories, [Gottfried and Abraham] quickly disassociate themselves [from these memories].
> Gottfried does it by giving too conclusive answers to questions which have no final answers. . . . Abraham tells us that he believes the future will be good for the next generation, but

his last sentences indicate that he cannot really believe that
whole-heartedly: "Can we ever free ourselves of the need to be
watchful? We must be ever watchful and not believe there exists a simpler answer 'Yes' or 'No.' If we do not succeed, what
may our children face?"

And he sums up:

"It is quite terrifying! There is no real sanctuary in the world
after Auschwitz," and then draws the analogy between our dialogue and building a house: "Unlike building a house, there
are many participants in this process. All these watchful eyes
and ears of the living and the dead, all with such extreme and
conflicting sensibilities that the possibility of failing is endless.
The original discourse of yesterday may easily become the
pseudo, 'as if,' discourse of tomorrow. How can we know?
How can we find our path?"[50]

Today my answer to this is clearer than in August 1993. The dialogue between Abraham and me is a continual process of learning
and maturing. Looking at the situation at that time, Dan Bar-On
was correct in his judgment. Today I—and probably Abraham
too—would answer Dan's questions quite differently. Based on my
experiences in our group, I would now evaluate more positively the
way the problems that have arisen for me through being a descendant of Nazi victimizers have been handled: even the longest path
through the darkness eventually leads to light.
    In 1995 Abraham wrote an article entitled "Germans and Jews
in Dialogue: Is There Anything to Discuss?" In it he said:

Yet half a century after Auschwitz an entire generation of Germans and Jews continues to share a legacy and a burden that
in the words of Sabine Reichel, born in 1946 in Hamburg, "is
like an historical umbilical cord that can't be cut off and that
pulls at the most unlikely moments."

At the heart of this cord is family history. It is an obstacle to both Germans and Jews. For Germans it remains the great divide between silence and dialogue. It is a diseased branch on the pages of far too many family trees.

Every well-meaning German wishing to engage in a frank discussion of German-Jewish relations (and there are quite a number) is nearly always reduced to tears or to silence when the inevitable question is asked: "What did your father or grandfather do during the Second World War?" To argue that he was in the German Wehrmacht or armed forces is no longer much of a rejoinder: the collaboration of the front-line troops with the racial ideologues of the SS in the murder of the Jews is by now a well-established fact.

Even more disarming is the question: "What did your parents or grandparents know about the Final Solution?"—the planned destruction of European Jewish life. Often the answer is one of genuine ignorance. German families in the main did not discuss this particular issue in the years after 1945. But we are beginning to learn that many more knew what was happening to the Jewish family who suddenly disappeared from their apartment building one day and never returned. Many more knew because their fathers, husbands, sons and brothers could not keep a *Reichsgeheimsache,* a state secret, which the Final Solution was always intended to be. In letters from the front, from the concentration camp, or in drunken, sometimes terribly guilt-ridden confessions while home on leave, these men told a great part of the home-front just what was happening in the "east" to the Jews of Nazi-occupied Europe.

But family history is also a problem for Jews. Children of Holocaust survivors, such as myself, have grown up in the eye of a hurricane, surrounded by the shadows of the Holocaust. We have grown up knowing that the Holocaust is a part of our being but often do not know why. Many have asked next to nothing about the suffering of our parents during the Holocaust years or the absence of murdered grandparents, uncles and aunts. These children of survivors fear the trauma inherent in their parents' reply.[51]

Perhaps it was my sensitivity to the sufferings of others which increased my need for justice and spurred me on to a greater degree of personal courage. I see Abraham and myself today more and more as witnesses of the second generation, who do not deny or suppress the fact that they are the children of Nazi victims and Nazi criminals. Describing us as "witnesses of the second generation," I see our special responsibility as being part of the present and the future, and that we are making our concrete contribution so that another Holocaust can be prevented.

How much there is still to do is illustrated clearly by events in Bosnia and Rwanda. But with this active, positive approach and commitment we will also be able to better come to terms with our personal fate. Today I no longer find it so terrible that "there is no real sanctuary in the world after Auschwitz." I am at home where people love, understand, or try to understand me. For me this is a release from the tradition of my family in Bayreuth.

Home for me as a cosmopolitan—husband of an Italian and father of a Romanian-born son—is first and foremost with my family in Italy. But as a nomad I can put up my tent anywhere in the world where a mutual acceptance of difference is regarded as enrichment.

Responsible conduct, in respect of others as well, makes my life meaningful. I acknowledge this despite all the uncertainty concerning my future existence and knowing that my thinking seems strange to many and is not necessarily beneficial to my career as a freelance director or as a journalist.

Discovering that I am constantly making mistakes also influences my life with my son. I am slowly trying to make him understand that my work in the Post-Holocaust Dialogue Group is a constructive part of my existence. Through the group, I learn to respect "being different" in a particularly intense way—an experience that I want at all costs to impart to my son. I hope he will understand someday why I refused to become a typical Wagner in Bayreuth, one who would have repressed memories of the Holocaust. This ethical position is obviously linked to my commitments in the Post-Holocaust Dialogue Group, and here Abraham and I are always in agreement.

Thanks to Sharon Gutman, a member of our group, the second international congress, Remembering for the Future, took place in March 1994 at Humboldt University in Berlin. We met after years of hospitality and superb organization in the United States. For Abraham and the other Jewish members, the choice of location was anything but problem-free: Berlin was primarily the capital of Hitler's Reich, and the nearby Wannsee Villa the place where, in 1941, the Final Solution was agreed upon for their relatives. Only a few steps from Humboldt University is the Opernplatz, scene of the book burning in 1933.

As part of the conference, we held a concert dedicated to the composer Viktor Ullmann, who died in Auschwitz. The music was preceded by a talk by Abraham and me called "From Monologues to Dialogues." Only a few people came to the round-table discussion in the university's Auditorium Maximum; yet those who did engaged in intense discussion with us. The hall was only half full for the concert, but we were not discouraged. Though the Holocaust and Ullmann lacked media and big-music-business clout, and this was clearly not an evening of German brotherliness between Christians and Jews, for those in the hall—who were mainly people with a Jewish history—our efforts had been worthwhile.

The program contained works by Ullmann, Weill, and Michael Shapiro. The months of preparation, the discussions on the organization, financial, historical, and linguistic details, and the content, bore fruit. Michael Shapiro, Abraham Peck, Sharon Gutman, Jan Colijn, Franklin and Marcia Littell and all the willing hands behind the scenes created a uniquely intense atmosphere onstage on the evening of 16 March, with the soprano Mildred Tyree, the pianists Jerome Rose and Michael Shapiro, and the cellist Ithau Khen joining forces for our Zero Hour of Dialogue in Germany. For us, the entire event will remain unforgettable. Whether our dialogue there can develop further remains to be seen. The difficulties facing a continuation of our work in Germany on a more regular basis are still enormous, but I firmly believe in a future for our group in that country too.

In accordance with the Post-Holocaust Dialogue Group statutes, great importance is given to dialogue between the different generations. This constant mutual learning process is very important, as illustrated by my discussion with the New York–based psychiatrist Yehuda Nir.

I met Yehuda briefly in March 1994 at the twenty-fourth Scholars Conference on the Holocaust and the Churches at Rider College in Lawrenceville, New Jersey. He gave me a copy of his autobiography, *The Lost Childhood*, published in 1989, which had been translated into nine languages. Yehuda's memories were very moving: a Polish Jew, he survived the six years of the Second World War with his mother and sister. I recall especially the sentence: "We were living in times when one had to be grateful to another human being for not exercising his option to kill."[52]

Despite the horror of what he experienced, he tells his story without hatred or prejudice, which particularly impressed me. After I read the book I kept thinking of the epigraph of his memoirs, from Samuel Beckett's novel *Malone Dies:* "Let me say before I go any further that I forgive nobody. I wish them all an atrocious life and then the fires and ice of hell and in the execrable generations to come an honoured name."[53] This epigraph confused me a lot, as at the time I found it in contradiction to the humane tone of the book, our friendly meetings, and international events we both attended. So in November 1995 I wrote to Yehuda and asked: "How can you manage to be my friend in spite of the motto of your book . . . and my family history?"

Yehuda answered: "Yours isn't an easy question to answer, but I'm happy that you asked, because it allows me to gain additional insight into my feelings toward the Germans; the murderers of my father when I was eleven years old. By quoting Beckett, I express what it means to have one's innocent father murdered when one is a child. It did not mean that I don't have hope, that I don't believe in the possibility of creating a better, peaceful world."

Referring to the Dutch edition of the book, with a special introduction for students, Yehuda continued:

My book intends to encourage young people not to be passive, to take charge of their lives as I did under German occupation. The Germans took away from me the ability to forgive, but I hope that my book will help young people create a world in which one can forgive. I see you, Gottfried, as a herald of that world. You are the Lohengrin who doesn't hide his past, the Lohengrin who says, "Please, Yehuda, ask me about what my parents did." You describe yourself honestly as "a child of perpetrators," born a "post-Holocaust German." You say that you have been crucified on the history of Germany, and I believe you. You don't even ask for forgiveness—all you want is to engage in dialogue to understand what has happened, how it happened, and to ask whether it is possible to prevent it from happening again. You are a German who can help create a world in which we, the Jews, can contemplate forgiveness.

With that letter, a great responsibility has been put on me.

A similarly strong effect was wrought on me by Michael Wieck's autobiography, *Der Untergang von Königsberg: Ein Geltungsjude berichtet* [The Decline of Königsberg: A German Jew Reports], which through its humanity became the basis of another important friendship in my life. I corresponded with Michael about many things, among them my relationship with my father. Like Yehuda, as child and teenage survivor, first of the Nazi terror and then of the Red Army terror in the former Königsberg in East Prussia (now Kaliningrad, Russia), he has a unique understanding of family and the historical dimensions of the consequences of the Nazi period. In addition, after an internationally successful professional life as violinist, this distant relative of Clara Schumann-Wieck is also able to appreciate the politico-cultural conflict arising for me as a Wagner and a German born after Hitler's death. After talks with Yehuda

and Michael, who met in 1995 at the premiere of my production of
Lohengrin, I know exactly why work in the Post-Holocaust Dialogue Group is meaningful for me.

During a short journey with the painter Toby Heifetz, niece of
the legendary violinist Jascha Heifetz, in autumn 1992, I learned
just how much art can help preserve human dignity in the shadow
of death and horror.

Our journey together began in Nuremberg with a visit to the
Dürer House and the site of the Nazi rallies, then moved to
Bayreuth and the Festspielhügel, with its busts of Richard and
Cosima, relics of Hitler's favorite sculptor, Arno Breker. *Götterdämmerung* was being performed that day, conducted by Barenboim. Toby wanted to see inside the theater and so at the beginning
of the intermission we went to one of the auditorium doors, where
we were immediately intercepted. The situation was unbearable,
and I said angrily to one of the attendants who would not let us
enter, "Either you let me briefly show Ms. Heifetz from New York
the auditorium, or I'll publish something about the police methods
on the Festspielhügel." We were granted five minutes.

It was a relief to leave Bayreuth and move on to the next stage of
the journey: Prague, the Jewish quarter, and then the citadel and
the Theresienstadt (Terezin) ghetto. Historical documentation can
only partially reproduce the area's witnessed hells, instead leaving
the intensity of the "forecourt to Auschwitz" to the individual feelings of the visitor. For me, the art exhibition in Courtyard 4, with
copies of drawings and paintings of the condemned Bedrich Fritta,
Leo Haas, Karel Fleischmann, Otto Ungar, Malina Schalkova, Hugo
Sonnenschein, Sona Spitzova, and Petr Kien, and in particular the
drawings of the Theresienstadt children, was a shocking experience. They were almost unbearably intense in their expression of
perversion in the Nazi city of Jewish culture, of the "Spa Theresienstadt for European Jewry," as a terminus or intermediate
station on the road to murder. Toby and I each photographed our
impressions from these pictures, the music and literature and these
were shown with critical commentaries in an exhibition, "From

Bayreuth to Theresienstadt," in mid-December 1992 at the German Industry and Commerce Congress.

In 1995 Abraham and I wrote an article for the American magazine *German Life* on the fiftieth anniversary of the liberation of Auschwitz. Abraham wrote about the problem of "silence and mistrust shared by Germans and Jews" and discussed our own efforts to engage in useful dialogue with one another. Our efforts, he admitted, came with many difficulties: "As Gottfried has stated, we have yet to reach the kind of 'objectivity' necessary to free us from the shadows of the past. He continues to feel shame at the thought of what happened to my family during the Holocaust . . . he feels angry and powerless at his inability to provide his family with the sense of mourning necessary to begin the steps toward understanding." Abraham spoke of my condition as one typical of Germans of my generation, who "suffer under the burden of history and the attendant sense of homelessness and rootlessness." For now, he writes, whatever our confusions or fears, we must continue to talk to one another.

He then questions the worth of our undertaking, "especially when so many Jewish friends tell me that there is absolutely nothing to say to Germans? I was never certain of this until I met Gottfried Wagner. . . . We tremble at the thought of all the shadows that lurk over us. But we also know that our post-Holocaust world has not changed enough to withdraw from the challenge."

He concludes: "The Holocaust has shaped us both. But we are responsible for helping to shape the way it is remembered by future generations, starting with our own children. Can we go beyond the hatred, guilt, and shame of our generation to leave a different world for them?"

In July, I received a phone call from Lara Nuer, whose mother, Claire Nuer, had founded the Institut Au Coeur de la Communication (ACC) in Paris, Montreal, and San Francisco. She had heard of my work and the Post-Holocaust Dialogue Group through Dan Bar-On and was planning an international meeting for August that year in Auschwitz under the slogan "The Turning Point." Rather nervously I asked Lara what my contribution could be to this meeting. She answered: "We of the ACC know your articles and the aims of your group. Like you, we want dialogue between perpetrators and victims and their children; not just between Germans and Jews, but between all essential conflict groups of past and present. Your aims are very similar to ours. We beg you and Abraham to come to Auschwitz as speakers at the three seminars."

I accepted without hesitation. Lara sent me the main questions for the discussion: "What created the preconditions for such large-scale destruction in the 1940s? What elements of general human behavior made the unacceptable possible? How does this type of behavior affect all sections of society?" Contemporary questions followed: "How can we avoid the large-scale destruction that could result from these conditions? How can we instead construct a healthy, sustainable society, beginning with our individual actions within our families, our own work and in smaller communities? How can our individual actions then be transmitted to all sections of society and gain influence?"[54]

Unfortunately, Abraham could not attend the meeting, but another member of our group, Tommaso de Cataldo, went with the ACC colleagues from San Francisco. For my part, I prepared various lectures, texts, sound and video material.

Driving past the watchtowers of Auschwitz-Birkenau, I was shocked by the incredible size of this death factory behind barbed wire. I thought of the words of my friend Harry Guterman from Tulsa, who had survived years in this hell: "It was all a lot worse than you can possibly imagine." Dazed, I entered the garden of the Catholic Meeting House, which is only a stone's throw from the barracks and crematoria of Auschwitz. The intensity and diversity of what I experienced in the next twelve days, in three seminars, can scarcely be described.

I shared a hotel room with Bernard Offen, who guided us through the concentration camps Auschwitz 1 and Auschwitz-Birkenau. A survivor of Auschwitz-Birkenau, Plaszow, Julag, and Mauthausen, he had been told of my background, although I never for one moment sensed any resentment against me. Before the start of the harrowing tours of the camps he gave me two tips that I will never forget: "What you're going to see now is difficult to describe in words. It will exceed your powers of imagination. Follow my personal fate in Auschwitz, which I'll be telling to all of you. Then six million murdered people will become conceivable to you again. Don't leave the group, because you should not try to come to terms with what you will see and experience there alone. Share your experiences with those who are near to you." I learned with time to follow his advice. But I had wildly overestimated my psychological strength. I had been convinced I could assist others, but now I myself needed help.

At the railway of death in Birkenau, Bernard told us how on 24 August 1944, his father had been selected to join a group of new arrivals destined for the gas chambers, while Bernard had been sent to the group who were to survive for the time being. At Crematorium 4, he described how the SS sent around two thousand people to their deaths at each gassing session. I started to cry. Bernard took my hand and silently we went, after saying a kaddish—prayer for the dead—for his father, to his former hiding place near the latrines. On the way Henry Knight supported me, having noticed that I could no longer cope with the situation.

I had imagined that on further tours I would be able to handle the confrontation better. I was deceiving myself. Every new tour through the two concentration camps became even more unbearable, as each time I realized more of the horror of the place. In the beginning I had hoped to be able to protect myself by acting as photographer. A vain hope. Bernard, who had lived through this hell, was like a father to me. Through his loving understanding I slowly started to grasp that realizing the horror of this death factory of the past was part of being human today. Only afterwards was I aware that the others were weeping as well.

I was further moved by Irit Weir, a young woman from Israel in her mid-thirties, who lives in Napa, near San Francisco. During the third seminar, after the renewed confrontation with Crematorium 4 and the murder of Bernard's father, the participants went to sit in the shade of a willow tree in front of the monument to Nazi victims. Suddenly Irit stood up and declared to all those present: "First of all

I'd like to thank Gottfried for kindly accepting me for who I am. Also, I'd like to tell him that here [in Auschwitz] we have switched roles. He is the victim and I am the criminal. He is the one who is suffering here. If we now want to go beyond not accepting the question of guilt [between us] and everything connected with it, as Claire [Nuer] suggested, then we must be more open with one another."

Claire threw in: "Take your time. Guilt does not stop us from being responsible in the correct way for what we want to create."

To which I responded: "I must point out that we in the Post-Holocaust Dialogue Group have been talking about guilt and shame. I am grieving. But guilt cannot automatically be passed on to the next generation, because this would start a tragic and terrible vicious circle. But to be here in Auschwitz means for me to feel deep shame. You have helped me replace the words 'guilt' and 'shame' with the word 'mourning,' and since yesterday that has been a new experience for me."

After the walks through the camps there were seminars and discussions with representatives of conflicting groups: Jews and Palestinians; Romanies and Sinti; a Serbian woman, a Croatian woman, and a Moslem woman. None of us—and we comprised people from thirty-three nations, all engaging in passionate discussion in a confusion of tongues—was seeking out a main culprit. It was much more a matter of creating, in Auschwitz, a higher degree of sensitivity for the suffering of all mankind.

The Germans I met in Auschwitz were people in shock, not ashamed of their tears for the millions of murdered Jews, Christians, Romanies and Sinti, and all the others. We kept asking ourselves: What can I, as an individual, and we as a group, do to fight forms of totalitarian behavior in and around us? There was talk of becoming human through the common experience of Auschwitz, but never of expecting absolution of redemption of one person by another.

When I landed at the Malpensa airport in Milan, Eugenio leapt into my arms and said, relieved: "Papa, thank God they didn't kill you there!"

I answered with a smile: "On the contrary, I made lots of new friends. We all just want to learn to live in peace with one another."

Notes

1. *Selected Letters of Richard Wagner*, edited and translated by Stewart Spencer and Barry Millington, J. M. Dent & Sons, 1987, p. 888.
2. Zdenko von Kraft, "Genius," in *Das Bayreuther Festspielbuch*, Bayreuth, 1951, p. 5.
3. Arnold Zweig, "Antwort an Béla Balázs," in *Weltbühne* no. 1 (1930), p. 618.
4. Dietrich Mack, "Das Trauerspiel der Macht: Miszellen zur Ring-Interpretation (nach Gesprächen mit Wolfgang Wagner, aufgezeichnet von Dietrich Mack)," *Rheingold* program, Bayreuth Festival 1970, pp. 3–12.
5. Richard Wagner, "The Jews in Music," translated by Stewart Spencer, *Wagner* [magazine] vol. 9, no. 1 (January 1988).
6. Richard Wagner, *Religion and Art*, chapter 1, "Know Thyself," in *Richard Wagner's Prose Works*, vol. 6, translated by H. Ashton Ellis, University of Nebraska Press, 1994, p. 274.
7. Friedrich Nietzsche, *Human, All Too Human*, translated by R. J. Hollingdale, Cambridge University Press, 1986, p. 80.
8. *Cosima Wagner's Diaries*, vol. 2 (1878–83), translated and edited by Geoffrey Skelton, Collins, 1980, pp. 772–3.
9. Houston Stewart Chamberlain, *Richard Wagner*, translated by G. Ainslie Hight, J. M. Dent, 1897, p. 176.
10. Houston Stewart Chamberlain to Adolf Hitler, 8 October 1923, quoted in Hartmut Zelinsky (ed.), *Richard Wagner: Ein deutsches Thema*, Berlin-Vienna, 1983, p. 169.
11. Winifred Wagner, "Open Letter," in *Oberfrankische Zeitung*, 14 November 1923, quoted in Zelinsky, op cit., p. 169.
12. Siegfried Wagner, letter to *Deutsche Zeitung*, Berlin, 6 June 1921.
13. Siegfried Wagner to Rosa Eidam, Christmas 1923, in Michael Karbaum, *Studien zur Geschichte der Bayreuther Festspiele (1876–1976)*, Part II, *Dokumente und Anmerkungen*, Regensburg, 1976, p. 65.
14. Adolf Hitler to Siegfried Wagner, 5 May 1924, in Karbaum, op. cit., p. 65.

15. Bayreuther Bund der Deutschen Jugend (BBdJ), "Proclamation," in Karbaum, op. cit., p. 74.
16. Winifred Wagner, *Meistersinger* program, Bayreuth Festival 1943, p. 11.
17. Friedrich Nietzsche, *The Case of Wagner*, in *Basic Writings of Nietzsche*, translated and edited by Walter Kaufmann, Modern Library, New York, 1968, pp. 638–9.
18. Foundation charter of Richard Wagner Foundation, Bayreuth, pp. 8, 10ff, and 4, quoted from Wolfgang Wagner, *Lebensakte*, Albrecht Knaus Verlag, Munich, 1994, pp. 446–463. (The statutes are omitted from English edition, *Acts*, Weidenfeld & Nicolson, 1995.)
19. Ibid.
20. Ibid.
21. Winifred Wagner in *Die Zeit* no. 19, 30 April 1976.
22. Ibid.
23. Josef Herbort, "Vom Junior Keine Konkurrenz," in *Die Zeit*, 3 June 1977.
24. Roy Koch, "Special" [report on the *Fidelio* premiere], *New York Times*, 30 May 1976.
25. Wolf-Siegfried Wagner, interview with Karsten Peters, in German edition of *Harper's Bazaar*, April/May 1985.
26. Immanuel Kant, *Critique of Pure Reason*, quoted in *Philosophisches Wörterbuch*, Stuttgart, 1969, p. 621.
27. Nietzsche, *The Case of Wagner*, p. 647.
28. Franz Liszt, "Chopins Individualität," in *Gesammelte Schriften*, vol. 1, Hildesheim–New York, 1978, pp. 94ff.
29. Uri Toeplitz, quoted in *Neue Zürcher Zeitung*, 8 February 1990.
30. Karl Lubomirski, *Die Zeitpendel (I pedali del tempo)*, Florence, 1990, p. 25.
31. Richard Wagner to Ludwig II, 14 October 1868, in Spencer and Millington (eds.), *Selected Letters of Richard Wagner*, p. 732.
32. Richard Wagner, "Hero-dom and Christendom," in *Religion and Art*, in *Richard Wagner's Prose Works*, vol. 6, p. 280.
33. Richard Wagner to Mathilde Wesendonck, 1 October 1858, in Spencer and Millington (eds.), *Selected Letters of Richard Wagner*, p. 423.
34. Karl Popper, *Alles Leben ist problemlosen*, Munich, 1995, pp. 158ff.
35. Wolfgang Wagner, *Lebensakte*, Albrecht Knaus Verlag, Munich, 1994.
36. Tilman Jens, "Der Erbfolgekrieg" [The War of Succession] in *titel, thesen, temperamente*, televised 10 November 1991.
37. Wolfgang Wagner, quoted in "Werkstatt Bayreuth im Wandel" [Workshop Bayreuth Undergoing Change], WDR Radio, 3rd program, broadcast 30 October 1993.
38. Gina Thomas, "Wagner vs. Wagner," in *Frankfurter Allgemeine Zeitung*, 15 April 1995.
39. Larry Mass, "Met Cancels Gottfried Wagner," in *Opera Monthly*, October 1992, p. 40.
40. Daniel Barenboim, interview in *Opera Monthly*, May–June 1993, p. 4.

41. Franklin Littell, "Confrontation in Bayreuth," in *Los Angeles Jewish Times*, 27 July 1993.

42. Alice Miller, *Breaking Down the Wall of Silence*, Dutton, Toronto, 1991, pp. 105ff.

43. Friedrich Heer, *God's First Love: Christians and Jews over Two Thousand Years*, translated by Geoffrey Skelton, Weidenfeld & Nicolson, 1970, dust jacket text.

44. Ibid.

45. Ibid., pp. xiv–xv.

46. Sidur Sesat Emet, Edition B (Jewish Bible), Psalm 142.

47. Ibid, Psalm 139.

48. Ilse Blumenthal-Weiss, quoted in *Heer*, op. cit., p. 2.

49. Hartmut Zelinsky, "Die 'Feuerkur' des Richard Wagner oder die 'neue Religion' der 'Erlösung durch Vernichtung'" [Richard Wagner's 'Ordeal by Fire,' or 'The New Religion' of 'Redemption by Annihilation,'" in *Musik-Konzepten* no. 5 (1978), Munich, p. 79.

50. Dan Bar-On, Introduction to Dr. Abraham Peck and Dr. Gottfried H. Wagner (eds.), *The Uses and Abuses of Knowledge*, texts submitted at the twenty-third Annual Scholars Conference on The Holocaust and the Church, 8 March 1993, in Tulsa, Oklahoma; Studies in the Shoah, vol. 17, pp. 428–30, University Press of America, Lanham, Maryland, 1993.

51. Abraham J. Peck, "Germans and Jews in Dialogue: Is There Anything to Discuss," *German Life* (April-May 1995), pp. 40–45.

52. Yehuda Nir, *The Lost Childhood*, Harcourt Brace Jovanovich, New York, 1989, dust jacket text.

53. Samuel Beckett, *Malone Dies*, John Calder, London, 1956, p. 2.

54. Information leaflet of the ACC, Paris, July 1995.

Index